FROM THE GAELTACHT
TO GALICIA

A Son's Tale

To Joe and Rosie,

¡Buen Camino!

Paul

x

Paul Murray

Honeybee Books

Published by Honeybee Books
www.honeybeebooks.co.uk

Printed in the UK using paper from sustainable sources

ISBN: 978-1-913675-16-5

Front cover main image: Major F.J. Murray at Chitose Aerodrome, Hokkaido, 13 Sep. 1945.
Front cover: Author in front of Santiago Cathedral at end of Camino Primitivo, Aug. 2009.
Back cover: Murray Spirit Grocer's, Oldpark Road, Belfast.
Back cover: Signpost at Portnoo, Co. Donegal

NOTE FROM THE AUTHOR

Any profit made from the sale of this book will go to NASS, the only
charity dedicated to transforming axial SpA (AS) care in the UK.

ACKNOWLEDGMENTS

BBC cameraman Ingo Prosser RIP first planted the seed for this book. I would like to thank an ex-colleague, Margaret Joseph, who was the first to suggest I write it, and subsequently my uncle, Fergus O'Kane RIP, who gave me further encouragement. Thanks also to John Northridge for his constant interest, my good friend Eddie Hughes who suggested a title, and another friend, Tim Hodgetts, for his research into the location of Akabira POW Camp and his flagging-up of the GHQ/SCAP records. I am most grateful to Anne Murray from Suffolk Archives for the link she provided to the trial of Lt Kaichi Hirate. A big thank you to Sally Dickinson from the charity NASS, Anna Foden who helped me plan my pilgrimage to the Far East, Jean Marshall RIP for sharing her stories of David, and Patricia Lee from the Oral History Unit of the Singapore National Archives for the interest she took in our dad's story when my sister and I were in the country. Particular thanks go to three journalists for their reporting – Adam Howlett from the *East Anglian Daily Times*, Melody Zaccheus from the *Singapore Straits Times*, and Daisuke Nakagawa from the Hakodate branch of the *Shimbun* newspaper. I had great help on Hokkaido from four men with unrivalled knowledge of the camps on the island – Masatoshi Asari, Satoshi Motono RIP, Hitoyasu Shirato, and Takahiro Haseyama. In England, particular thanks go to Lizzie Oliver from the Researching FEPOW History Group for giving me the opportunity to publicise Dad's story at a recent workshop, and to Ken Hewitt for his help with Dad's liberation questionnaire as well as his interest in the Leicestershires who were imprisoned with him. Thank you also to the Imperial War Museum in London for allowing me to reference G.A. Sketchley's article about his imprisonment in Japan, to Valeda Andler for permitting me to use extracts from the book she edited about her husband's diary, and to Crowood Press for permission to quote from R. Keith Mitchell's book on his experiences in the camps. Sincere thanks to Chella Adgopul and Helen Baggott from Honeybee Books for all their assistance in designing and checking the book. In Ireland, I am most grateful for the help of Paula Harvey from the Donegal GAP Heritage & History Group and her amazing knowledge of local history. Lochlann McGill kindly allowed me to use extracts from his authoritative book on the history of west Donegal. Aodh MacRuairí, the former manager of the Ranafast Community Centre, gave me invaluable help with people's names in the village as did Liam Andrews and Róise Ní Bhaoill with accurate spellings. Thank you also goes to Emilio Martín Bauza for helping me unpick and translate some of the more illegible text from a 16th century letter in Spain's Archivo General de Simancas where the National Archives' staff were most accommodating. To Diane Bayliss and Hazel Wilding for contacting me about their uncle, Pte Raymond Suttle, thank you. A huge thank you to two women, Sonoko Gauci and Miriam Davis, who painstakingly translated Japanese newspaper articles and extracts from Hitoyasu Shirato's book as well as replying promptly to every query I had. I would like to pay tribute to two special people in Japan – my guide Taeko Sasamoto, and my interpreter Chris Holmes. Without their help, I would never have discovered so many details about Dad's time in the camps on Hokkaido. Thank you to my sister Villana for accompanying me to Singapore and for being there when I needed her most. A heart-felt *gracias* to eight pilgrims – Anne, Eugen, Mario, Chule, Javi, Bea, Pierre, and Jolanda – for the special moments they shared with me in Spain. Thank you also to my brother-in-law Arthur Roberts and my son Andrew for helping to check through my early drafts of the book. A very special thank you to my wife Jan for her endless patience and technical assistance while I researched and wrote it, and for her understanding during my special pilgrimage to Singapore and Japan. Finally, I would like to pay tribute to my brother Carl for the vast amount of research and the meticulous transcribing he has done of both our parents' stories over the last 40 years. It is mainly thanks to him that our dad's story is now receiving the recognition it deserves.

This book is dedicated to Jan and Andrew,
the two great loves of my life.

This book is also dedicated to the memory of Alan Froud
(1947 – 2020).
You taught me never to fear the high mountains.

One further dedication is to Fergus O'Kane (1927 –2021).
"Everything in moderation."

PHOTO ACKNOWLEDGEMENTS

The author and publishers wish to express their thanks to the following sources of illustrative material and/or permission to reproduce it. (In the cases of 6,7 and 15, contact proved impossible):

1. p.88 Fr F.M. Browne SJ Collection / Davison & Associates

2. p.88 Niall Sloan of Coláiste Bhríde, Ranafast

3. p.89 Seiji Taninaka, curator of Muroran City Folk Museum

4. p.89 Diane Bayliss

5. p.90 Hoshinofurusato Centennial Museum, Ashibetsu

6. p.90 *Yokohama B and C Class War Crimes' Trial watched by American Interpreter* by William Osuka

7. p.90 *Biography of Shigeo Emoto, My Mentor* by Kazuyoshi Yoshimura

9. p.91 Josette, Ray and Phillip Sellings

10. p.91 Julie and Catherine Davies

13. p.93 *Think You Are From Portnoo* Facebook

14. p.93 Jan Murray

15. p.93 *Treasures of the Armada* by Robert Sténuit, Cardinal edition published in 1974 by Sphere Books Ltd.

16. p.94 Montreal Museum of Fine Arts

18. p.94 BELUM.BGR.6, No Tengo Ring, Spanish Armada Collection, copyright National Museums NI, Collection Ulster Museum

19. p.94 BELUM, BGR.431, Cross of a Knight of Santiago de Compostela, Spanish Armada Collection, copyright National Museums NI, Collection Ulster Museum

20. p.95 Archivo General de Simancas, Spain, Ministerio de Cultura y Deporte, EST,K,1570,7

26. p.96 Edmée Murray

CONTENTS

INTRODUCTION

This book covers a very broad spectrum of themes. At the heart of it is a love story involving two teenagers which began in an Irish-speaking community in 1929. It covers my parents' formative years in Belfast and the role played by one of my mum's relatives in the 1916 Easter Rising in Dublin.

I have provided glimpses of my dad's time in a rural hill station in India, preparations for war in Malaya, and his transfer to Singapore prior to the Japanese invasion. There he joins the thousands of other POWs in Changi, is transported by 'hellship' to Japan, and endures six further camps on the northern island of Hokkaido. Throughout 42 months of incarceration, he distinguishes himself in his role as a medical officer and, in three of the camps, as the commanding officer of the British contingency of prisoners. He survives thanks to his love for my mum and his Catholic faith. Based on his secret daily diary to her, the book provides insights and specific details about the conditions suffered by the prisoners of war of some of the 'forgotten army' in the Far East.

My own pilgrimage in 2017 to Singapore and Japan to follow in his footsteps included hearing the story of Singapore's first chief minister from his widow. Her husband has a special link with my dad. I honoured the memory of the 13 POWs who died on my dad's watch. They are all buried in the Commonwealth War Cemetery near Tokyo. On Hokkaido, I learnt more about the POW camps and, in particular, about two Japanese officers who played vastly different roles in them. My visit to both countries led to moments of great poignancy.

Further themes cover his subsequent work as a Belfast GP in the newly created National Health Service, and my siblings and me growing up during the Troubles in Northern Ireland.

I have linked my interest in long-distance walking pilgrimages in Spain and, to a lesser extent, my parents' multiple pilgrimages to Lough Derg with Dad's imprisonment in terms not only of their respective physical challenges but also the desire to subsequently change how we treat our fellow human beings. In recounting some of my experiences on three pilgrim routes, I have grown increasingly aware of the value of prayer.

I visited Japan in a spirit of reconciliation which stemmed from my experience one evening with a Japanese family in the pilgrim hostel I help to run in northern Spain.

I hope that my pilgrim stories may inspire some readers to follow the ancient pilgrim trails in a country whose people have always made me feel at home in terms of their friendship and generosity of spirit.

I have drawn a parallel between the admiration towards my dad felt by the British prisoners under his command, and the high esteem in which the crew of three Spanish Armada ships held their captain – the second-in-command of the fleet – over three and a half centuries earlier. The area in Donegal in north-west Ireland associated with the wreck of his second vessel, the *Duquesa Santa Ana*, has suffered much with the decline in visitor numbers since the boom years of the 1960s when my family used to holiday there. In highlighting the area's historical Armada links and the story of an ancient bell and shrine associated with a nearby tiny island, I draw attention to a part of Ireland that deserves recognition not just for its isolated beauty, stunning beaches, and impressive mountain walks.

I would like to raise awareness of the painful arthritic condition of axial spondyloarthritis which I inherited from my dad. I offer advice on coping strategies that work for me.

It is my hope that any reader with a particular interest in one of these themes will perhaps discover aspects of some of the others that may relate to their own life's journey.

Paul Murray,
April 2021

PROLOGUE

"Are you up for crossing the bridge?" asked Chris, my interpreter on the Japanese island of Hokkaido. He, together with Taeko my guide and I, had been alerted to its existence the previous day by the curator of the local museum. It was our final day together and a special one in that I was finally out of the glare of the Japanese media which had followed me throughout my stay on the island. We had already clambered round the side of the barrier meant to deter visitors from the structure, following the damage to it from a typhoon the year before in 2016. One look at the gaping holes where some of the missing slats had stood made my mind up for me. My one-year-old prosthetic knee would not have easily forgiven such a rash undertaking! I contented myself with taking some photos, though I must confess we did transgress just beyond some yellow no-crossing tape.

Our decision to explore the environs of the bridge before we all went our separate ways was not one on which we needed to consult each other. We were all of a mind that this peaceful setting, surrounded by the stunning autumn colours, was symbolic in a way epitomised by the much more famous bridge over the River Kwai, thousands of miles to the south in another ambit of the war. I had only just learnt from the same curator that the final POW camp where my dad had been incarcerated after 42 months of imprisonment by the Japanese was not Nishi Ashibetsu, as indicated not only in his secret diary but those of all the other British POWs' accounts I had read, but rather a place called Raijo. On Tuesday 5 June 1945, his fellow British, Dutch, and a handful of American POWs marched the three miles upstream from Mitsui Ashibetsu Railway Station, crossed this bridge over the Ashibetsu River, and made their way to their new camp. Each day until their liberation that September, the same slave labourers would have crossed the bridge again, on their way to and from the coal mines.

I can't recall the exact date when I said to my dad what a horrendous event the dropping of the atomic bombs on Hiroshima and Nagasaki marked in the history of the world. I suspect it was around September 1973 when, as an impressionable 19-year-old undergraduate at Queen's University, Belfast, I was outraged at the overthrowing of the democratically elected Chilean government of Salvador Allende in a repressive military coup led by General Augusto Pinochet. What I do vividly remember, however, was Dad's reply: "You listen to me. You would not be alive today if the Americans hadn't dropped those bombs. The Japanese would have killed every POW." I had no reply. It was a seminal moment in my life and it taught me the lesson that there are, indeed, two sides to every story.

CHAPTER 1

"SWEET SIXTEEN"

*"I was so excited and I got up and we danced that dance
and every dance for the rest of the week in Ranafast."*

(Our mum's recorded thoughts on meeting our dad for the first time)

The lyrics of the James Thornton classic ballad, 'Sweet Sixteen', made famous by the traditional Irish folk group, the Fureys, have always resonated with me. Our dad, Francis Murray but known by his family and friends as Frank, and our mum, Eileen O'Kane, met in the Irish-speaking community of Rann na Féirste (Ranafast) in the summer of 1929. Both were brought up in working-class areas of Belfast, Dad born in December 1912 and Mum the following month. This was a matter of months after the sinking of the Titanic, historically one of the city's most famous claims to fame as it was built at the Harland and Wolff Shipyard. Rann na Féirste is a village situated on the Atlantic coast of Donegal, Ireland's most north-westerly county. They were 16-year-old school pupils learning the Irish language in rural areas known as the Gaeltacht and normally to be found in more isolated communities in the west of the country. To this day, they continue to be subsidised by the government to encourage the speaking of the language.

Coláiste Bhríde (St Bridget's College) was the venue for morning lessons in the language and for evening *ceilidhs* (dances). The hall which still stands today was where they met aged 16 on the first evening of these nightly socials. Before the dance, Mum and her three room-mates eagerly chatted about the dresses they would wear. Her mother had adapted a blue one belonging to our Auntie Meg by lengthening the hem at the bottom with some white fabric. She described the scene of a cluster of boys gathering at the back of the hall and all the girls sitting along one side. They were very excited as this tall, slightly stooped but very handsome youth with dark, curly hair made his way down the line. For Dad it was love at first sight but for Mum, who was not feeling in the least attractive, there was surprise when he stopped by her and asked "*An ndéanfaidh tú an damhsa liom?*" (Would you like to dance with me?). They never met during the day but danced together every evening for the rest of their stay.

The dances put me in mind of the opening of the first act of part two of the theatre show *Riverdance*, not so much in the sadness of the young lovers on their last night before the young men emigrate to America but rather in the simple, romantic setting of an encounter at an Irish cross-roads. Sadly, Dad did not live to see the seven-minute interval performance at the 1994 Eurovision Song Contest which was held in Dublin. I am sure he would have shared the immense pride of a nation finding itself, perhaps for the first time, on the European stage in hosting an event which spoke volumes about a country moving slowly but steadily towards a new millennium. On a more poignant parting note, I think of the many thousands of Irish people who emigrated to America at the time of *An Gorta Mór* (The Great Famine) in the mid-19th century. Harsh economic times precluded any possibility of a return. I vividly recall seeing a young Liam Neeson in 1976 tread the boards of Belfast's Lyric Theatre in the lead role of Gar O'Donnell in Brian Friel's play *Philadelphia, Here I Come!* on the eve of his departure to a new life across the Atlantic.

Looking at their respective backgrounds, I am again indebted to my brother who had the immense foresight to record an interview with our parents in their home in Newcastle, Co. Down back in the '80s. The information that Carl elicited has added significant detail to our family history that would otherwise have not appeared in my book. Our paternal grandfather, Charles, bought a shop at 155 Oldpark Road, Belfast in 1896 along with his brother Daniel. They made it into a 'spirit grocer's' which I can still recall today in the hands of a cousin of our dad's as an ordinary grocer's though the building was subsequently converted into a look-out post by the British Army during the Troubles. Its strategic position on the bend of a main road commanded views both up and down the Oldpark. Daniel soon sold his share of the shop to set up business as a publican in the docks area of the city, while Charles and our grandmother, Margaret McGrane, along with our dad and his two brothers and five sisters, continued to live above the shop. In one of the many links to the theme of pilgrimage in this book, our grandparents had met at Pettigo Station on the way to making their own pilgrimage to Lough Derg (of which more later). They married in 1905.

This period before the partition of Ireland in 1922 witnessed years of great unrest, particularly in Ulster where the majority Protestant population were fearful of Home Rule in Ireland which some, in turn, equated to

'Rome rule'. On the afternoon of 28 August 1922, one of our dad's cousins and his friend were shot while working in the shop. Our grandfather was also hit by a bullet which struck him just below the knee while returning one evening to the home the family had recently purchased on the nearby Cliftonville Road. During the recording, Dad vividly recalls watching from the first floor above the shop a line of British soldiers pointing rifles at a Protestant mob who were intent on attacking the nearby Catholic Sacred Heart Church. His memories of those troubled times put me and my four siblings in mind of growing up during some of the worst days of the Troubles in Northern Ireland in the early '70s.

Our grandmother came from Clones in Co. Monaghan. Educated partly in Dublin, she learnt as a teacher to play the violin and was an avid reader, mainly of the classics, a love which she passed on to Dad and his seven siblings. (When it came to emptying our family home in Newcastle in 2007, we were amazed at just how many books our grandmother had amassed.) During the period of the Great Depression in the '30s, she carried food and blankets to the poor of the area "often to the detriment of her own family" in the words of our dad.

His early schooling was in the Marrowbone area of north Belfast which has come to be known as the 'Bone'. (Little did he realise that he would return there and set up as a family doctor after the war ended.) He also spent two years at the non-sectarian Jaffe School, established by Sir Otto Jaffe, a German-born Jewish businessman who was twice elected lord mayor of Belfast. There is, therefore, a precedent for Lagan College in Belfast which in 1981 flew the flagship as Northern Ireland's first integrated school in the modern era. The trend has continued to grow steadily ever since. These schools are breaking down the barriers between Catholic and Protestant communities and are contributing to a greater understanding of 'the other side', given such momentum since the 1998 Good Friday Agreement. By way of an aside, meeting my fellow students for the first time at Queen's University, one of the very few integrated institutions in the province in the '70s, invariably led to an exchange of questions about respective secondary schools should our names not elicit 'what foot we kicked with', i.e. what religion we were.

Our maternal great-grandfather came from a slightly more affluent Catholic family. He was a building contractor and helped to erect a number of terraced houses in streets like Kashmir Road and Cawnpore Road in the Lower Springfield Road. There was even a street named after him

– Kane Street – though it has since disappeared. He lost a finger while helping to build the Stoneyford Waterworks on the outskirts of the city. He had enough money to afford one of the first cars in the city, an Argyll. Like our dad's family, Mum was also born above a shop – at the corner of Clondara Street and the Falls Road – before her family moved to a detached house at 195 Springfield Road. Her father, Hugh O'Kane, later purchased a pub in Leeson Street in the Lower Falls. He enjoyed some success playing Gaelic football, represented his county of Antrim between 1908 and 1913, and played in the All Ireland finals of 1911 and 1912. Our grandmother, Ellie Murphy, played camogie, the female equivalent of hurling, and they probably met in these sporting circles. They were to marry in 1910. Hugh was later to change the family name from Kane to O'Kane in his desire to place a greater emphasis on his Irish ancestry. In fact, Fergus O'Kane, the youngest of our three maternal uncles and three aunts, has told me that the name Galway University were using when he enrolled for his degree in the late '40s was still showing as Kane. So it seems that it was not actually official years later though the family never used any other name than O'Kane.

Our dad's family came predominantly from the townland of Cullion near Draperstown in Co. Derry and he spent every summer there with his brothers and sisters when they were "packed off…armed with cricket bats, tennis racquets and footballs". On a more sinister note, four of his uncles used to take to the hills in the vicinity each night in the early '20s to escape from raids by the Black and Tans, the ill-disciplined British military force recruited into the Royal Irish Constabulary. They were drawn from the ranks of soldiers who had survived the Great War and were infamous for their reprisal attacks on civilians.

The story of a maternal aunt of our mother's, Kathleen O'Kelly née Murphy, and her small part in the 1916 Easter Rising in Dublin, is one of which I had been totally unaware until recently and which is worth recounting[1]. She was a member of Cumann na mBan, The Women's Council, a paramilitary organisation created in Dublin in 1914 to support the cause of Irish liberty. Along with five other women who included Nóra and Ina Connolly, two of the daughters of James Connolly (one of the founders of the Irish Citizen Army and commandant general of Dublin District during the Rising), she caught the midnight train from Dungannon to the city, arriving at 5 a.m. on Easter Sunday. Their purpose was to inform Connolly that there was support in the north for a rebellion. They duly made their way to Liberty Hall where Nóra insisted to an armed guard that she be permitted to speak to her father immediately. After much argument, the guard allowed her to go to his bedroom whereupon he came downstairs to address the six women and sent them to the nearby hotels where the other leaders were staying. A long meeting on the Saturday evening had not long broken up but Connolly insisted that the women should gain access to the men to inform them of the mobilisation they, the women, had witnessed in Co. Tyrone the previous day. Furthermore, they carried orders from him for them to return to Liberty Hall for another urgent meeting.

Kathleen, for her part, was sent to the hotel near the General Post Office where Joseph Plunkett[2] was staying. All the women were accompanied by Citizen Army soldiers. The porter's refusal to admit her was explained by the fact that Plunkett had recently had an operation on his neck and "was a very sick man…The Citizen Army soldier produced a gun and demanded that I should see Mr Plunkett as a matter of urgent military importance." This did the trick and she was admitted to his bedroom where she found him hastily wrapped in an overcoat covering his night attire.

After helping, along with the other women, to prepare breakfast later that Easter Sunday back at Liberty Hall, they met a uniformed Countess Markievicz[3]. It had been an exhausting two days. Kathleen borrowed the countess' fur coat and lay down to sleep on a floor of the hall with it draped over her. Later Connolly asked her to take a photo of him with the countess and her dog "for attachment to a poem he had written which he intended sending to America." All the women slept that night at the countess' home which was a mass of rebels preparing for the Rising the next day. She wrote "Beds were used in relays and were warm from previous use when I got into my bed."

Before returning north to Dungannon on the 9 a.m. train that fateful Easter Monday morning, Connolly showed the six women the Proclamation of Independence which was hot off the printing press. He initially asked Kathleen, being the tallest, to carry it concealed underneath her blouse but changed his mind when he realised the extreme danger it would put all of them in were it to be discovered.

By a remarkable coincidence, especially given the fact that it occurred in a large city like Belfast, our parents' families actually knew each other long before Mum and Dad ever met in Ranafast. When Dad's father

13

Charles first came to the city as a young man, he found employment in a bar in the Short Strand, a Catholic enclave in east Belfast. The bar was owned by the man who was to become Kathleen Murphy's father-in-law, Eamon O'Kelly. To test his honesty, Eamon placed half a crown somewhere in the bar area. Charlie, as everyone liked to call him, returned the coin to his employer thus passing the test with flying colours. It was with sheer delight that Kathleen greeted the news from our grandparents that there was a romance between our mum and Charlie Murray's son.

NOTES

1. *See Kathleen Murphy, Bureau of Military History 1913-1921, W.S. 180, dated 16-10-48.*

2. *I recently discovered that the subject of the ballad '***Grace***', sung with their trademark beautiful harmonies by the Irish folk group the High Kings, recounts the wedding of Grace Gifford to Joseph Plunkett in Kilmainham Gaol on 3 May 1916. He was executed a few hours later for his part in the Easter Rising.*

3. *Countess Markievicz was an Irish politician, revolutionary, and socialist who served as Minister for Labour in the Irish Dáil. She was the first female MP to be elected to Westminster though she refused to take up her seat.*

CHAPTER 2

"RETURN TO RANAFAST"

"I am thinking of St Patrick's Day and ceilidhs and Ireland and you, my darling today. Please God we shall spend the next one together in Dublin and go to the Mansion House and dance all the dances I have loved. I want to see you do a hornpipe again and sing a Gaelic song – how I loved you for them both. I shall always love you, Eileen. God bless you."

This was Dad's diary entry from Muroran Japanese POW Camp on Hokkaido on Monday 6 March 1944. The twin pillars of his love for our mum and his religious faith which enabled him to survive three and a half years of captivity are perfectly epitomised in this extract.

My brother and I had both accompanied our mum on separate visits to Ranafast in the years following Dad's death in 1993 but it was 2011, the year of my retirement from teaching, before I began a concerted attempt to follow in his footsteps. On our annual bed and breakfast stay in Donegal, my wife Jan and I have become good friends with an English couple called John and Mary. Mary is a huge fan of Ireland's favourite 'crooner', Daniel O'Donnell. One wet evening at the end of the summer, John and I dropped the ladies off at a massive marquee tent in the village of Kincasslagh from where Daniel hails and headed further up what is now part of the newly designated Wild Atlantic Way. We were heading for the village of Crolly.

John was a particularly interesting companion to have for the evening as he is a railway enthusiast and was able to point out the embankment above the village where the now disused line would once have passed. Enquiries at the local pub led us to the former railway station, now a private house. Mum and Dad had often spoken about their separate journeys on the Londonderry and Lough Swilly Narrow Gauge Railway. The story went that passengers had time to descend from the carriages and pick flowers before clambering back onto the moving train! Although they had danced together every evening, our dad's shyness meant that he chose to wait close to Crolly Station to catch a glimpse of our mum on the day of her departure, smiling at her as the train went past. Perhaps a good vantage point would have been the nearby railway bridge.

While researching this book, I discovered that the original bridge was dismantled in the early '20s by a local IRA unit using picks and crowbars. This was to prevent the advance of British troops in the area. One member of the unit who, coincidentally, departed from the same station in 1926 to emigrate to America was John Óg Devenney, a native of Ranafast and the paternal grandfather of General Martin Dempsey. The latter was appointed by Barack Obama in 2011 to lead the Joint Chiefs of Staff of the US Army[1].

Sharkey's Pub in Annagry, a veritable shrine to the footballers of Glasgow Celtic, was our next port of call in my attempt to discover the location of the two private houses which accommodated Mum and Dad in 1929. A young local man had heard of Teach Eoghain Mhóir[2] (literally Big Owen's House) where Dad had stayed though follow up emails failed to elicit its exact location. Suitably refreshed, John and I headed along the minor road in the shape of a horseshoe linking Ranafast with the main coast road at Annagry. I suppose part of me thought that the two houses might just reveal themselves through the gathering dusk via a name on a front door but that proved too unlikely. At least I had made a start in my quest.

Returning to Sharkey's for a pint the following year but this time in daylight and with Jan, the man serving us behind the bar said he hadn't heard of the houses but pointed to a local man along the counter who readily offered to take us not just to one but to both! I was so excited that the two houses were still in existence over eighty years later but respectfully kept my distance to let him finish his drink in peace. We then followed his battered red Mini to the property on which Teach Eoghain Mhóir was situated. He gave us directions to the nearby second house and I thanked him profusely for all his help.

I tentatively knocked at the front of an immaculately painted white house with its grey-trimmed door and windows. Nóra McGarvey opened it and, when I explained our reason for calling, she readily invited us in and introduced us to her husband Paidí. As a linguist, I was fascinated by Paidí feeling more comfortable speaking in his native Irish. As we sat having a welcome cuppa, Nóra would periodically translate for him the background to Mum and Dad meeting in much the same way I frequently interpret Spanish for those who do not speak the language. As well as confirming that Teach Eoghain Mhóir was still on their land, they said that they continue to accommodate undergraduate students from

Queen's University in Belfast who come to the Gaeltacht to learn Irish. Nóra estimated that around 30 families in the village still open their doors to secondary school-age boys and girls from all over the country during the summer holidays with the aim of them learning the language. Furthermore, Coláiste Bhríde was still the venue for the youngsters' Irish classes.

Nóra was keen to know how we had tracked down their house. I replied that I thought the red Mini driver was called Greene and, as is the way in country areas where everyone knows everyone else, she said that that would be Philip. Pointing Jan and me down the hill below their house, we found ourselves staring at a derelict, relatively small two-storey building with a ground floor extension to the left. The tethered goat on some outside steps leading to a loft took a keen interest in us! On closer inspection, the house contained a motley collection of farm implements and partially used buckets of paint. It was difficult to envisage how Dad and the other boys would have shared the house with a family all those years before. What did strike me, however, was that this unpretentious dwelling was very much in keeping with the modest personality so much admired by everyone who knew him.

Thanking the McGarveys for their special Donegal hospitality and promising to keep in touch, we walked back towards the centre of the village, past Coláiste Bhríde and on to a bigger house – Teach Phaidí Sheáinín Pheadair – where Mum had stayed. The house is owned by an actor in the Irish language RTÉ television soap, *Ros na* Rún. Apparently it enjoyed the nickname 'The Gresham' as in the luxurious hotel in central Dublin. Still today, nearly a century later, it offers accommodation to college students.

At this point, it is worth digressing and looking at the logic behind the names of the houses. In a similar way to *'Casa'* appearing in Spain to identify many houses in rural areas and being called after their current owners, in 1929 Paidí (Paddy) would have owned the house, Seáinín (wee John) would have been his father and the previous incumbent, and Peadar (Peter) would have been Paidí's grandfather and the owner before that. Aodh MacRuairí, the former manager of Áislann Rann na Féirste (Ranafast Community Centre), researched two generations further back and added Conall and Seán (John) to produce a full five generation lineage and give the exact house name as Teach Phaidí Sheáinín Pheadair Chonaill Sheáin. What a mouthful if our mum had proffered this on Carl's taped interview! And would her faultless pronunciation have wavered let alone her always excellent recall of names? I doubt it.

Two things struck me about the naming of the houses. Firstly, and influenced by these days of equality of the sexes, I noticed the absence of a female name. This is in contrast to my experience of Spain where women's names figure just as frequently as men's in the naming of houses. Secondly, the lack of any need to insert a surname. Most of the family names at the time were restricted to a small number like the derivative MacGrianna and the same can still be said for many rural communities nowadays. In fact, Aodh told me that, in a recent publication by a native of Ranafast, the first inhabitants to settle in the area in 1736 were the MacGrianras which subsequently became McGrenra, then MacGrianna, and finally the anglicised form Greene, as in the name of our original car guide. On a personal note, I had not realised that Aodh (pronounced 'ee') is Irish for Hugh. This is indicative of my barely scraped pass in O level in the language! As mentioned in the previous chapter, Hugh was also our maternal grandfather's name. It appears on a commemorative Gaelic football medal awarded to the descendants of the successful 1911 and 1912 Antrim teams in a glitzy evening a few years ago at the Waterfront Hall in Belfast. The county team were runners-up both years in the All Ireland Final. A maternal aunt, Josephine Scullion, was its proud recipient and my cousin Roisín has since passed it on to me.

Adding another famous Ranafast resident to that of an ancestor of General Martin Dempsey is the name Seosamh (Joseph) MacGrianna. The finest work produced by this author who wrote in Irish is *An Druma Mór* (*The Big Drum*) which tells the story of the rivalry between two marching bands in the area spanning the years 1912 to 1917[3]. The plethora of first names and total absence of family names reflects my research, and reading the novel had me constantly referring back to the name of Mum's lodging to see if I could make a match. Seosamh, however, was careful not to identify by name any of the inhabitants of the village he fictitiously called 'Ros Cuain' but which in reality was Ranafast. This proved to be a wise step as the book was banned due to libel when it first appeared in 1935 and did not see publication until 1969. The description of a dance in the old school struck a chord when I read the following: "Finally one man turned around and pointed his hand to a girl who was sitting three yards from him and crooked his finger. The other men did likewise and the women got up with a short, sudden, submissive stumble and walked to their sides, and the dance began."[4]. Although the ritual intrigued me, I must confess that I never saw our dad crook his finger at anyone in such a gesture of inflated superiority!

One further link to a surname that in my youth I had only ever heard in football circles when watching on television the Glasgow Celtic and Scotland left-back Danny McGrain was the discovery that our own paternal grandmother who hailed from Clones in Co. Monaghan was called Margaret McGrane.

Jan and I wandered down to one of the many nearby sandy coves. Was this the one where Dad used to trace Mum's name on the damp sand each afternoon? Neither of the outdoor settings for the two old black and white photographs from 1929 which I had unearthed revealed their exact whereabouts. Not surprisingly, our parents did not appear together, Dad posing in the company of three other young men and no less than nine young women! All 13 had wonderfully happy expressions and must have had some fun lining up excitedly for the picture. A stone's throw across the bay now lies the picturesque location of the county's small airport where another bevvy of beautiful young women fly in each year at the end of July to attend the Mary from Dungloe Festival. By contrast, the picture of Mum with two female friends sitting on some rocks at the time of a swim portrays slightly more subdued countenances.

NOTES

1. Donegal Airport magazine **Take Off**, 2011 edition, pp. 56-57.

2. Owen (the anglicised form of Eoghan) Mór is also the name of the nursing home in Derry where Northern Ireland politician, John Hume, spent the final two years of his life. He died in the summer of 2020. He was one of the key figures behind the Good Friday Agreement and enjoyed universal admiration for his adherence to non-violence. In a further coincidence, it was said at John's Requiem Mass that he met his wife Pat at a dance and that they honeymooned in Dublin. Our parents chose the same city for theirs.

3. **An Druma Mór (The Big Drum)** translated by A.J. Hughes, Ben Madigan Press, Belfast 2009.

4. The Big Drum, p.23.

CHAPTER 3

"PASSAGE TO INDIA AND MALAYA"

"We talked of everything but war – nobody was worried about war in those early days, it was all so unreal and far off. War did not worry me in the least – it was all an adventure and besides, I was only a doctor!"

This was how our dad described his voyage on one of the Heysham boats which had been dismantled for use as a troop carrier as it made the crossing from Southampton to Cherbourg on Wednesday 10 January 1940. (The description is contained in a summary he began writing on 12 November 1942 whilst in Changi POW Camp and covered the period December 1939 to April 1941. He entitled it 'My Career as a Medical Officer'.) Having dumped their bags on the train at the port's railway station as there were no left-luggage facilities, the men had the day to themselves to explore. Their youthful exuberance with any thoughts of war far from their minds is further conveyed by his description "Off we ran to see Cherbourg and fill empty stomachs!" There then followed a railway journey through France to Marseille, and a sea crossing on HMT *Ettrick* via Malta, the Suez Canal, Aden, and their eventual arrival at Bombay. How totally arbitrary then that their destination be decided by drawing names out of a hat. Dad had the good fortune to be posted to a hill station above Rawalpindi in the spectacular foothills of the Himalayas where he was to spend the next 14 months caring for patients from both British and Indian regiments in his various ranks as a lieutenant, captain, and acting major in the Royal Army Medical Corps.

Why did a young Irishman from a nationalist background enlist in the British Army in the first place? Carl explores this in the website he has set up[1] with a reference to our dad being influenced by one of his patients in Birmingham. Fr Johannes Messner was an Austrian exile who had fled the country following the German occupation in 1938. Another clue appears in a diary entry on Sunday 1 October 1944: "Darling, it is a good thing, in a way, that I went to war. It will not do any harm to the Catholic cause in Northern Ireland, to have had Catholics doing something in this war."

I know that both my brother – in connection with the website containing the POW diary, our dad's account of his career as a medical officer, and his letters from India and Malaya – as well as myself in re-reading them in advance of writing this book, have been really struck by the tremendously engaging tone of our dad's narrative. He inherited his love of reading from his mother and always encouraged my siblings and me to read. A long career in teaching sadly did not leave me with the energy after a day's work and five evenings a week of preparation and marking to sit down and enjoy a good book. I have tried to remedy this since my retirement in 2011. Recently I read somewhere that a Japanese officer at Changi POW Camp in Singapore arranged for thousands of books from a library in the city to be made available to the prisoners to take their minds off their incarceration. Dad does not mention the circumstances surrounding this benevolent gesture. The first of the books mentioned in his letter dated Friday 30 April 1943 is *The Courts of the Morning* by John Buchan. There then follows a great array over the following 29 months of 57 books – an average of two per month – most of which are novels but also include a small number of plays. The last of these is *De Profundis* by Oscar Wilde and is dated Wednesday 11 July 1945. The Irish playwright's account of his imprisonment at Reading Gaol would seem an appropriate choice.

It was in the area of Barian, Murree, and Khyra Gali located in the hills high above 'Pindi where he was allocated a bungalow and a man-servant named Yassin. The ritual of being assigned a servant would not have met with his approval nor would that of Stephen *Paddy* McElligott, his Irish batman in Changi and the majority of the camps on Hokkaido. Dad was captivated by the beauty of his idyllic surroundings though the utter peace and tranquillity were interrupted by two very annoying cicadas who would "for hours on end scream forth their awful din" from a huge tree that occupied most of his front lawn. Into this world cocooned from the impending nightmare of a world war there arrived one day a cable from his father telling him of the news of the death of his mother on 13 January 1940. I cannot imagine how lonely and distraught he must have felt. "It just broke my heart to think that my beloved mother had died and I so far away from home". His angst must well have been compounded by there being no reference in the cable to the cause of her death at the age of 59. Sadly he was never to learn this.

Alongside the many vividly painted descriptions of landscapes in the diaries and witty, though at times caustic, descriptions of his fellow officers and spouses encountered at the local hospital and officers' club, his friendship with one young English family stands out. "But my best friends were Major Paul Gleadell, and Mary not to mention Virginia, their daughter. I had never met Mary before but on first acquaintance I thought she was the most charming little wife I had ever seen; that was only confirmed by time. I spent many happy evenings with them. It was the happiest home I have ever been in – they were both good Catholics. Somehow they were always smiling – and it was not pretence, there was something good about them that outshone anything I had ever encountered in a married couple before".

Dad's first Christmas Day away from home in 1940 began with Midnight Mass on a bitterly cold evening. "Oh what a lovely scene that was; I was sad unto tears and yet I was happy in a way. I felt so lonely sitting there thousands of miles from home and very little chance of getting back soon…. Paul and Mary greeted me outside when all was over and that made my heart glow." Before retiring to bed on that most blessed of nights, he biked to the Gleadells' home to carefully place Jennifer, a toy dog, on their verandah for baby Virginia before slipping off into the night. He was invited to Paul and Mary's for Christmas dinner but, in typically modest fashion, it was many days before he revealed to them the identity of the purveyor of the gift.

Paul subsequently returned to the war in Europe and was promoted to Lieutenant-Colonel of the 12th Battalion of the Devonshires, leading them during the Rhine Crossing on 24 March 1945. Mum and Dad visited him in England when he was seriously ill in July 1988, the two friends' first reunion since their time together in India. Paul died the following month. On the same visit to England and our home in Gloucester that summer, Dad expressed a wish to meet Virginia who, by coincidence, lived in nearby Cheltenham. The links between our two families continued when, years later, Virginia mentioned that her daughter Karina wanted to send her eldest son to the school I had been teaching in, St Peter's Catholic High, in Gloucester. Not only did Jordan come to our school but he was placed in my tutorial group for five years and I taught him Spanish in his first year. I have to admit that the topic of conversation at parents' evenings with his mum at times strayed from my pastoral brief!

Jordan and his younger siblings read beautifully at their beloved grandmother's Requiem Mass in 2008. During the service Dad's link to the family was recalled in a tribute by one of the family when he updated Jennifer's whereabouts almost 70 years later by saying that the boat taking the Gleadells back to Europe was torpedoed and she now lay at the bottom of the South China Sea! (It may, in fact, have been the Indian Ocean.)

I am convinced now, more than ever, that Dad, whether subconsciously or not, used the model of Paul, Mary and Virginia as the archetypal Catholic family on which to base his own when he and mum raised my four siblings and me. Karina has even gone so far as to suggest that I was named after Paul, her grandfather, a theory to which I would be honoured to subscribe.

Returning to our mum and dad's romance, 11 years had passed since their meeting at Ranafast when dad got in touch from faraway India. They had both attended Queen's University, Belfast – Dad to study medicine and Mum geography. He adored her from afar but suffered from shyness and also felt unworthy of joining her on the pedestal he had placed so high for her. They had both made a career for themselves: Dad practised as a GP in a working class area of Birmingham for two years from October '37 until the outbreak of the war in Europe while Mum became a secondary school geography teacher in the Loreto Convent School in Omagh, Co. Tyrone. Dad was about to receive a temporary promotion to the rank of major in the Royal Army Medical Corps and to become second in command of the 27th Field Ambulance, a unit who were attached to the Indian 11th Infantry Division. He resolved to re-establish contact with Mum and sent her a Christmas card. Mum replied four days after Christmas and he was overjoyed to receive this, signed with love, two months later in February '41. Dad's response was to reply with "eight long tightly packed pages, full of love and joy". In a shortened version of his diary written in 1988, he describes the renewal of their relationship thus: "It was a sort of miracle – and it was this miracle that was to give me hope and courage to survive for the next four and a half years."

Training with the 27th was by now taking on a greater urgency. "We tramped the countryside by day in the heat of the day, over dusty dirt roads and through sleepy little villages and there we saw the real poverty of India's people. They had little water, no education and awful hygiene which led to much disease. The nights were cold under canvas; and the days hot (102 F)." After many months of preparation, exercises and route marches "The 27th was ready to go to war." The men entrained at 'Pindi on 5 April '41. He had no idea where he was headed. (If any destination was uncertain, he always used to say to us "I know not where".) A train journey followed to Hyderabad and Madras. Then the penny dropped – it was to be Malaya. The crossing by boat to Penang took three days. There then followed spells at Ipoh, Keroh and Kuantan which were interspersed with a proposal of marriage in a letter dated 18 May. The suspense ended seven weeks later with a telegram from Mum to the affirmative. He was quick to give thanks to the *Almighty* as he had spent ten years praying that this day would arrive and, in a typically amusing aside, notes that "He must have grown tired of me..."

For the first time in his experience, censorship precluded him from naming his whereabouts in the Malayan Jungle where he trained with the men. It was 11 June '41. He was mightily impressed that, as stretcher bearers, they were carrying patients up and down a hill a couple of hundred feet high, a task he could not match despite his 12st 10lbs frame. During summit rests he was fascinated at how the men could sit without moving a muscle as they surveyed the dense foliage below. Their impenetrable faces did not reveal any of their thoughts. Back at their unnamed tented compound, he would insist they frequently wrote back to their families in India to whom they would send nine tenths of their pay. Numbering 100 in all, he much preferred socialising with them than his fellow officers and "talked to them as equals....The lowest among them in caste had a smarter salute from me than I have ever given to any general." I guess he could well empathise with them in their alien environment hundreds of miles from home. Acutely aware of malaria being transmitted by mosquitoes, he took to smacking any bare arms and legs on view with a stick each evening when he conducted his rounds.

Turning to leisure pursuits, Dad organised several hockey matches for the men though he found the game more difficult to play than his native hurling! In the days before mail oder, I have often asked myself how on earth, in the middle of the Malayan Jungle, he managed to acquire a full green and white football strip for the men. It was no coincidence that these matched the colours of Belfast Celtic[2].

On 7 November, he and six of his sepoys finished earlier than expected digging a bore hole for water and they indulged in one of Dad's favourite sporting pastimes...swimming. As the huge breakers rolled towards them, they held hands, were scattered like nine pins and "after each submersion I had to carefully count the six black heads around me and make sure that none were missing." A clue that their whereabouts was on Malaya's east coast is provided when the men innocently quizzed him as to whether the land they could see from the beach was India to which he replied that the country far over the seas to the north east was Japan and that their homeland lay, in fact, behind them to the north-west.

He was to enjoy other swims on the rare occasions when he escaped the camp to indulge his passion. He was a strong swimmer but the warm though dangerously choppy tropical waters in which he revelled were only ever remotely matched at one location back in Ireland. That place goes by the name the locals at Malin Mór in south west Donegal give it – the 'Silver Strand'. On one holiday, Carl and I were determined as teenagers to swim out to a prominent rock in the bay. Our parents stood helplessly on the beach following the sort of risky venture Mum in particular had protected us from throughout our formative years. She taught all five of us to swim but neither Carl nor I were particularly strong swimmers. As I recall, we took a lengthy rest at said rock and returned unscathed to shore. Carl told me recently that Dad accomplished an even more spectacular swim to another rock beyond the confines of the bay, an impressive achievement for someone in their 50s by now unaccustomed to any form of endurance swimming. It was, however, with considerable disappointment in his later years that he described one visit to the local swimming pool at Downpatrick as his last as he could no longer co-ordinate his strokes.

We were all brought up as Catholics. Returning to Malaya, he makes a distinction in his nightly prayers between grown-up ones enunciated on his knees and, curiously, two he called 'baby ones': "As I lie down to sleep, I give my soul to God to keep…" and "Infant Jesus meek and mild, look on me a little child…" These he said in bed in the same manner his mother had taught him and which I, in turn, would say to our young son Andrew when he was a child. There is something magically innocent about them which has remained with me to this day.

Barely three weeks later, he wrote a reassuring letter to Mum in an attempt to allay her fears for his safety as the threat of war approached: "during this war I am a non-combatant and have special privileges under Article 21 of the Geneva Convention and am under the protection of the International Red Cross. I am not allowed to fight, nor is the enemy allowed to fight me; I can be taken prisoner but the enemy must treat and pay me as an officer! They can only use me as a doctor in whatever way they wish but they cannot compel me to do any other work. However it remains to be seen whether the enemy will carry out all these things to the letter." He was certainly correct in being sceptical as to the Japanese subsequently adhering to the terms of the Geneva Convention. At least this letter confirms the reasons behind our dad's reply to Carl and me that he never killed any of the enemy as this was the burning question we wanted answers to as young boys. He did, however, carry a gun and writes on Sunday 7 December 1941 "My little automatic is with me day and night, but I know I shall never use it."

Within a matter of hours, the Japanese attacked Kota Bharu in Malaya and Pearl Harbor on Hawaii. Two days later he wrote: "We were bombed and machine-gunned by Japanese bombers this morning for hours. This was my first air raid and strangely enough I was not afraid in the least; I carried my sergeant pilot on a stretcher into a trench with the other patients. There we were for ages looking up at those huge planes, first in formation at 10,000 feet and then just above the tree tops when they machine gunned our hospital." Three mementoes from Mum were to give him immense inner strength – a lock of her hair, a tiny photo of her which he placed inside an empty cigarette case, and the miraculous medal from her that hung round his neck.

A new posting as commanding officer to a British unit and, this time, a permanent promotion to the rank of major with responsibility for 50 ambulances meant a sad and tearful farewell to his Indian unit who, on his departure, hung a garland of flowers around his neck. On Sunday 18 January 1942, he arrived in Singapore.

NOTES

1. *For further details and access to correspondence between our parents, a time-line, and photographs and illustrations of our dad's time in India, Malaya, Singapore and Japan, go to the website that Carl has created – www.thebelfastdoctor.info*

2. *Belfast Celtic were one of the most successful football teams in Ireland. They subsequently withdrew from the Irish League following an attack on the pitch at the ground of one of their rivals, Linfield, in December 1948.*

CHAPTER 4
"THE FALL OF SINGAPORE AND CAPTIVITY IN CHANGI"

"The worst disaster and largest capitulation in British History."
Winston Churchill

The sinking of the Royal Navy battleship, HMS *Prince of Wales*, and the battlecruiser, HMS *Repulse*, by Japanese long-range torpedo bombers on 10 December '41 left Singapore defenceless and, more significantly, brought an abrupt end to the long-held belief that the colony was invincible. In a book about David Marshall, a fellow prisoner of Dad's and later to become Singapore's first chief minister in April '55, its author, Chan Heng Chee, expresses the following psyche among its inhabitants: "British officials and businessmen had come to believe in their own propaganda that Singapore was an impregnable fortress, the *Gibraltar of the Far East*, and in turn transmitted the air of invincibility to the population at large."[1] In another reference to the effect on the European community, the author adds "It was an enlightening experience for Marshall as he saw at close range the Europeans unmasked, no longer protected by a cloak of privilege which had elevated them above the Asians over which they ruled." Adding fuel to this overwhelming idea of superiority there was even a widely held belief that the Japanese could not see at night, making an invasion after dark unlikely! Such naivety in many ways mirrors the conviction by Lt General Arthur Percival, the British general in charge of Malaya Command, that the enemy would invade from the east. Japanese field intelligence thus shifted their attention to the more sparsely protected north-west of the island as they planned for the invasion.

Both Dad's letters to Mum prior to the fall of Singapore as well as his daily diary written to her every day for 42 months following the colony's surrender on 15 February '42, followed a pattern of not wanting to alarm her as well as not being over-critical of the enemy in case they were discovered. This included his subsequent incarceration in mainland Japan where the conditions of the prisoners were much more primitive than Changi POW Camp. With no reference to the worsening situation, he mentions the verandah of a Chinese school in which he was billeted

27

eight days after reaching the colony. This was probably Nanyang Girls' High School (now Nanyang Primary School) on King's Road in the Bukit Timah area of Singapore which ceased lessons in late '41 in order to be used by British soldiers and then by the Japanese as a military hospital. He comments nostalgically that "it is not the same as my stretcher bed in the jungle" but that "those grand days…will come again when we push the Japs back up through Malaya again." This mixture of optimism and defiance proved to be somewhat premature. They were also days when he first met Australian troops whose 22nd and 27th Brigades of their 8th Division were the main defenders of the north-western coastal area. "They are grand soldiers and a very happy crowd." By a happy coincidence, his grandson Chris, my nephew, married an Aussie girl, Anna, in 2015. They live in Perth, Western Australia.

On the day of surrender itself, he was heartbroken in the knowledge that he would have to burn all Mum's letters "with every single word of them so precious to me." He was by now billeted in the grounds of St Andrew's Anglican Cathedral whose nave served as a temporary operating theatre. The building was also used as a casualty clearing station and became very overcrowded. The day had fallen on a Sunday and he attended Mass and received Holy Communion at the nearby Catholic Cathedral of the Good Shepherd. The next day he was lucky to escape serious injury when a huge piece of shrapnel fell at his feet following the accidental explosion of an ammunition dump.

The Tuesday saw the first of the many 14-mile marches by approximately a third of the 52,000 captured Commonwealth prisoners. One of the routes was from the centre of Singapore along the Indian district of Serangoon Road, past the end of the Lavender Street red light district, out through the outlying district of Bidadari and the more rural Paya Lebar and eventually to Changi. Ronald Searle, more famous for his subsequent comic creation of *St Trinian's*, was one of this defeated army. His superbly drawn sketches depicting the cruelty of the enemy and the bravery of the POWs[2] is mirrored in the vivid verbal account of R. Keith Mitchell[3] of the Royal Signals. Mitchell's Far East imprisonment journey is almost identical to that of our dad and his book has been invaluable for me in how it complements Dad's writings. The two men met up shortly after my wedding[4] in the summer of 1983 at the home of my sister's in-laws in Shoreham. By now, Dad was in his early 70s. Josette recalls the disturbed nights which ensued for our dad as the memories of his time in the Far

East, seemingly for the first time, returned to haunt him.

In researching this book, I read a moving and incredibly dignified account by Andy Coogan, the great-uncle of GB's Olympic cyclist Sir Chris Hoy, whose description of his march to Changi evokes the horror of one particular deterrent by the enemy. "When I first saw a clump of heads on poles, I didn't realise what they were, as they were completely black. Then, as we marched past them, the great swarms of flies that had settled on them lifted to reveal the shocking sight of several heads with tongues protruding and eyes rolled back…The air was thick with the smell of decomposing flesh and the stench from the bloated headless bodies, burst sewers and burning buildings hung in our nostrils. Our spirits sank even lower and we were suffering badly in the scorching sun. We were dehydrated and suffering from a maddening thirst. Every now and again, very brave Chinese women would risk a beating to come out of their homes and offer us water."[5].

For Dad, the uncertain period of limbo between surrender and incarceration ended the following Saturday. He chose to march proudly with his men rather than accept the offer of a lift in an ambulance car. On the eve of the march, it was with a peculiar combination of relief and pride that he wrote "My darling, at last I am to become a real Prisoner of War." He had not the slightest idea that he would not see freedom for another three and a half years. His deliberately understated entry for the day was "My darling, I shall never forget that march as long as ever I live. I was very fit and in good marching condition; heaven only knows what some of the others felt like at the end of the march! We were a weary lot when we reached here; we kept in perfect line the whole way, there was no straggling (and we were the exception)."

The following month, Dad was appointed as the medical officer to the 81st Anti-Tank Regiment. Both he and Andy Coogan mention a fellow RAMC officer of Dad's, Capt. Peter G. Seed. A first visit by me in 2016 to the research room of the Imperial War Museum in London uncovered the transcript of an interview with Seed conducted in 1977[6]. (I have to say, in passing, that such a grandiloquent name for a museum conjured up for me the idea of some jingoistic edifice, even in the mind of an Irishman who has lived in England for some 40 years, but this pre-conceived notion could not have been further from the truth.) Andy recalls Seed's especially sad reflection as MO when incarcerated in Taiwan where the men were forced to work in the infamous Kinkaseki Copper Mine on

Formosa. He felt that it was the younger rather than the older POWs – those who had no girlfriends, wives or children – who died first. This was a view that Dad shared in his subsequent role as chief MO but even more as unofficial confidant to his men. His knowledge that Mum was waiting for him back in Ireland gave him enormous comfort and enabled him, in turn, to offer both mental as well as physical support to the men in his charge.

As I read Andy's autobiography, I realised there was a second prisoner who figured very prominently in both his book and Dad's letters. Fr Richard Kennedy was a Dublin Jesuit priest whom Dad first met when he was appointed CO of a motor ambulance convoy in Singapore. He was a Catholic chaplain and, apart from Dad gravitating towards any fellow countryman, he would have definitely approved of the priest's black humour in a reference to the troops' new-found interest in religion: "He says it is amazing the amount of good a few bombs have done to many souls in this war!"

After the move to Changi, one of Andy Coogan's officers from the 155th Field Regiment Royal Artillery of the Lanarkshire Yeomanry asked him to look after Fr Kennedy who had volunteered to join up with the regiment. He became his batman and accompanied him on his regular visits to Roberts' Hospital, formerly Roberts' Barracks, to comfort the sick and the dying. Dad himself was hospitalised for six days with rheumatic fever a mere three days after the march to Changi and again, this time for nine days, in May with dysentery-type symptoms. A familiar friend, Capt. Seed, visited him on 17 May bearing a gift of two bars of chocolate.

In the interim, he was allowed outside in his role as anti-malarial officer with a small party of men to spray the many swamps in the vicinity of the camp. Fr Kennedy enlisted his help and that of Andy in scouring the coast for any debris which could be used in the construction of a Catholic chapel. This was duly inaugurated on Saturday 13 June and included a large crucifix for the altar which Dad had proudly donated. A signboard bearing the name 'Catholic Church of St Ignatius of Loyola, erected by the Prisoners of War, 11 Division, Singapore' was placed above the door but sadly nothing remains of the improvised chapel nor have I been able to find any photographs of it.

Dad does not mention Andy in his letters but they would have known each other to see. They also appear to concur on a highly distressing incident when Fr Kennedy was punched in the face by a Japanese officer for not saluting the Japanese flag being displayed on a passing vehicle. Andy was also hit and then, unbelievably, ordered to punch the priest which the latter was forced to do in return. This humiliating ritual continued much to the Japanese officer's entertainment for five minutes. On Saturday 25 April Dad describes what was probably the same incident: "I had the awful experience of seeing a priest's face slapped today and I could not do anything about it and neither could he." Given that Dad mentions no other priest during his time at Changi and that he would always use the word 'minister' to refer to a non-Catholic cleric, I would be very surprised if the priest in question was not Fr Kennedy. Again he would not have mentioned him by name in order to preserve his anonymity in the event of the discovery of the letters.

I had the immense privilege of speaking to Andy and some members of his family over the phone in April 2015, two years before he died. I was struck throughout our conversation by his unswerving positivity and will always remember his understated remark "I didn't enjoy that holiday." The penultimate paragraph in his remarkable memoir contains the lines which perfectly resonate with the philosophy behind my own journey to the Far East: "I have always believed that bitterness and hatred are self-destructive emotions. I forgive the Japanese people but I cannot forget the awful cruelty of the Japanese army."[7].

The last day in August saw the prisoners refusing to sign a document swearing not to attempt to escape. This enraged their Japanese captors who proceeded to execute four recaptured men on Wednesday 2 September after they were forced to dig their own graves at the nearby beach. To reinforce this dictate, some 15,000 of the prisoners, a figure which represented the vast majority of the Changi POWs, were ordered to report with all their kit to the confined space in front of Selarang Barracks. No other single event in the 15 months of Dad's imprisonment in Changi affected so many men at the same time. It came to be known as *The Selarang Barracks Incident* and the stand-off lasted for three days in the most appalling sanitary and overcrowded conditions. On the second day, the Thursday, he wrote "We have been literally sleeping on top of each other! I shall never forget what I have seen today – it is indescribable. It's like the Black Hole of Calcutta and American Civil War." Ironically, he had been delivering a lecture to the 81st a few days before about vitamins, food, beriberi and dysentery. It was a fear of the latter as well as an outbreak of diphtheria that led to the men eventually signing the notorious document on the Saturday. It reads more like a certificate relating to a vow taken by a chivalrous knight of the Middle Ages. "I, the undersigned, hereby solemnly swear on my honour that I will not, under any circumstances, attempt escape."[8].

Meantime, Mum has no news of Dad since his last letter which was posted on 2 February, a full two weeks before the fall of Singapore. She receives word from the War Office on 21 September that a card, written by him and confirming that he is a POW, is in transit to her from Lourenço Marques (nowadays Maputo, the capital of Mozambique.) Her relief is manifest when the "precious postcard" finally reaches her on Monday 19 October: "In a word, I am walking on air."

Before Andy Coogan's regiment was sent to Formosa in October, the Japanese asked for volunteers to go up north to a 'holiday camp' where they would work for only three days in the week. Fr Kennedy advised him against it and he decided not to go. Work had begun on the notorious Burma 'death' railway the previous month but reports about the terrible toll of casualties and atrocious working and living conditions had obviously not filtered back to Changi by the time Dad's request to be transferred up country was rejected. It was Sunday 9 May 1943. The horrific death toll of Allied POWs over the 13 months it took to construct the railway is estimated at between 12,000 and 16,000 in addition to around 100,000 civilian labourers. On that day he wrote "I went to the DDMS [Deputy Director Medical Services] in the afternoon but he could not help because two other doctors had been already nominated. I am furious about it all because I want to be with my pals." Being third on the list of candidates might well have saved his life. Barely a week later on Saturday 15 May he was abruptly ordered to leave Changi in a crowded lorry to embark on the *Wales Maru* prison ship bound for Japan. J Force, as they were called, consisted of 600 British, 300 Australian and 50 Americans POWs.

NOTES

1. *A Sensation of Independence: A Political Biography of David Marshall* by Chan Heng Chee (1985).

2. *To the Kwai-and Back, War Drawings* 1939-1945 by Ronald Searle, Souvenir Press (2006).

3. *Forty-two Months in Durance Vile* by R. Keith Mitchell, Robert Hale (London 1997).

4. *Jan and I were married on 6 August 1983, the 38th anniversary of the dropping of the atomic bomb on Hiroshima. I now have two reasons for never forgetting the date.*

5. ***Tomorrow You Die*** *by Andy Coogan and Graham Ogilvy, Mainstream Publishing Company Ltd. (Edinburgh 2013), pp.151-152.*

6. *Imperial War Museum London, ref.1615, photocopy of p.57, transcript of an interview given by Seed in May 1977 to Dr Anne Wheeler whose father, Major B. M. Wheeler, was imprisoned with Seed and in which he describes his experiences in the RAMC.*

7. *As note 5 above p.252.*

8. *See p.89, note 2 above.*

CHAPTER 5

"HELLSHIP TO JAPAN"

"We were packed so tightly in the hold that on the first night not everyone could lie down….The depression in our chest filled with sweat which woke us when we turned over. If we touched a neighbour, both would wake."

These words penned by Sapper Gerald A. Sketchley of the 560th Field Company, Royal Engineers come from by far the most evocative account of those that I discovered at the Imperial War Museum which relate to the journey by sea and subsequent incarceration in Japan[1].

Mitchell shared the smaller of the two holds with Dad and 380 other men during what was to be a voyage lasting over three weeks. The nickname 'Mucky Maru' for the *Wales Maru* in part derived from the latrine facility on deck which consisted of wooden seats with board rails. Bowels were emptied over the sides and the rolling hull became extensively stained. He describes Dad in his book as "a most excellent doctor from Belfast who was to prove a tower of strength in the difficult years ahead"[2].

Food consisted of rice and fish heads' stew but the cramped and insanitary living conditions with very limited access to exercise in the fresh air up on deck, in addition to the presence of rats and flying cockroaches, in fact produced no fatalities. This is partly explained by the following account. My siblings and I all agree that it is the story which most fills us with pride about our dad and is recounted in chapter 13 of Mitchell's book. Curiously, but in keeping with his modesty, Dad does not include it in the love letters but the two men's meeting in 1983 must have triggered his memory. Dad was responsible for the issue of cigarettes to the men. To combat boredom but, more importantly, to reduce the risk of dysentery due to the rising infestations of flies, he announced that one cigarette would be issued for every 10 dead flies brought to him. These had to be whole and he kept strict accounting so that a proportion of the 10 killed on one day could be carried over to the next. The burials at sea via the emptying of a large screw-topped jam jar were conducted daily by him so there was no possibility of illicit recycling! Mitchell's hilarious description of "a new hazard" in the hold of men falling over themselves and anyone else that happened to get in the way "in reckless pursuit of some luckless fly" will remain with us forever. He concludes thus: "This simple inspiration was a godsend, for it gave prisoners an objective in life, and within a few days they had reduced the fly population of the ship to the point where it no longer threatened to become a problem." Many times I have watched, in admiration, our dad in the kitchen of their bungalow in Newcastle where he and Mum saw out their retirement as, with an incredibly swift flick of the wrist, he would trap and crush an encroaching fly in his hand. I guess he had learnt numerous such techniques as he sat in the hold of that hellship. (A diary entry later that year records a count of 50 which he killed in two minutes. If true, this must be some sort of record!)

Unbelievably, in the midst of these chaotic, dingy surroundings, he managed to read Shakespeare's *The Merchant of Venice* and to begin *As You Like It*. The ship headed north east, anchoring at Saigon and then Takao on Formosa. On Sunday 23 May, he movingly wrote "I am going further and further away from you, my darling, but I am coming nearer and nearer to your heart."

The ship, along with the whole convoy of boats steaming towards Japan, did not carry any identification features. A torpedo from an Allied submarine that narrowly missed the bow on 5 June was therefore a result of 'friendly fire'. (The *Tsushima Maru*, however, was hit though the torpedo failed to explode.) Panic ensued among the guards on deck who began firing guns and dropping depth charges. The men in the hold were terrified. The ship began making zig zag movements and increasing speed. When they were eventually allowed back on deck, it was to find that the ship was now totally alone. Gregory F. Michno in his book *Death on the Hellships* clarifies the lack of damage to the ships by the culprit, the USS *Tinosa,* by stating that the torpedoes were, in fact, duds as the American navy were experiencing problems at the time. There must have been even greater panic in their isolated position the next morning when the guards opened fire on a so-called sub which turned out to be driftwood.

Lt Oswald Wynd was the British officer who was the interpreter at the camps in Japan. His father had been a Scottish Baptist missionary in Japan where the boy grew up in the 1920s. He therefore had dual nationality. He too travelled on the *Wales Maru*. After the war he had a successful career as a novelist under the pseudonym Gavin Black, most notably with *The*

Ginger Tree which was adapted by the BBC and Japanese NHK TV into a four part series in 1989. Wynd penned a book he entitled *The Forty Days*[3] which tells the story of the fictitiously named hellship, the *Oshima Maru*, upon which the journey to Japan was based. There is only one character on board whose name bears any resemblance to the people mentioned in Dad's letters. Major Eichi Hirado is the sadistic Japanese officer who is responsible for the POWs. His name is remarkably similar to that of Lieutenant Kaichi Hirate, the commander of two of the Hokkaido camps. There is a jeweller among the men in the novel called Smith. This was also Mitchell's profession. A number of the men in the hold were from the Suffolk Regiment which was the case of many of those on the *Wales Maru* and who, sadly, figure among the 13 who died on Dad's watch.

I was most interested in 'Wyndo's' description of the doctor as Dad worked closely with him in two of the camps. ('Wyndo' was the nickname given to Lt Wynd by the POWs.) This character is ascribed the name Carter and his first appearance goes like this: "an angular man wearing a pair of outsize slacks gathered in at the waist, and nothing else. He had a good deal of brown hair, but very little of this was on the top of his head. His face was long, ending in a slightly prognathous jaw which gave him the look of a depressed horse. His humour was flavoured with the morbid."[4]

I couldn't imagine Dad ever being stripped to the waist or imbuing his humour with a sense of morbidity as he would have tried to keep the men's morale up at all times. The word "prognathous" had me scrambling for a dictionary to discover it means 'protruding'. I find this adjective somewhat dubious but Wynd definitely hit the spot at Dad's sensitivity right up until his later years at being follicly challenged.

By the time the ship reached the southern tip of Japan at Moji on Monday 7 June and J Force prepared to disembark, the high tropical temperatures were a distant memory. The men would have to adapt to freezing sub-zero temperatures over the two bitterly cold winters that lay ahead.

NOTES

1. *Imperial War Museum, London, ref 7770, **The Captive Guest** by Ichy San Ku Ray (number 1390) G.A. Sketchley, p.43. The article is 92 pages in length. The "guest" in the title is an ironic reference to the Japanese Emperor Hirohito.*

2. ***Forty-two Months in Durance Vile** by R. Keith Mitchell, Robert Hale Limited, London 1997, p.91. This and the quotes from the following paragraph are the*

first references to Dad in Mitchell's book.

3.   ***The Forty Days***, *a novel by Oswald Wynd, William Collins Sons & Co Ltd, St James's Place, London 1972*

4.   *See note 3 above, p.54*

CHAPTER 6

"HOKKAIDO – FIRST CAMP HAKODATE, SECOND CAMP YAKUMO"

Signalman Stan Faunch, Royal Signals. Died 24.6.43 aged 21.

He was the first of 13 men to die on Dad's watch. He was also the youngest.

It took three days for the remainder of J Force, by now reduced from 950 to 300 due mainly to transfers to other camps, to travel by ferry and train through Honshu, Japan's main island, to Aomori, the ferry port at its northern-most tip. The men were held in a school for many hours before being paraded through the town "with crowds on either side of us laughing." The pride that Dad felt marching at the head of his men into captivity at Changi was now replaced by humiliation in the country of his captors on this day, Thursday 10 June.

The four-hour ferry crossing to the port of Hakodate, the site of the first of Dad's six camps on the island of Hokkaido, was followed by a one-hour march through the town and arrival at the camp at midnight. One of the inmates of Hakodate Camp, Dan Brown, was so impressed by the news he heard from the latest arrivals that he wrote in his diary "no deaths were suffered on the ship."[1]. At least some of the credit for the survival of the men in the hold on the *Wales Maru* must go to Dad.

He was up by 5.30 the next morning after a night on the floor and spent the next two days until nine at night caring for the sick. The conditions in the camp came as a shock: "The horrors I have seen among the British troops (RAF) here cannot be described. Plenty of human skeletons."

Departure to a second camp for 200 of the 300 as well as the 10 accompanying officers was a mere six days later on Wednesday 16 June, 100 remaining behind to work in the town's cement factory though Mitchell states that they rejoined the main group on 22 June. Their new destination was a two-hour train journey around the bay to Yakumo. The men had to wait patiently in a field while a large stable was converted into living quarters by carpenters. They were to spend the next four months constructing a nearby airfield.

It took three weeks of intensive care of the sick before a more manageable routine could be established. One entry from 18 June mentions rain pouring through holes in the stable roof as he lay on his bed after an exhausting 16-hour day. Surprisingly, in view of the fact that it was summer, he comments on the intense cold, presumably because the men were still wearing clothing more suitable for the tropics. By Thursday 21 October this was to get far worse: "Almost frozen in bed last night with cold – never felt so cold in all my life. And winter has not come yet. I did not thaw until the afternoon."

Both Mitchell and Sketchley confirm Dad's brief reference to the most brutal of the guards, Sadao Watanabe, in an affidavit he wrote after the war. He was nicknamed the 'Basher' about whom Dad wrote "on one occasion [he] lined 30 men up in a barrack room and knocked each man down with his fist." Mitchell was convinced that Watanabe, along with several other guards in the camps, had been moved to less front-line duties due to the mental scars they suffered in combat. Their contempt for their prisoners who had surrendered, in addition to their vindictiveness, helps to explain this brutality. Sketchley heard the guards use the Japanese word *namakemono* (lazy person) to describe the POWs. He recalls the 'Basher's' use of his leather belt to flip it at their cheeks. To save his strength, he would modify the approach Dad had observed by getting 20 men to line up and hit each other[2]. When Sketchley's turn came, he would swop hands to inflict equal pain on both sides of the face of the man opposite: "I always tried to even out the pain to my fellow by working from the top of his head downwards to his neck." Sadao Watanabe was committed to trial in late July and early August '46 in Yokohama and received a sentence of 30 years' hard labour[3]. As with all the non-hanging sentences, this was substantially commuted as the country recovered from war.

We never heard our dad swear so, even if he had ever spoken to me and my siblings about the guards in the camps (and he never did), he would not have used Sketchley's nickname for another brutal guard, this time a Korean. Mitchell names the 'Black Bastard' as Namamoto. (The U.C. Berkeley War Crimes Studies Centre does not list this name among the accused). In the midst of my angst at reading Sketchley's graphic account in the Imperial War Museum in London, I was struck by his poetically morbid turn of phrase: "He was dressed all in black which, we all agreed, matched his countenance and his black heart."[4]. His favourite ploy consisted of hitting the men with his stick as they relieved themselves. The blows were all the more painful as they had little flesh on their bones.

Sketchley himself was on the receiving end of one such attack when he could no longer control his bladder and, unknown to him, was followed by 'Blackie' (yet another nickname for the guard) to an area of open ground where he was mercilessly thrashed. He concludes his portrait of the 'Black Bastard' by wryly commenting that "in a literal sense [the name] was a disservice to all love children."

It is interesting to note that Sketchley's sentiments exactly mirror those of Andy Coogan in his assertion "As for the enemy, my duty is to forgive but, dear friends who perished, I shall never forget."[5] On a personal note it is one thing for me to share such tolerance as one who never experienced what these men went through. However, it is quite another to have been mercilessly brutalised and yet still have the capacity to forgive.

As the work on constructing the airfield at Yakumo continued, Dad was allowed to swim in the sea where he accompanied his patients who suffered from skin infections. There is definitely a feeling of greater well-being in his descriptions of this camp which is wholly absent from the other five. He is fascinated by the capture of a bear nearby in mid-July. A Japanese MO gives him some pictures of the local Ainu people. Sunday was traditionally the *yasume* (rest day) for the prisoners and on 26 September he, a Capt. Maloney and Lt Wynd (accompanied by the camp commander Lt Kudo and four guards) are, unbelievably, allowed to go on an eight-mile walk in the hills. He indulges in dreams of his rural homeland: "There were Irish glens and running brooks. There were delightful little farms, larch woods, silver birch, ferns, and a marvellous Volcano Bay. We gathered wild grapes." He ruefully adds "No bears available" but perhaps that was just as well!

His optimism on Sunday 21 August is sadly misplaced. "Glorious news about Europe in *Nippon Times* – Sicily nearly finished; Mussolini kicked out, Russians advancing, Americans doing well in Pacific and China. I'll soon be home to you, darling." It was to be 27 months before he could make this promise a reality.

As already mentioned, our dad wrote a shortened and more reflective version of his POW diary in 1988. None of the self-imposed constraints of the original diary are evident. Carl then word-processed it and bound it in book form for me, our three sisters, Carl himself and our mum. Dad wrote a dedication in each of the six books which we all treasure. This journal has a sarcastic entry in June related to Lt Kudo whom Mitchell describes as having a permanent fat grin hence his nickname the 'Cheshire Cat', or 'Kudo the Cat' or simply the 'Cat'. "The Japanese refused to send any POW sick to hospital. They must die here. The generous camp commandant gave a quarter cup of milk to one of the very ill. This baby-faced young fat lieutenant is a ruthless cruel beast. He had been an analytical chemist in civvy street."

Before moving on to the third camp on Hokkaido where 12 of the 13 men who died on his watch passed away, I must outline the sad fate of the youngest of the group. Curiously, I am not using Dad's diary as source material for what happened to 21-year-old Stan Faunch. His entry on Thursday 24 June only makes reference to "a patient very ill with septicaemia" but, there again, he may have wanted to spare Mum the fact that Faunch died, in addition to the gruesome circumstances surrounding the disposal of his body. However, the 1988 version contains no references to this sad case either.

Faunch was in the same regiment, the Royal Signals, as Mitchell who gives the cause of death as meningitis. This does not correlate with Dad's nominal roll entry as "acute cellulitis of the face." Mitchell's description of his friend's death, vigil and burial all make for distressing reading. "His body, wrapped in straw sacking, was carried out of the barn at early *tenko* [roll call] and placed in a small storeroom at the end of the second barn. I caught a brief glimpse of his fair curly hair as the little cortège moved past our silent ranks, the last I was to see of a brave young man, a friend who had died, not in battle, but from inhuman neglect in a Nipponese hell-camp. He was our first loss on Dai Nippon. How many more would follow? That night a vigil was mounted over the body in the rat infested storeroom and I was allowed to do the first hour of this. In the afternoon of the following day he was jammed in a foetal squat into a square packing case and carried off for burial. I could not go but Paddy Byrnes, who had wangled the job of batman to the 'Cat', told me that the guards had broken knee and hip joints to force the body into the required sitting position in the crude coffin."[6] I wonder now if it was this tragic recollection that triggered Dad's nightmares in August 1983 when he met Mitchell for the one and only time after the war.

Two incidents epitomise Dad's life-long devotion to equality and fair play. Again, it is Mitchell's observations that fill my family with pride. The first was when another major from the second barn came to ask for more vitamin pills for the officers' mess. Mitchell aptly describes Dad as "God-fearing" and "normally very much in control of himself" but he clearly lost his temper this time and retorted "Not another vitamin pill goes down your bloody throat until I get the medicines I need for the men!"[7] The second was Dad's recommended treatment for a Japanese guard suffering from pneumonia by strapping a poultice of hot rice wrapped in a towel on his chest. Using food as a method of curing his disease apparently terrified the guard who rejected it. He died a few days later. When the men questioned Dad's offer of help to their captors, he was quick to quote the Hippocratic Oath.

Two planes landed on the completed runway on Friday 1 October. It was now time for the men to be moved on yet again. On Friday 22 October, three days before their departure, Dad summarises his frustration to Mum thus: "My patients all doing well, though I have no means of diagnosing many of them. I have to rely solely on my hands, eyes, ears, and touch. No X-rays, no urine or stool tests, no dentist – no anything."

NOTES

1.   See Dan Brown's diary published by his son Nigel on www.nigelbrown.me.uk

2.   Imperial War Museum London, ref.7770, **The Captive Guest** by G.A. Sketchley, pp. 49-50.

3.   Yokohama Reviews, University of California, Berkeley War Crimes' Studies Centre, ref. Watanabe Sadao.

4.   Imperial War Museum, Sketchley, pp. 45-46.

5.   Imperial War Museum, Sketchley, p.7.

6.   **Forty-two Months in Durance Vile** by R.Keith Mitchell, p.123.

7.   As above Mitchell, p.134.

CHAPTER 7

"HOKKAIDO – THIRD CAMP MURORAN"

Wednesday 22 December 1943. "One of our men was carried into hospital unconscious today from the guardhouse: been there for 10 days without blankets – he was stone cold and will die soon."

Thursday 23 December 1943. "I was forced today at bayonet point to omit the cause of death of Suttle."

Of all the letter entries during the entire period of Dad's incarceration in both countries, the two above make the most impact on me. His outright criticism of his captors is very rarely recorded for the reasons I have already given so to read these, particularly the second one, comes as a huge surprise.

The tragic death of Private Raymond Suttle, 23, of the 4th Suffolks, occurred in Muroran, the third of the six camps where Dad was imprisoned. The affidavits of Dad and seven other POWs are recorded among the thousands of other testimonies used by the GHQ/SCAP (General Headquarters/Supreme Commander Allied Powers) in the war trials that took place after the war, not just in Yokohama, Manila and Singapore but also at Nuremberg, in convicting Japanese and German war criminals.

Dad was interviewed back in Belfast on 11 January 1946. The disadvantage was he would have been recalling events, as in the case of Suttle, from just over two years before but at the same time I was finally reading what he really felt. The extra detail is startling in its brutality and total lack of humanity. "Suttle...was sentenced on 18 December 1943 to 10 days' detention by the Japanese in the guard room for stealing a piece of fish out of the cookhouse. He was put in the guard room without any blankets in mid-winter and no medical attention. On 23 December 1943 he was removed from the guard room in extremis – his feet were gangrenous and he literally froze to death and died one hour after entering hospital. This was the responsibility of the camp commandant."[1] Dad was forced to enter the cause of death as "croup pneumonia" but in the nominal roll he recorded it as "exposure and neglect after detention." Mitchell's recall of events includes the observation that "He [Suttle] was hauled out each day to stand in deep snow for further beatings and abuse."[2] I shall return to the fate of the camp commander, Lt Kaichi Hirate, in a subsequent chapter.

Monday 25 October was the day of the move to their third camp further round the bay at the port of Muroran. The name derives from the Ainu *Mo Ruerani* meaning 'the bottom of a little slope'. This is borne out by the camp being constructed at the foot of one such hill in the northeast of the city. It was here that the men were to spend by far the longest amount of time in any camp – 20 months. Lt Kudo formerly handed control over to Lt Hirate whom Mitchell describes as being "very much under the influence of the guards he was supposed to control…"[3] Never was a truer word spoken as I was to learn in my own pilgrimage to the Far East 74 years later when I went to Muroran.

The POWs worked as slave labourers in the nearby Wanishi Iron & Steel Works (now the Nippon Steel & Sumitomo Metal Corporation) and each day had to cross the railway line to enter the foundry. The work was exhausting and it was in this camp that the Yakumo prisoners, when added to the British already there and now totalling 370, joined 350 Dutch POWs. The number of British officers was 19 and the Dutch numbered six. Dad was the senior officer in the makeshift hospital in the camp and, in this capacity, was allowed to sometimes accompany the remains of the surprisingly low number of British prisoners who died in that period on their journey to the town's crematorium. The first of these was Pte Robert Bivans, 25, of the Beds and Herts Regiment. He died of dysentery on Saturday 13 November.

A typical day for Dad as a medic he describes on Tuesday 2 November: "Cold and wet for the men working. We have a bath every three days. Get up at 5.30 a.m.; P.T. and roll call at 6 a.m.; hospital food; breakfast; hospital rounds at 8 a.m.; wash; dressings at 10 a.m.; hospital lunch and my own at 11.30; reading; dressings at 5 p.m.; hospital supper and mine at 5.30 p.m.; sick parade 6.30; roll call 8 p.m.; bed. God bless you."

Mitchell provides a sketch of three of the six camps. I suspect that his one of Muroran has the mortuary doubling up as the small chapel to which Dad makes reference as the resting place for the ashes of the men who died. Apart from Raymond Suttle, there were two pairs of men who died on the same day in the space of five weeks at the end of '43 and the beginning of '44. This is a terrible coincidence and one wonders if some subconscious pact was formed between them. Pte Thomas Mayes, 39, of the 5th Suffolks, died on Wednesday 1 December of pernicious anaemia and, on the same morning, Pte Roland Braysher, 34, of the 4th Suffolks, passed away. He had chronic dysentery. Dad's poignant letter that day includes the words "They said for a long time that they *wanted* to die – I knew they would not last the severe winter." What must the feelings of the men have been on that very day when the Japanese celebrated the first anniversary of the opening of the camp? In a bizarre gesture, the prisoners were all given special meals which included six loaves each as well as a drink of sake.

A concert was cancelled on Christmas Day due to the extreme cold and this after the men worked an extra hour at the iron and steelworks, though Mitchell claims they worked half an hour less. Their Christmas treat was a present of one apple. Dad described the day as "the worst I have ever known."

The second pair to die on the same day, in this case Monday 3 January 1944, were Sapper Ernest Glover, 39, of the Royal Engineers, whose leg was gangrenous and who died of acute osteomyelitis, and Private Francis Bond, 27, of the 2nd Loyals, who had dysentery. Both in the letters and the affidavit, Dad lays the blame squarely on the shoulders of Hirate and Staff Sgt Kuniichi Araki, a member of the medical staff, for refusing to allow Glover to be treated at a fully equipped hospital outside the camp or even to supply him with the instruments to improve his patient's condition. In a story submitted to Wakefield Library in Yorkshire, the county of Glover's birth, as part of the 'We Will Remember Them Project'[4], an account of the ultimately fruitless vigil that his mother kept for two years during which she had received two cards stating that he was well and hoped to be home soon ends with the news of his death in December '45. She had redecorated the house and rarely left home expecting his arrival at any time. As with all the relatives of the 'Thirteen', with the exception of Suttle, I have to date been unable to contact any of their descendants.

The affidavit from Dad criticises Araki for often sending the sick men out to work and for making a point of beating someone every day, usually with his fists. On one occasion he splits a prisoner's head open with his sword scabbard. The verdict at the Yokohama War Trials was for him to be hanged but this was commuted to 20 years' hard labour, only a fraction of which he would have served. Dad's 1988 shortened version of the diary includes a small but quite hilarious retribution which he takes on this most violent of medical staff: "Well, all my patients in hospital are infected with lice; so every morning I collect a handful of lice and put them down the Jap's neck as he bends over his desk at the hospital!" Amusing it may be though I imagine he would have suffered a severe beating if discovered. He adds that Araki profited financially from his position by stealing the POWs' drugs and selling them outside the camp.

In February Dad is photographed along with the other British and Dutch officers in a propaganda picture taken next to American Red Cross boxes, the contents of which were partially retained by the Japanese[5]. This was a pattern repeated with subsequent deliveries. The photo includes Major Stewart of the Manchesters who was the senior officer commanding the men in the first two camps. When the latter was moved later that month, Dad takes command of all the British POWs in Muroran. The Catholic chaplain, Fr O'Mahoney, who also appears in the photo, is moved along with 15 officers to Niigata Camp on Honshu on Monday 21 February. I remember an emotional reunion of the two men in our home in Belfast in 1966. I was only 12 at the time, too young to appreciate the significance of such a visit though curious to meet for the first time someone who had spent time with our dad as a POW.

One prisoner whom Dad never spoke about but who appears extensively in the letters was his batman, Paddy McElligott, a gunner in the 155th Field Regiment of the Royal Artillery. Older than dad at 48 and at times affectionately treating him like his son, his next of kin was his wife with an address in Princes Risborough in Buckinghamshire. He was attached to Dad for over two years from their days at Changi through to February '45. In the diary to Mum dated Saturday 26 February '44, he writes "My darling, should anything ever happen to me I want you to look after my batman, Paddy. He has been so good and devoted to me; he has nursed me and spoiled me ever since I have known him. All I can say is Thank God I have such a man with me." A reference to them reminiscing about their favourite beaches in Ireland, Dad recalling Bundoran in Co. Donegal and Paddy, Ballybunion in Co. Kerry, led me to look on-line for Paddy's ancestry in the Listowel area of that county. Unfortunately, I naively fell into the trap of thinking that Paddy was his Christian name when it was, in fact, his nickname and he was actually called Stephen! At my request, a local newspaper in Kerry ran the story featuring the name 'Paddy'. Unsurprisingly, it got no responses.

In his memoirs, Gerald Sketchley describes Dad as "the most outstanding character in the camp at Muroran." It is with immense filial pride that I am quoting from his article to illustrate Dad's treatment of one of the brave men in his care. Sketchley begins with the horrendous daily dilemma facing Dad: "Among his other duties he had the onerous task of deciding which of several sick men must be chosen to make up our workforce! What a terrible job for him. I have seen men helped on their way out of the camp by their colleagues. What on earth they did to escape the *Hanchos* (foremen) on site I cannot imagine, or how they got through the day. As far as the camp officials were concerned they were happy since they had sent the full quota…The sick paraded every night after work; but there was little in the way of equipment. A talk with the medical people was always good for morale and they always did their best with what they had…While on the job of loading pig iron I developed *blind boils* on my back. The *Hancho* noticed that I was not working hard enough and started a tirade against me, "*mirru mirru*" I said pulling up my shirt to show him. "*Dammin dammi*" (you are a bad worker), he told me before hitting me with his stick. Thank goodness he didn't hit those boils!…I had an arrangement with the MO that as far as possible my boils would be lanced following an infrequent soak in the bath. When it came for treatment I was advised to "get set". I would spread my legs and grip a shelf. A pair of sharp pointed scissors would then be pushed into the boil to relieve the pressure. For a little time afterwards I would feel very sore and physically sick. While being treated one night a Nip medical student bent his head to watch my reaction. I was so angry that I barely felt the pain. I hope I looked inscrutable. I certainly tried!…In themselves, of course, the boils were not serious, but their effect in that forced labour camp could be quite devastating…I dreaded them more because I couldn't see them, but my friends kept me informed of their progress. They just seemed at the time to keep coming and coming, and most had to be lanced to allow me to work the next day…Our medical officer certainly did his best for us and we held him in the highest regard."[6]

The eighth man to die on Dad's watch was a young 27-year-old corporal, John Lumbers, of the 5th Suffolks on Thursday 9 March. Mitchell witnesses him keeling over opposite him at breakfast time and being carried to the medical room. His problem stemmed from ingesting a hard soya bean which had caused an abscess which had then burst[7]. Dad records the cause of death as haemoptysis due to tuberculosis. Along with others unnamed, he is allowed to accompany the body to the crematorium the next day but the lorry is stranded in the snow and the men are forced to carry the coffin over half a mile through deep drifts.

Mitchell is grateful for Dad's advice to the POWs to keep exercising all parts of the body during these particularly cold winter months. The signs to look for were pain in the body's exposed extremities giving way to a painless, translucent look with the possible onset of gangrene. The men's poor diet would have provided little protection against this horrific condition.

A new nationality, albeit a small group of five, arrives in Muroran from a camp on the Philippines on Monday 27 March '44. This party of American medical staff is led by Lt Max Andler. Although they were to have occasional differences, the two men developed enormous respect for each other and quickly became good friends. Coincidentally, Dad suffered a bout of rampant diarrhoea at the time of their arrival. Max was a neurosurgeon living in Los Angeles who subsequently attended Senator Robert (Bobby) Kennedy in hospital in 1968 as he lay dying following the assassination attempt on his life. Max was the only prisoner with whom Dad maintained regular contact after liberation. Our parents visited him and his wife Valeda at their home in Beverly Hills in the summer of 1967 when they toured America, and again some 10 years later. After his death, his widow published a compilation of the letters he wrote during captivity to his mother, brother, and a college friend[8].

Early in April, Max contracts fever which, by Monday 10 April, Dad suspects is typhoid. He is now "his nurse all day long". He makes a remarkable recovery and the bond between the two men grows. By the 20th, he is assisting Dad to fix up a man's broken collar bone, much to the admiration of the Japanese.

Pte Sidney Quarterman, 28, of the Royal Army Service Corps is the next to die on Friday 5 May. He had pulmonary oedema. Sadly, for the third time, Dad records in words totally devoid of any positivity "He wanted to die".

On a lighter note, the warmer late spring weather brings with it leisure activities such as baseball with the American medical orderlies. It is with some nostalgia that Dad recalls playing a similar game on the strand at Ranafast, presumably rounders, in front of an admiring Mum in 1929. There is even a game of football, a cross between rugby and American football, involving two Japanese sergeants and American and British POWs. Volleyball, table-tennis and putting the shot are also mentioned. '*Yasume*' days coincide with the occasional walk beyond the camp fences in the countryside for both officers and men.

The British and American MOs' relationship with the Dutch officers is put under strain when the latter insist on speaking in their own language in the officers' huts, a situation which is never totally resolved in Muroran. I have often accompanied my students on exchange visits to stay with families across northern Spain and those with less linguistic capacity can often feel that their exchange partners are talking about them in their own language. This can lead to some serious misreading of situations. I can well imagine the officers feeling uncomfortable when mixing with their bilingual Dutch counterparts speaking in their own language but can also appreciate the Dutch stance in all of this. Naturally they would have felt more comfortable communicating with each other in Dutch.

Amidst these slightly more relaxed conditions, a Scottish prisoner, Pte William Jardine, 32, of the Royal Army Service Corps, was the next to die on Monday 22 May. He had tuberculosis and his death Dad describes as "a happy release after six months in bed with fever every day."

One wonders yet again at the basic medical implements at their disposal when, five days later, Dad is assisted by Max in managing to sew back on a man's toe which was almost cut off after being crushed under pig iron in an accident at the works. On Monday 10 July, he successfully performs three lumbar punctures first time.

When I first read Dad's letters, I remember being struck at the Japanese cataloguing the characteristics of the officers in the camp. I had never heard of this in other camps but presumably it would have been a widespread procedure in getting an important handle on the personalities of the POW leaders. He tells Mum on Monday 24 July that they describe him as having "Great faith, but sometimes lacks harmony; eager for business but no humour." I think my siblings and I would agree with the first and third of these but would not recognise the second and fourth in our dad. Incidentally, the adjectives they ascribe to Max are "mild and prudent", and to Oswald Wynd, "good and co-operative."

The regular beatings continue, again overlooked by Hirate. A guard sergeant, Eiji Asari, owned a metal-studded belt which he used to whip prisoners about the face. He was tall and had scars across his own face which led to the men nicknaming him 'Al Capone' or 'Scar-face'[9]. His laughable defence at the War Trials states that he violated regulations for the POWs' "own good". His "incomplete education" led to his ignorance of the customs of foreigners[10]. He was sentenced to 25 years which would, again, have been dramatically reduced. A Japanese military doctor, Sgt

Tsutomi Shiba, in similar fashion to the other medical officer convicted of brutality, Sgt Araki, is described in Dad's affidavit on one occasion when "he lined up all the sick men of the camp in the snow and kept them on parade for two hours and beat everyone across the face. He said there were too many sick in the camp and did this to discourage sickness." Incredibly Shiba was sentenced to a mere five years of hard labour.

The eleventh fatality was a Welsh sapper from the Royal Engineers, 29-year-old Richard Richards. He had dysentery and died on Saturday 26 August. Two days later, Dad was again allowed to accompany the body to the local crematorium but this ironically burnt down in a fire the day after. Fortunately Richards' body was still intact and had not been cremated so a party including Dad, a Royal Army Medical Corps sergeant called Comber, Max, and another American MO, Sergeant Matuozzi, set out on the Wednesday to collect his remains in a lorry for cremation in the town's main crematorium. This was his first opportunity in 10 months to view the town as the journey took them along the coast to a building on top of a little hill that "ran down steeply to a pretty little cove". My pilgrimage to Hokkaido in 2017 indicated that this was probably Itanki Beach. As I stood for a few quiet moments by the shore line, I prayed for the souls of some Chinese prisoners whose bodies, I was told, were buried under the shale of this and similar beaches. The antipathy that continues to the present day towards their near neighbours was a feature of the Japanese of which I was unaware until my visit.

En route to the crematorium, Dad comments on his first sighting of a member of the indigenous Ainu people he had initially heard about back at Yakumo Camp. He spots a woman completely naked to the waist walking on the beach with a huge moustache tattooed across her upper lip. This was a feature of adult Ainu women.

As for the ceremony itself, he is fascinated by the chanting of the monks and the dull tolling of the temple bell accompanying the various cremations of Japanese citizens. A small bowl of rice is placed in front of each coffin, the atmosphere made heavier by the burning of incense. The small bleary-eyed Buddhist monk who greeted the party on their arrival bows deeply to them on their departure, a notable and humble gesture of respect in Japanese society. As the crow flies, it is a short journey back to the camp and the lorry takes a short cut through the factory while also passing a playground full of young boys parading in uniform. This leaves Dad despondent as does an entry on Saturday 7 October when he is permitted to bid farewell to Lt Wynd at the town's railway station where young girls are acting as porters and lifting heavy boxes.

At this point I should state that Dad never actually describes a cremation, only the accompanying of some of the bodies to the crematorium. A copy of a letter given to me in Japan and written by C.E.A. Ripley, the British consul in Tokyo in 1986 and an ex POW, reveals the logistics behind the recovery of the men's ashes: "We always left the barrel (this would have contained the corpse crushed into the foetal position as described in chapter 6 by Mitchell) outside one of the doors [of the crematorium], a few days later we would return for the ashes and take them to a Buddhist temple and hand them over to the monks." Presumably the urns would have all been collected before the departure from Muroran.

In typically modest fashion, Dad's letter on Tuesday 5 September '44 devotes a mere two lines to Max's and his successful attempt at curing the hysterical paralysis of Welsh aircraftman C. Price of the RAF. This was by no means an isolated case at the time and reflected the mind-set of some of the men who could no longer face the hard labour of the iron and steelworks. Max goes into more extensive detail about their 'alternative' treatment for paralysis in his letter written on 10 September[11] involving pressurising certain nerve centres, poking the man's backside, and slapping him across the back of the legs. The two doctors then position themselves at opposite corners of the room to force the patient to walk from one to the other. In his abridged 1988 version of the diary, Dad makes two interesting asides. The first is of Pte David Marshall's appalled observation through a window of the procedure undergone by his Welsh friend. (Dad and Mum visited David and his wife Jean in Singapore in 1977. The bill for their accommodation at Raffles Hotel was generously paid for by David. Carl and Mum subsequently visited the couple in 1995 and, along with my sister, I had the enormous pleasure of meeting Jean and her son Jonathan in 2017 in her home in Singapore.) The second and more poignant point Dad makes is of the many Dutch POWs lying paralysed in the makeshift hospital. They are subsequently stretchered out of the final camp at liberation.

The mistrust between the two nationalities would not have made for sharing best medical practice but the fundamental differences in attitude towards their Japanese captors is far more revealing in Dad's liberation questionnaire. I am indebted to Ken Hewitt who is compiling a detailed history of the Leicestershires for showing me the form on his lap top during an interval at the Researching FEPOW History Group's 5th International Conference at the Liverpool School of Tropical Medicine in 2015. Of course I recognised Dad's immaculately neat handwriting straightaway but my tears prevented me from deciphering the five concluding lines until Ken kindly forwarded me the link the following week. This is what Dad wrote: "British troops behaved magnificently. They persistently refused to do any skilled or technical work for the Japs unlike their Dutch fellow prisoners. They preferred doing heavy labouring jobs in appalling climatic and working conditions rather than help the Japs in any expert capacity. They were baited with extra food and better conditions but they refused. Their morale was always high." His explicit observation of the survival instinct at all costs of the Dutch POWs does not at first sight appear to be confirmed by the statistics compiled by the POW Research Network Japan which lists the deaths of 13 British and 40 Dutch at Hakodate Branch Camp 1-B (the name given to Muroran)[12]. However, apart from one death in May '45, all the Dutch fatalities take place prior to the arrival of the main contingency of British prisoners in October '43. The better diet and reduced manual labour for the Dutch from this time onwards must have contributed to this dramatic drop in their casualty rate. On the other hand, in correspondence with my guide Taeko two years after my visit to Japan, she gives an alternative explanation for the figures in that more favourable treatment was given by the Japanese to the original occupants of any of the camps. She illustrates this by giving the example of Sumidagawa Camp in Tokyo where American and British POWs fared better than the Dutch and Canadians who were later arrivals. Although Dad's concluding remarks in no way detract from the men's refusal to 'kow-tow' to the Japanese, there is no doubting the old adage of there being 'two sides to every story'. I should point out, in passing, that one British death at Muroran is recorded before the new influx, that of Cpl George Smith of the RAF on Wednesday 10 March '43. Dysentery was the killer yet again.

The two most frequent questions I am asked by friends as I write this book are firstly how did Dad manage to hide his letters from the Japanese and secondly how can the low death rate be explained. The former we should have quizzed Dad about long before his passing in 1993 but alas we never did. As for the latter, 19 of the most seriously ill men were moved back to the main camp at Hakodate on Tuesday 19 September '44.

In addition to Dad's many other roles in the camp which included the supervision of food distribution at meal times and lay chaplain, he would have been acutely aware of the need to maintain personal hygiene, albeit in the most appalling conditions. Mitchell recounts the story of him as sanitary inspector one cold *yasume* day in the winter of '44/'45 ordering all the men to take it in turns for two minutes each to break up the frozen mass of excrement under the 12 *benjos* (toilets) adjacent to the British huts[13].

Beatings such as that of the aforementioned Comber for stealing a sheet on Friday 10 November were extended to the whole camp by forcing the men to parade in the snow for 90 minutes. Mitchell adds that medicines made available to the medical staff would be withdrawn if camp rules were infringed, a most vindictive way of Japanese authority being imposed.

It is around this time that Dad becomes friendly with two new arrivals, an Indian from Malabar called Krish Nair of the RAF, and a Dutch POW, George Reuneker. One of only four photographs I have seen taken inside the camp is explained by the fact that they were all carefully used for propaganda purposes. It shows Dad dressed as Santa Claus in his cotton wool beard on an improvised stage giving out prizes at the end of a Christmas pantomime in December '44. Mitchell recalls a few rousing choruses of 'Aye aye yippi yippi aye', a firm favourite of the Japanese guards who are also in attendance. One wonders if any attempts were made to adapt the lyrics to the occasion! Dad generously gives his copy of the photo to Reuneker later the following month while Paddy is gifted the group photo of the pantomime cast.

New Year's Day '45 is a Monday when the snow falls constantly all day. Dad has no need to improvise a speech to the men as he is handed one to be read out by Hirate. It is both fascinating and a source of immense pride to quote from Mitchell's description: "Couched in stilted, formal English, this document ordered us to be obedient prisoners, to honour Emperor Hirohito, to work hard and well for the Nipponese Greater East Asia Co-Prosperity Sphere, to forget our homes and our loyalties to our own countries, and so on, and on, and on. Major Murray read this nonsense in a loud clear voice, without faltering, apparently telling us again and again to forget homes and families and to commit treason against our homelands. With the camp commandant and the Nip interpreter standing immediately alongside him the MO had had little choice but to comply with their order. We stood in stunned silence and heard him through to the bitter end. Doc Murray, of all people, could not possibly have gone *Nip-happy*. At last he came to the end of the diatribe. He paused and looked around the assembly and added in an even louder voice: You will *not* do any of these things! This defiance echoed back from the hillside behind the camp and was greeted by gasps of amazement, and then by laughter and shouts of approval. Neither Lt Hirate nor the [new] interpreter had been able to follow the reading and they were obviously non-plussed when we laughed and cheered the Major. He had taken a risk, but it was a smaller one than if he had refused to co-operate. Had he refused we would most certainly have lost him. This way our greatest asset, the excellent British MO and senior officer, was not taken out of circulation"[14]. It was indeed fortunate that Hirate, a French scholar at Osaka Foreign Language School (now Osaka University), had, along with his interpreter, a poor grasp of English. Whatever the reason for not making an example of Dad after this, he was able to proudly boast to Mum at liberation that he had never saluted a Japanese officer. A throwback to his days in the army came in my early-years right through to adolescence and beyond when he used to give me a salute when confirming something was OK. I became accustomed to this gesture in the privacy of the family home but, curiously, seldom associated it with his time in the army.

He rarely, if only briefly, complains of feeling unwell but a frost-bitten right thumb nail he gets on Thursday 8 February '45 is the one physical manifestation that as children we all remember. This is a particularly cold month with blizzards and gales as the norm and a brief entry the day before shows his morale at its lowest: "My own darling, I know now that if I am not a free man in a few months' time I shall never see home again – what an awful thought, Eileen. To think that I might never see you or home again. Good night and God bless you, Eileen." He does derive comfort in the midst of his pessimism by Mum's promise to return to Lough Derg on pilgrimage. Each of our parents visited St Patrick's Sanctuary on the lake on 11 separate occasions, Dad six and Mum five. On Carl's tape-recording Dad reminisces about his parents meeting each other for the first time around the turn of the 19th century on the platform at nearby Pettigo Railway Station, the traditional arrival and departure point for pilgrims right up until its closure in 1957.

As news of Japanese reversals in the war spreads round the camp (mainly through Dutch Ensign Jan Jongsma who operated a secret radio and also translated Japanese newspapers), Dad orders the men to each set aside two tins of meat from the latest Red Cross parcels in the event of a mass break-out[15]. Better they make a run for it than be lined up and shot.

This was the POWs' expectation of their captors.

Dad enjoys the daily stimulation of conversations with Nair and Reuneker and is impressed by a wonderful essay the latter has written about Asia. He describes him as a dreamer and an idealist and would have been drawn to George as a kindred spirit in those far off days when he dreamt of freedom for an Irish nation.

On Monday 26 February a British POW returns to the camp at 10 a.m. with a badly crushed right foot. Max and Dad are astonished to hear that their request to treat Tommy Kime from the Royal Artillery at a hospital in the city is granted. This is more likely due to the interest on the part of the Japanese medical staff in the operation which is observed by four or five doctors and nine nurses[16]. The small white surgical gowns prove a tight fit and, although Max manages to put on the wooden block slippers, they do not fit Dad and he stays in bare feet throughout on the wet tile floor of the operating room. He administers the spinal anaesthetic and assists Max who eventually decides against amputating any of the toes.

The real drama occurs on the journey back to camp at 2.30 p.m. when one of the three wheeled motorbikes overturns on a snowy bend and Dad lands on his head in a four-foot-deep canal and is momentarily unconscious. The others who include an American MO, Sgt Stevens, as well as the patient himself, escape with minor bruises. Max inserts two stitches in Dad's head-wound back at the camp. As for the motorbike, a crowd of some 50 Japanese school children assist in pulling it out of the ditch before the driver uses a hammer to knock the fender back in place.

On Friday 18 May a Cpl Porter has his chicken pox diagnosed as a potentially deadly case of smallpox. The projected move to another camp in the interior of the island is now postponed as two weeks of quarantine are imposed while Porter is moved to a Japanese hospital in the city. To fill the long days, Dad takes on yet another role in the camp, this time of PT instructor, for two half-hour sessions at 5.30 a.m. and 1 p.m. He conducts this from one of the two watch towers and the fact that there are 420 men exercising indicates that some of the Dutch are also included. However, his comment to Mum on Tuesday 22 May reveals an anxiety that is gnawing away at him: "Still examining the men daily. I am the most dangerous contact in camp because I handled the patient up to the last moment of leaving camp. It was my duty – I could not ever be afraid of any disease." [As I write, such sentiments are particularly poignant in these times of the Covid-19 pandemic when health workers throughout the world selflessly expose themselves on a daily basis to the virus.] Pte Finucane of the RAMC who replaces his erstwhile batman, Stephen 'Paddy' McElligott, remains in Muroran with Porter. The patient eventually recovers and they re-join their comrades at the fourth camp on 18 July[17], unlike the last two POWs to die on Dad's watch who are killed in the most tragic of circumstances on Sunday 3 June.

Mitchell states that it was an unusually wet day with a cold, westerly gale. The men are ordered by the Japanese to remove furniture and stores from the camp in preparation for their departure to a new camp two days later. This involves the relatively short walk via an unfenced level crossing towards railway wagons in a siding of the steelworks. Cpl Alec Angell, 29, of the 1st Battalion the Cambridgeshire Regiment, and Warrant Officer Edward Durrant, 43, of the 2nd Battalion, are at the front of a small column of men, no doubt with their shoulders hunched and their collars up, waiting for the passing of a long goods train on the far line towards the west. The noise of both this train and the wind combine with their stooped posture under the weight of goods and their facing away from the direction of the wind and driving rain to prevent them from hearing or seeing an eastbound passenger train. It swings round the shoulder of the hill on the near line heading for Muroran's main station and crashes into the men. Multiple injuries to Angell's body mean there is nothing that Lt Andler can do to save him. Such is the force of the impact on Durrant that he is catapulted into the adjacent canal where the rescue party, which includes Dad, wades through the muddy waters for almost an hour before discovering the gruesomely decapitated body[18].

Mitchell goes on to say that Dad makes a strong protest to Hirate at the lack of guard supervision but that the commandant, incredibly, views the cause of the deaths as suicide[19]. There is no mention of the latter in Dad's letters though I am sure he wanted to keep the horrific details brief. The 1988 version, however, despite his anger, makes no reference to the camp commandant's ludicrous interpretation of the event.

There is a small assembly hall at the southern end of the camp where Dad conducts the funeral service the next day for the two men in front of all the British POWs. Two crudely made deal coffins decorated with spring flowers contain the corpses and Mitchell describes the ceremony as "simple but moving"[20]. A few hymns are sung as the men remove their caps and the bodies are loaded on to a lorry for the journey to the crematorium.

NOTES

1. *This extract is taken from the US National Archives' GHQ/SCAP records. The 'Supreme Commander' was General Douglas MacArthur. The section related to south-east Asia was copied onto microfilm by Japan's National Diet Library and made public, possibly in the 1980s. The testimonies of thousands of POWs have been transcribed from interviews and are of particular interest to researchers as the Japanese burnt all POW camp records at the end of the war. Taeko Sasamoto, my guide in Japan, made several records available to me.*

2. **Forty-two Months in Durance Vile** *by R. Keith Mitchell, p.158.*

3. *As above p.145.*

4. *Visit www.wakefield.gov.uk/libraries-and-local-history/local-and-family-history/we-will-remember-them/stories/south-elmsall/ernest-glover*

5. *Mitchell incorrectly dates the photograph which he reproduces in his book as December 1943.*

6. *Imperial War Museum, London, ref.7770 The Captive Guest by G.A. Sketchley, pp.57-58.*

7. *Mitchell, p.187.*

8. **Letters Home, A Reflection of a Man's Survival**, **Maxwell M Andler Jr., M.D.**, *edited by Valeda Andler (The Center Press 2005).*

9. *Mitchell p.151.*

10. *Yokohama Reviews, University of California, Berkeley War Crimes Studies Centre, ref. Sergeant Eiji Asari.*

11. *As in 8 above,* **Letters Home,** *pp.110-111.*

12. *For detailed lists of Japanese POW camps, visit www.mansell.com*

13. *Mitchell p.220.*

14. *As above pp.212-213.*

15. *As above p.221.*

16. *As in 8 above,* **Letters Home** *pp.155-156.*

17. *Mitchell p.249.*

18. *My interpretation of this terrible tragedy is based on a combination of Dad's diary entry, his 1988 abridged version, Mitchell p.234, and Andler p.168, together with my own observations when I visited the level crossing in October 2017.*

19. *Mitchell p.235.*

20. *Mitchell p.235.*

CHAPTER 8

"HOKKAIDO – FOURTH CAMP NISHI ASHIBETSU/RAIJO, FIFTH CAMP UTASHINAI, SIXTH CAMP AKABIRA"

Wednesday 15 August 1945 (Assumption). "The Emperor made a speech at noon today and oh it meant a lot....Darling, I diagnosed that the war was over! Oh what wonderful news if it is true."

The date of Angell and Durrant's funeral coincides with the departure of all the Dutch and 30 British POWs. On Tuesday 5 June, the remaining prisoners leave Hakodate Camp 1B for the last time. It is 4.40 a.m. and their march to the city's main railway station inevitably takes them past the scene of the terrible accident. Dad describes the journey to Ashibetsu as dull with the blinds deliberately lowered, presumably so as not to give the men any idea of their surroundings. However, their mood must also have been so sombre as they reflect on the needless deaths of their two companions. He ascribes the adjective "terrific" to the size of the crowds at the station to "greet" them, in stark contrast to the mocking animosity the men had encountered at Aomori before they crossed over to Hokkaido two years before. A much more basic train which reminds him of the Lough Swilly Narrow Gauge transports the men to the smaller town of Nishi (literally west) Ashibetsu. As already mentioned in my prologue, all accounts I have read of their final camp use this name which makes for confusion as the town has its own POW camp which is officially numbered 4B. As a lover of nature, Dad felt much more at ease in the beautifully wooded surroundings of Hokkaido's interior as the men tramp the three miles up the Ashibetsu River together with four horses and carts carrying the heavier goods. Their final destination is Raijo and the wooden bridge is duly crossed.

Although the air is fresher, Dad is concerned by the latrines and work places as they are positioned indoors while Max complains about the only source of water as being 150 yards outside the camp. This necessitated the arduous task of each detail of men taking an hour to fetch water for the preparation of one meal. The management of bath time is an even more daunting task.

I would be surprised if it wasn't Dad who ordered the excavation of a deep latrine trench. He first refers to it on Thursday 21 June and takes his turn over the following four days until the cover of the pit is completed. The work proves even more arduous in rainy conditions and stretches down to seven feet before the men hit rocks. He seeks sympathy from Mum by describing his "tiny hands" as "blistered". Mitchell's sketch of the camp shows the latrines at the back of the camp beyond the hut that houses mainly the British POWs[1].

The heavier daily work involved the walk back downstream to the coal mines at Nishi Ashibetsu, the site also of a Chinese POW camp. There was, however, lighter work at Raijo consisting of clearing the immediate undergrowth in preparation for planting seeds but this was basically a waste of time as the season was too far advanced for an autumn harvest. I recently revisited an online account by another Irish POW, Joseph Dunne[2], who was detailed to join the gardening squad. He describes food rations as being "at an all-time low" and expands this by saying "In desperation the cooks added mulberry leaves and dandelion to make up the morning and evening stews. Lunch was a bowl of rice sprinkled with fish flakes."

A change of camp makes no difference to the Japanese insistence that the sick are made to work. On Monday 18 June Dad is unspecific about "more trouble" that he faces by refusing to send sick men to work and, as usual, those that need what little nourishment is available are on half rations. (Point 8 of the 10 that Dad makes in his affidavit after the war is worth quoting here: "Anyone not working for the Japs e.g. medical orderlies, sick men, shoe repairers etc. received far less food than the normal working parties. This was particularly hard on the sick, especially hospital cases who needed the extra food.") Is it the defiant stance that he takes in standing up for the sick that leads to his sudden transfer to a fifth camp only three weeks after the move to the interior? Max's same request the previous month to be transferred to another camp where more medical work is available[3] is met with the response that other camps have more MOs than the current one. Therefore it would be highly questionable if Dad's medical experience was required elsewhere. As he is the only prisoner to be transferred, is his removal, rather, a punishment? In another of his recorded interviews, Carl visited Dr Andler in his home in California in the summer of 1995. The thing that most stands out from his conversation with Dad's old friend is Max's belief that "he [Dad] refused to go along with some experiments that the Japanese lieutenant medical officer tried to carry out." This begs the question what could these have been?

Whatever the reason, he hastily makes preparations for departure at one hour's notice. It is Tuesday 26 June. Not surprisingly, it is a move tinged with great emotion as he has been with the majority of the British POWs since the voyage on the hellship two years before. Those that are in the camp at midday line up to shake his hand and back down the valley at Nishi Ashibetsu the men in the mine break loose and climb out to add their goodbyes. His reaction is brief: "It broke me up." I cannot imagine how lonely he must have felt, especially when he is now deprived of the two notable friendships with Krish and George. Two days before, he relishes the challenge of helping to teach Reuneker English and talks to Mum in glowing terms of someone in a camp to whom he can open his heart.

Fortunately his fifth camp, Utashinai Camp 3B, is only a short distance away and he has met many of the 150 British troops before in Changi. He describes the camp as "a foul place – stinking and in a hollow" and doesn't even bother to identify it for Mum. The men work in a coal mine beside the camp. It is four days before his kit arrives with his precious diary still undiscovered. He is unspecific about how he "goes for" a guard who is beating up an American POW on the evening of Friday 29 June. Perhaps this is an indication that he feels he can verbally or, indeed, physically confront his captors now the war is nearing its end.

Only 12 days pass before he is moved yet again (and once more on his own) to the last of the six camps. Akabira Camp 2b is a short two kilometres away. It is Saturday 7 July. The majority of the POWs are British, 167, and the remainder American, 114. The former include four RAMC orderlies. There is also a Capt. Lynch from the Royal Canadian Army Medical Corps. Dad is now the senior officer in the camp as confirmed on the website of the North China Marines[4]. As at Utashinai, the men are slave labourers in the mines. He is encouraged by the news they bring from their previous camps in Hong Kong, Shanghai and Peking of Japanese reversals. One week later he has dramatic evidence of this as all the men are confined to a barrack room all day because of American air raids.

On Monday 23 July he puts six stitches in a head wound of an American POW, Corporal Timpany, who is injured in a mining accident. He gets on well with the Americans who are generous with their gifts of clothing to the British as more of their supplies arrive daily. On Tuesday 7 August he censors his one line account of volunteering to break into a store in the camp the night before to retrieve an American secret radio by writing about it to Mum in Irish: "*Oídche indé chuaidh mé isteach ins an seómra agus stole an radió.*" (Fluent Irish speakers will recognise the anglicisms but there is more than enough for Mum to get the gist. It translates as "Last night I went into the room and stole the radio.")[5] In the reflective 1988 version of the diary, he retells the drama in more detail. After dark, he crawls along the floor and, following detailed instructions and with several Americans on the look-out for any passing sentries, finds it carefully concealed at the bottom of a trunk. The whole incident would have made riveting listening for our young minds but I don't recall Dad ever recounting to us such a daring deed. There must have been subsequent transmission problems as no news is forthcoming of the dropping of the atomic bombs on Hiroshima and Nagasaki.

The first inkling that anything has happened comes at noon on Wednesday 15 August when the camp commandant, Jiro Tendo, and the guards gather round their radio to hear Emperor Hirohito make a speech. Another senior officer, Capt. Francis, and Dad are then summoned to the office to be told that the mine work would cease forthwith due to a typhus epidemic in the district. Ever one for exercising his wit, Dad "diagnoses" that the war is over. I am indebted to Vicki Hamilton, the daughter of the British POW Pte Rowland Nelson, who shared her father's diary with me, for his account of the event: "He said he [Dad] felt immediately that there was something funny about the typhus excuse for he said it is a winter disease caused by crowded louse-bound conditions and under-nourishment, it was impossible for it to be present in that part of Japan in the middle of August." Nelson trusts Dad's interpretation of the order. The previous morning Dad had aspirated fluid from his chest to alleviate the most serious symptoms of his pleurisy. News of the Japanese surrender quickly spreads round the camp.

There is a dramatic change in conditions for the men. Dad would not have been alone in suddenly receiving mail from home. He gets four cards from Mum dating back to before Christmas. Vitamins are available daily as are Red Cross parcels. On Sunday the 19th the medical office and store are handed over to him and, as a result of his indictment of the Japanese medical staff, they disappear from the camp. The 21st brings official confirmation that the war is over but all he wants is for Mum to have news that he is safe. On the 24th, there are unfurling ceremonies of

61

the Union Jack and the Stars and Stripes as well as gusty renderings of God Save the Queen and the Star Spangled Banner. Bizarrely, Tendo calls for a toast with sake wine to which all bar one man agree and the return of the popular erstwhile second commander of all the camps on the island, Lt Colonel Shigeo Emoto, to address the men is warmly greeted. This too may appear perplexing but the background to this remarkable anglophile and English-speaking Japanese officer is one to which I will devote a full chapter.

Rowland and Dad disagree on the casualty numbers crushed by the dropping of food, clothing and medical supplies from American B29s. Aerial reconnaissance photographs taken by aircraft from the USS *Hehenta* [Nehenta] Bay on 10 September 1945[6] show a fascinating outline of the camp with the fast flowing Sorachi River forming a natural barrier on one side. The decision to reduce fatalities by placing POW signs on the far bank leads to some of the men having to swim across to retrieve the drops. They get into difficulty and find themselves stranded by the current on the far bank. The dramatic diary entry for Wednesday 29 August includes our dad as one of the rescue team: "I volunteered to swim across with three other boys with a line. We reached them in spite of the terrifically strong current; however the line broke and I was swept downstream with another boy clinging to the line. Can you imagine such force which made it impossible to hold on to the line? All this time I was filling up with water! I just made the near bank in the nick of time – exhausted."

NOTES

1. See Mitchell, p.240.

2. See www.jbdunne.co.za

3. **Letters Home, Maxwell M Andler, Jr.**, p.163.

4. See www.northchinamarines.com/id28.htm This website includes a photo of a group of American POWs, among whom is Timpany, taken at Akabira Camp.

5. The POW diary section of my brother's website contains the transcript of several other occasions from June '44 onwards when our dad used Irish to prevent his captors from deciphering what he was writing.

6. See note 4 above.

CHAPTER 9

"LIBERATION AND JOURNEY HOME"

"I shall be like a fish out of water for some time, but you will understand as you always do. You have been my guiding star and you always will be."

Manila, Sunday 23 September 1945

A brief return for the day to his men at Raijo on Saturday 1 September brings a great welcome and shaking of hands all round. Hirate's insistence via a sergeant he dispatches to Akabira that Dad be transferred back to Raijo results in a permanent return the next day. Efforts to ingratiate themselves with the ex-prisoners by the Mitsui Mining Company after whom the Nishi Ashibetsu Railway Station is also named include invitations to Dad, Max, Krish and Capt. Borski, the senior Dutch officer, to dinner at the company's club in the town. This was by no means exclusive to this select group as evidenced by a photo taken on 20 August of another group of Australian and American officers outside the same venue[1]. On another occasion Hirate bizarrely presents each officer with a present of a picture in a red lacquer frame. This is one detail that leaves me flabbergasted. It is as if he is officiating at a passing out ceremony and the officers are rewarded for completing the course. The whereabouts of the frame that none of my siblings or I have ever seen is unknown, an indication perhaps of what Dad thought of the so-called gift.

One gift that Dad would certainly have welcomed comes from Medical Sgt Umeki. This officer who gives Dad a fan was appointed to Muroran in the February and moved camps with the POWs to Raijo. Significantly, he speaks good English and would have endeared himself to Dad by telling him his best friend hailed from Belfast. His background is that of a ballet dancer in Tokyo. Mitchell says that he became a valuable friend and adds that he was born and brought up in San Francisco. He definitely does not fit the profile of any other Japanese officer in the camp and, in fact, is one of only two who, whether by choice or invitation, pose in Raijo for a photo with the British, American and Dutch medical staff on Monday 3 September. It is Umeki who purchases a 700 yen Samurai sword for Dad in a visit to Sapporo with Max. As children, we used to stare at it on the wall in the hallway of our home in Belfast, never daring to unsheathe it for fear of the dreadful consequences of severing one of our limbs! (It was, however, used by burglars one night to cut a panel out of a solid wooden door of a downstairs room in our home.) A number of group photos are taken that day which, as well as giving a wonderful impression of the joy of the liberated men, also offer a vivid picture of the lush surroundings of inland Hokkaido.

On the Wednesday at 5 p.m. Dad is the centre of attention when he is presented with a giant scroll of tribute by the 350 British and five American POWs. He calls it "the proudest moment of my life". To this day it is the most treasured possession in our family. Below is the wording on the scroll whose original size measures 70 cms by 50 cms. (The "absence" referred to in the opening paragraph is explained by the fact that the wording was composed at a time when the men did not know if they would be reacquainted with Dad.)

Dear Major Murray,

In this moment of release from the purgatory of Japanese incarceration, we feel your absence and wish you were here to share our happiness as you shared our want and humiliation till seven weeks ago, when you were removed from this camp.

The great majority of us have known you for over three years-since the "Mucky"Maru of May 1943. You were our only Medical Officer at the Prisoner of War Camps at Hakodate, at Yakumo and during the worst period at Muroran. Since early last year you have been Officer Commanding British and American Prisoners of War and Senior Medical Officer at Muroran and here. During these two years - the blackest period of our lives - you were at all times and in all places a genuine friend to each and all of us.

Your quiet and indomitable struggle for our health and welfare in the face of obstructive and often vicious Japanese inhumanity; your tenacity in carrying on though it fell to you at times to watch, helpless, the suffering and dying for want of food and simple but essential medicines and surgical instruments; your dignity in dealing with the Japanese and patience with their interfering swashbuckling medical orderlies; the tonic of your dry humour which exorcised any tendency to self-pity; your extraordinary memory and intimate knowledge of every one of sometimes more than one hundred men; your ability to maintain discipline, without force to back you, in very trying living conditions, your understanding of and forbearance with the occasional aberrations of some of us, which we now sincerely regret; the reforms you introduced and vigilantly enforced to ensure honest distribution of the little food and Red Cross supplies available, the utilisation of your private funds for the benefit of the sick; your unwearying patience with each of us according to his needs; all this, and much else, we shall never forget.

Many of us would not be alive at this happy moment but for your care; from the point of view of health all of us owe you more than we can express. You have been an inspiration to everyone and to very many of us a source of spiritual refreshment and courage.

Whatever wider recognition you may, as we hope, ultimately receive, we all, the men of the British Navy, Army, Air Force and Mercantile Marine and the American Army now in this camp want you to know that [it] is with feelings of profound gratitude, respect and affection that we say

God Bless You, Sir

Nisi-Asibetu. Japan.

August 1945

Sketchley remarks that the presentation "was in recognition of his general concern for our welfare as shown by his outspoken confrontations with the Japanese Camp Commandant."[2] Max had received a similarly ornate scroll containing the signatures of all the men in a ceremony two weeks before. A third tribute to the Dutch went not to Capt. Borski, their CO, but to Ensign Jan Jongsma in recognition of his invaluable role in keeping the camp informed about the progress of the war through his secret radio and the theft of the occasional Japanese newspaper. Max identified the talented calligrapher as an unnamed British cook whom he had previously chided but it was not until years later that we were to discover the author of the incredibly moving tributes to the three officers. A recent analysis by Carl of the signatures of the British POWs accompanying Dad's tribute has thrown up the strong probability that the calligraphic was produced by a British prisoner from the Royal Army Ordnance Corps called Harry Southall.

On Friday 7 September Dad makes the first of four visits to the Chinese POW Camp at Nishi Ashibetsu. He is appalled by the conditions and writes "Those poor creatures were so glad to see us." Sketchley, who must have worked down at the adjacent mines, refers to the ritual of corpses being removed on stretchers held at shoulder height by fellow inmates. Dad demands that the camp be handed over immediately to the Chinese officers. Sgt Eric Davies' daughter, Elizabeth Hallett, provided me with her father's diary with its startling statement that 30 per cent of their prisoners died in the previous 18 months. No Red Cross medicines had been released. Thirty British POWs return to the camp the next day with clothing, canned meat, cigarettes, sweets and other supplies which are duly unloaded in the camp square to the absolute delight of the inmates. Dad visits their hospital with dressings and medicines and "fixed them up as best I could." He ensures that all remaining food from the Raijo Camp store in addition to old British Army greatcoats are given to the Chinese before the Allied soldiers leave the camps in the area. He comments that the Japanese were "furious" at this generous gesture towards foreign nationals who they treated with contempt.

He takes immense pleasure from the ceremony on Saturday 8 September as the Chinese, now resplendent in their uniforms, officially take over the camp: "Then we had the flag ceremony when 400 Chinese in perfect order lined up with their officers and NCOs in front; 30 British with myself in front. All saluted as the flag was slowly hoisted. Chinese then sang their national anthem; gave three cheers. All were then dismissed amid great jubilation." In highlighting the abject conditions of the Allied POWs, the fate of the Chinese and Korean prisoners in their camps in Japan is often overlooked. (I have not mentioned that there was a Korean camp opposite the one at Yakumo). These prisoners were often subjected to even greater brutalised treatment. In October '46, Dad would have been so pleased to receive a letter from Ki San Lee, the Chief of the General Affairs Section of the local Hakodate Branch of the Chinese Association, thanking him for his efforts in contributing towards the regaining of health of the former Chinese POWs, most of whom had returned to their homes in China.

I find Sketchley's description of his departure from Raijo particularly poignant: "As we walked slowly up that mountain, I turned to look back on the camp. Now silent and damaged on the outside, [this may be a reference to the air drops of relief supplies] it still represented for me a former lifestyle of horror. I wanted to hurriedly get away in case it proved to be just another of the thousand 'freedoms' I had experienced at night as a POW – dreams of home which could, on the instant, change to dreadful nightmares." [3]

Reciprocal help is supplied by 200 former Chinese prisoners on Dad's longed-for day of departure from Raijo, Wednesday 12 September, as they assist in the loading of supplies initially by truck before the train journey to Chitose Aerodrome near Sapporo. Dad is in the lead truck with British and American flags flying in an evident gesture of triumph. "Oh what a wonderful feeling this is now. I am really *free* at last." Photos taken at the airfield by a Lt Edmunds of the Royal Marines show our smiling dad though it is a shock to see his uniform hanging limply from his body. He now weighs nine stone (57 kilos), a startling loss of over a quarter of his weight during his 42 months of captivity. Six American pressmen surround him to ask "awkward questions which I was forbidden to answer" (1988 version of the diary). Incredibly, also in attendance are Hirate and some of the guards as well as the subdued-looking figure of Lt Colonel Tokuro Hosoi, Emoto's successor, appointed in May as high commandant of all the Hokkaido camps. A huge plane transports Dad on his inaugural flight along with 40 others to Yokohama. In dry humour so typical of him, he writes "Men were vomiting all over the place but the trip left me unmoved!"

It takes nearly two months for him to complete his circumnavigation of the world with stops in Okinawa and Manila, a traverse of the Pacific on HMS *Glory* via Honolulu to Victoria in western Canada, and a short stay, in Dad's case, with the family of Helene Rae in Vancouver in order to build up his reserves of strength. Sketchley writes that he too was 'farmed out' to another family in the city. Eventually he crosses the Atlantic from New York on the *Queen Mary*. The ship docks at Southampton, the same port from which he had embarked almost six years before. It is Sunday 18 November.

Mum has waited patiently until letters arrive, frequently months after being written. Those far-off days, years before the invention of social media and instant communication, are virtually impossible to appreciate in the tech-savvy age of the 21st century. News of his status as a POW did not reach her until a full seven months after the event and one letter from her he ruefully remarks has taken 18 months to come! Often word has got back to each other through tenuous contacts with intermediaries such as priests and chaplains or friends who also have a relative who is a POW. The painful uncertainty must have been unbearable for all the prisoners and their loved ones.

A cheque from him posted days before the fall of Singapore has enabled her to buy a three-stone diamond engagement ring. The visual bond between them is eventually maintained through an exchange of a few black and white 'snaps' (photographs) though the only one Dad had when he first went to the Far East was one given to him by his sister Una who appears with Mum and the rest of the team in the camogie kit of St Mary's Teacher Training College in Belfast. Mum resigns her post as a geography teacher at the Loreto Convent School in Omagh to do "office work" during the academic year '42/'43. It is only after the war that she reveals to Dad that this was in fact postal censorship, a job she confided in us subsequently that she absolutely despised.

In an amusing turn of phrase, Mum responds romantically to Dad's "fish out of water" simile in a reply that October: "Well darling, if that is the case we shall take two headers into the water together." She also was a strong swimmer and this seemed a most appropriate image given their mutual love of sports. In a further letter written by her during his crossing of the Atlantic, she takes advice from a recently repatriated prisoner from Hong Kong to Omagh, a Sgt Tommy Cunningham of the RAMC, not to journey to Southampton for their great reunion. He describes the scenes at the port as "pathetic" as families chaotically attempt to find their men. Apart from this, travel for civilians in England he terms as "impossible".

Mum receives three offers of a lift to Larne to meet the ferry from Stranraer and accepts the one from Dad's best friend, Gerry McGuinness. It is Tuesday 20 November 1945. In his reflective summary of the diary written 40 years later, he vividly recaptures the moment thus: "and there on the dock she stood. When I had disembarked we ran with arms outstretched and cried with joy in that wonderful embrace. At last I was home; and here in my arms was the one person who made my home-coming possible. It was Eileen's love, her faith and prayers, her steadfastness that gave me hope in my direst moments as a POW; I could never have survived without her."

Postscript: On 27 October 2013, Jan and I were privileged to attend a service at the Church of St Michael the Archangel in Southampton prior to a short parade down French Street to Town Quay Car Park near the docks where a black granite memorial plaque was unveiled to commemorate those who survived the war and returned across the Atlantic to dock at Southampton. The order of service included a moving address by FEPOW Maurice Naylor CBE, formerly of the 135th Field Regiment:

"Sixty-eight years ago, in the period between October and December 1945, over 38,000 Far East prisoners of war and civilian internees arrived

back in Southampton and Liverpool to the sound of ships' sirens and the cheers of multitudes of well-wishers. I was one of the POWs and the welcome is one of my fondest memories.

We had endured, for most of three and a half years, appalling conditions of untreated disease, neglect and brutality. Sadly we had left behind 12,500 or more of our comrades and fellow prisoners who died during their captivity.

Those of us who survived, and our families, then had to contend with the long-term physical, mental and emotional effects of captivity; many died prematurely as a result. There are not many of us left now to tell the tale and soon there will be none.

I feel very strongly that the FEPOWs who suffered and died and those who also suffered but managed, against all the odds, to survive, and their families, should not be forgotten."

The memorials to the survivors at Southampton and the Pier Head in Liverpool, along with the recognition Maurice gives to the role of their families in helping them come to terms with their ordeals at the hands of the Japanese, put me in mind of the uplifting Howard Goodall musical composition *Eternal Light A Requiem* which he composed in 2008 "to provide solace to the grieving". Coincidentally, as I write these words, my choir is rehearsing Brahms' *Requiem* which Goodall goes on to compare to his own work in that they both offer "a Requiem for the living, addressing their suffering and endurance, a Requiem focusing on the consequences of interrupted lives."[4] Maurice sadly died on 17 October 2019.

The birth of his five children and later his three grandsons as well as his love for Mum undoubtedly helped our dad to face the challenges posed by his new life as a 33-year-old in the years post 1945.

NOTES

1. See Australian National War Memorial website www.awm.gov.au/collection/ C254381

2. Imperial War Museum, London, ref 7770, **The Captive Guest** by G.A. Sketchley p.58.

3. As above, p.74.

4. See foreword to musical score of Howard Goodall's **Eternal Light a Requiem,** Faber Music, London 2008.

CHAPTER 10

"RETURN TO CIVVY STREET"

"The essence of a satisfactory health service is that the rich and the poor are treated alike, that poverty is not a disability, and wealth is not disadvantaged."

Aneurin Bevan writing about the creation of the
National Health Service on 5 July 1948[1].

Three men from the camps establish contact with Dad. Pte Tom Finucane, an Anglo-Indian from the RAMC and his second batman, spends a few days in early December at our family home on the Cliftonville Road in Belfast. Dad finds it difficult to entertain him, a situation compounded by Finucane's insistence on wearing his army uniform, thus making a trip to Dublin out of the question. His ignorance of the provocative nature of his military attire is quite incredible. In the middle of the month, Fr Richard Kennedy has a hospital appointment at Moira near Belfast and the rugby-playing priest purchases two tickets for Dad and him to watch a match at Ravenhill, the home of Ulster rugby. In what proves to be a busy month for reunions, Sgt Roy Evans of the RASC invites Dad to his wedding to a Carrickfergus girl in the town on New Year's Eve.

Our parents' own wedding on 4 February 1946 is a joyous occasion though Dad must have greatly felt the absence of his mother who had died in 1940 of pulmonary tuberculosis while he was in the Far East. It is only after the war that he learns of her abiding wish for him to marry Eileen O'Kane. Fr Joe Murphy, Mum's uncle, is the officiating priest. They honeymoon in Dublin. In what turns out to be their one and only visit to a racecourse, they have a flutter on the 12/1 shot Cool Customer which wins the Leopardstown Chase on 16 February.

After the wedding Mum moves in to the Murray family home where they live with our grandfather. The latter makes Dad the generous offer of using the floor above the shop on the Oldpark Road as a doctor's surgery. A desk, couch and chairs are purchased and our grandfather is not slow in exhorting any customers with ailments to "Get up the stairs!" or "Go and see himself!" An elderly woman is his first patient. He charges half a crown for treatment and three shillings and sixpence if it includes medicine but any patient unable to afford the charge pays when they can. Mum comments on Carl's taped interview that the money he makes is barely enough to secure their future. It is two and a half years before the NHS is launched but, in a letter to Mum years before from Malaya in November '41, he accurately predicts the introduction of the ground-breaking health care system: "When this war is over, a state-controlled medical service is sure to come into force and, though this has many disadvantages, it should suit us very much. It may abolish the old idea of a family doctor but the patients will get better attention than ever before. I shall be able to visit poor patients more frequently because it will not cost anything for them for extra visits and special attention. That's what I loved about the panel system when I was working in Birmingham; I did work hard for those poor people in the slums and it brought me great joy. It is part of the glory of a doctor's life – one feels that one is doing something useful in life without gaining anything from it by way of recompense except great consolation and happiness – and what better reward could one ask." In the taped interview, he explains that there was no work in Belfast when he qualified as a doctor in 1937. That year, he heard about a vacancy across the water in Birmingham at Dr McSherry's practice on Summerhill Road with an annual salary of £312. In addition, he was given responsibility for difficult maternity calls, often occurring at night, which he attended on foot or by bus for the more distant cases.

Six months after the surgery is up and running, our grandfather sells the shop for £500 to our dad's cousin. However, there is an urgent need for more help so Dad employs a couple as caretakers. They are friends of Mum's Auntie Kathleen, yet another fortuitous link between the two families. The Donnellys move into the two upper floors of the building and rear a large family of 10 children. Mrs Donnelly also takes on the job of receptionist. In typically humorous fashion, he writes to her after his retirement that she be considered as a recipient of the Victoria Cross. His admiration for her whom he always addressed as "Mrs Donnelly", never Edna (my siblings and I never knew her first name until we renewed contact with her and her family many years later), is manifest in a letter dated Christmas '85 which her daughter Aileen photocopied for me: "How grateful I am to you for all you have done for me over many years while I was in practice. You were always my front-line of defence in those days, you made my work so much easier. Apart from the practice, it was a tonic to hear nothing but laughter echoing down from your rooms." Aileen tells me that their living room and kitchen were, in fact, on the same floor as the surgery. Dad would loudly say good-bye to his final patient whilst simultaneously knocking the adjacent door to give her siblings and her the all-clear to raise the volume again!

The unique access via the diary and letters to our parents' thoughts abruptly ends at this point as their married life together begins. Inevitably, my recall of events is now subject to personal experience and the recollections of my three older sisters and younger brother. There is no doubt, however, that the regular income afforded by the introduction of the NHS made the future a more certain one for our mum and dad.

One of my sisters, Josette, recently told me a funny story overheard by Mrs Donnelly of a conversation between two female patients one day in the surgery waiting-room when one quizzed the other as to why she hadn't seen her there the previous week. Her next question was "Were you sick?" Indeed Dad used to say that a lot of his patients regularly came for "a wee chat" which made them feel a lot better as they descended the steep stairs out onto the crowded thoroughfare of the Oldpark Road and back to their busy lives. This was especially true with the arrival of the Troubles in 1968 when many of them suffered greatly from their nerves. I am again indebted to Carl who discovered a website called Belfast Forum. One particular conversation thread has some moving tributes to both our dad and the other GP in the practice, Dr O'Gorman[2]. (Since the report on BBC NI news on the eve of VJ Day in 2020, a number of ex-patients have contacted Carl on the website he has set up. My four siblings and I will always treasure the admiration with which they recall our dad as their GP.)

These were the days when his weekday mornings were spent treating his patients at the surgery while afternoons and Saturday mornings were filled with 'calls' (home visits) in his Austin Cambridge around the city. As civil unrest grew and the enforced relocation of families from both sides of the religious divide to more outlying areas of the city, his remit of a relatively small area of north and west Belfast grew bigger meaning he often did not return home until well after tea-time, our evening meal which we usually ate around six o'clock. How things have changed for general practitioners nowadays when they rarely visit patients in their own homes as they are expected to make their own way to surgeries and clinics. I did enjoy accompanying him on his calls on the occasional Saturday morning in the days before I discovered football and preferred a kick-about with my friends at the Grove Playing-fields on the shores of Belfast Lough.

Another story, this time from the horse's mouth, was the impromptu organising of street parties whenever one of his patients contracted German measles. A vaccine to prevent it had not yet been created and, mindful of the danger that the disease, also known as rubella, carried in leading to miscarriage or birth defects, he would ensure that as many people as possible were exposed to an outbreak. I failed to ask him how he kept already pregnant women from attending such outdoor gatherings nor did I ask him if the General Medical Council, had I known the existence of such an organisation at the time, approved of such an unorthodox procedure for reducing the risk to the offspring of mothers-to-be. I would love to hear from anyone who took part in such bizarre but eminently practical social gatherings.

Apart from the continued correspondence by letter with Dr Andler, the giant scroll of tribute in prominent display in our home and Dad's already-mentioned deformed thumb nail, there was little else to remind us as children of his time in the camps. He did, however, experience poor circulation in his feet every winter due to beriberi reducing his levels of vitamin B. It was taken as a given that we always finished the food that was on our plates though there was never any stated compulsion for us to do so. This was not his way. He never talked about his experiences and this was how the POWs were encouraged to deal with the past. Nor did he join any ex-servicemen's clubs though this probably had more to do with him not wanting to draw attention to himself as an ex-Irish officer in the British Army. His war medals were carefully put away as was his military MBE certificate signed by King George VI on 6 June 1946 and received through the post.

Josette did tell me recently that, out of the blue, as the seven of us sat down to dinner at the home of the Donegal farmer's family where we holidayed every July in the late '50s and '60s, he suddenly mentioned the war. The context was a pleasant one. He said that he now felt more physically fit than at any time since his imprisonment. She and the girls remember being so surprised to hear him mention the war.

There were, however, a few linguistic reminders of his time in Japan. Being a linguist, this is an area that fascinates me. Our adored golden cocker spaniel he named Joto after the Japanese for 'first class' though I have since discovered from a fluent speaker that the word was *jootoo*. He taught us how to count up to 10 but my memory stops at eight, I suspect due to its similarity with the English word 'hatch'. I instantly recall them, 'one' and 'two' the most amusing and always bringing a smile to my face as they return me to my childhood: 'ichi', 'ni', 'san', 'shi', 'go', 'roku', 'shichi', 'hachi'. The prisoner number he was given and would have uttered at the daily *tenko* roll calls was 'ichi', 'ichi', 'rei', 'ni' (1102). Sapper Gerald Sketchley's account in the Imperial War Museum archives is entitled *The Captive Guest* by Ichy San Ku Ray which equates to his number – 1390. I doubt if any of the veterans ever forgot theirs.

Another word he always used to say was my old *jidosha*, this being the Japanese for car. I guess the sound of the word appealed to him. A legacy of his time in India, probably when Yassin was his man-servant, was *Effendi* (Master), a throwback to the time of the Ottoman Empire.

His knowledge of Latin from his schooldays undoubtedly helped his studies of medicine at university. In retirement, he attended adult evening classes in Spanish and often made the link between this Romance language that is my passion and its Latin roots. I am not so sure if I would ever contemplate beginning to learn a new language in my 70s but I remain immensely impressed at his efforts even if they only had one outlet abroad in a summer holiday to Tenerife. I still treasure his meticulously scribbled notes on a variety of key communication phrases in his recycled 1973 Wellcome medical diary which share the pages with adverts for the likes of Septrin, Otosporin and Migril.

Regarding his attitude to the Japanese, it was unsurprising that he never wished to go back to the country. It was not in his nature to embark on any diatribe against its people but, at the same time, he steadfastly refused to buy any products from the country. When I returned from a summer French language course in the Pyrenees in 1976, I remember how his interest in my enthusiastic stories about my fellow foreign students suddenly waned when I mentioned a Japanese lad called Tomoyuki. My siblings and I were curious to see if he would follow the '72 Sapporo Winter Olympics from Hokkaido with special interest but he made no comment. On a trip with Mum across Canada in 1981, another of my sisters, Villana, was puzzled at his quiet outburst in Banff: "They're everywhere." "What do you mean, Dad?" she asked. As he pointed out the presence of hordes of Japanese tourists eagerly enjoying the beautiful attractions of the resort in the Rockies, she realised that it must have been many years since he had seen so many in one place. He was obviously feeling ill at ease.

On one visit to England, he arranged an appointment at the Liverpool School of Tropical Medicine to gain a better insight into his beriberi but nothing came of it. He preferred not to make a fuss and was reluctant to make further hospital visits across the Irish Sea. The final weeks of his life were to bring back the full nightmare scenarios of his captivity.

NOTES

1. *See Chapter 5 **In Place of Fear**, Aneurin Bevan's 1952 essay on the NHS.*

2. *See www.belfastforum.co.uk/index.php?topic=44943.0*

CHAPTER 11

"THE TROUBLES"

"What kind of Ulster do you want? A happy and respected province, in good standing with the rest of the UK, or a place continually torn apart by riots and demonstrations, and regarded as a political outcast?"

Terence O'Neill, Prime Minister of Northern Ireland,
appearing on local television in December 1968.

Any account of Dad's life back in Belfast would be incomplete without reference to the Troubles. They were to affect the lives of every single person in Northern Ireland and unresolved legacy issues still continue today, 50 years on. Back then, frisking of everyone entering the ring of steel gates in Belfast city centre, the daily bomb scares, evacuations of buildings, and re-routing of traffic were all daily occurrences. The event that most turned the spotlight on the country, due to its extensive coverage on television and in the newspapers, was the NICRA (Northern Ireland Civil Rights Association) march in Derry on 5 October 1968. The images of the police brutality in dealing with the marchers were beamed around the world. O'Neill could never have imagined as he uttered what came to be known as the 'crossroads speech' that civil unrest leading to over 3,700 deaths would continue unabated for the next 30 years.

I was 14 when it all kicked off, only slightly older than Dad when he witnessed the sectarian strife in Belfast in the early 1920s. Carl and I had elected not to follow our three sisters to boarding school not, I hasten to add, to feel safer but because we were 'home birds' and preferred the familiarity of a home routine. I was in the first cohort of pupils to move school in 1968 from St Mary's Christian Brothers' Grammar School at Barrack Street in the city centre where our dad had also attended school back in the 1920s out to a new purpose-built school on the Glen Road on the outskirts of the city below the towering bulk of Black Mountain. It was a novelty taking a second bus each morning even though the low ceilings of the old red trolley buses forced me to bend my head as I boarded and looked for a seat. This was their final year in service and it was with great delight that we anticipated arriving at school late when the poles occasionally detached themselves from the overhead wires. The conductor then proceeded to extract an enormous bar from a cavity that ran the entire length of the trolley bus. This he expertly manoeuvred high above his head to hook the poles back on to the electric cables.

August 1969 saw the first deployment of British troops and the erection of 'peace-lines' in Belfast to divide Protestant and Catholic communities in flash-point areas. The general atmosphere of civil unrest increased in 1971 with the introduction of internment without trial. I vividly remember a hoax telephone bomb warning given by a pupil in my Spanish O level class one lunch time so as not to have to sit our regular Friday afternoon vocabulary test. The whole school was promptly evacuated until the army carried out a search. These were the days before coded warnings were introduced. It seems incredible now to recall the interruption to our French O level dictation when the IRA were firing at a British army helicopter from one of the roofs of our school. I use the word "interruption" to refer to the sounds of gun-fire, not to the pausing of the cassette by our teacher as he carried on regardless!

The day after 'Bloody Sunday' in January '72 when 13 unarmed civilians were shot dead in Derry by members of the Parachute Regiment following another march by the NICRA was a day I will never forget. I was 17 and about to enter my final five months of formal schooling before sitting my A levels. Huddles of boys gathered in classrooms and corridors exchanging thoughts. Feelings were running high and the looming prospect of public exams could not have been further from our minds. There were more important things in life, things which, even though we were young adults, we tended not to discuss with our parents. There was talk of a strike among us on the following day though nothing came of it. One of my three A levels was history and the events of Sunday 30 January put the whole story of British rule in Ireland in context. I remember at the time railing against the limitation of an option paper we were preparing for being confined to Irish history up to the late 19th century. Was this some sort of conspiracy by the Northern Ireland Education Board to prevent us from studying modern Irish history? My interest in world history and particularly in conflict resolution has continued to this day. As a footnote, some quick mathematical calculations put the age of my history teacher at the time, Dan Cashman, as in his late 70s or early 80s! I know this as, incredible though it may sound, he also taught my dad and there are 42 years between me and him. Dan was a passionate teacher with a great love for his subject and revelled in relating little exposés on epoch-changing periods of history. I never took notes but was mesmerised by his delivery.

Returning to our lives at home, the worsening security situation in the city resulted in Contactors' Bureau, the doctors' organisation who were paid by GPs in the city like our dad to cover night calls, refusing to go out after dark. Carl and I watched helpless, unable to comfort Mum, as he would take his turn, usually two nights a week, at going on call to patients' houses all over the city. Army check points demanded that car headlights be turned off so as not to make them a target for terrorists. There were no stickers issued to doctors to reduce delays while number plates and driving licences were checked. His trusty black doctor's bag that sat on his front passenger seat was further proof of his identity. Mum never slept during those nights until his safe return.

A confidential phone number was widely publicised on posters giving a number to ring if people wanted to anonymously pass on details about suspected terrorists to the authorities. One afternoon we found ourselves on the receiving end of a malicious one. The first Carl and I knew that anything was happening was when a group of British soldiers appeared from nowhere at the back of our house while we were playing football. Without telling us what was going on, we were made to stand against the yard wall with our backs to them. At least five minutes must have elapsed before they left and we ran into the house to find out what on earth was happening. It transpired that they had had an anonymous tip-off that there were guns in our home. Dad was at work but Mum had angrily drawn their attention to the giant scroll of tribute on our dining-room wall. They immediately left with a profuse apology. Dad was livid and the following day, still irate, he made a visit to the nearby fortified army/police station to make a formal complaint.

One evening in April 1973, a suspect car was spotted by the army parked outside our house. As it had been reported as stolen, the presumption was that it was either booby-trapped or about to be used in a bomb attack. Instead of evacuating our home while they carried out a controlled explosion, the army told us to move to the rear of the building. When the explosion came, it shattered many of the front windows. Glaziers were impressively on hand first thing the following morning to board up the windows before returning shortly to replace the glass. We suffered no physical or mental scars from the small explosion unlike many people in

Northern Ireland who were much less fortunate.

The sound of what seemed like nightly gun battles between the British Army and the IRA was magnified as it carried from the area of the Old-park Road across the open expanse of Cliftonville Cricket Club's grounds and to our home which lay directly opposite. The clubhouse was burned and looted in August 1972, and thereafter came to be known as the 'People's Park'. To this day, the sounds of exploding fireworks at Halloween and New Year's Eve involuntarily take me back to those dark days when I lay in bed trying to sleep. Although I still have periodic nightmares about our home on the Cliftonville Road which are always related to our vulnerable mum and dad living there helplessly on their own, I no longer worry when a car pulls up slowly behind me or feel the need to sit in a bar with an unhindered view of the main entrance in case gunmen burst through the doors.

However, there was one event which directly affected Dad. Once again it was 1972, the worst year of the Troubles when the death rate reached almost 500. Along with his partner Dr O'Gorman, he took the decision to vacate the old surgery. The shop on the ground floor had long since ceased trading and the whole building had become a British Army observation post. The new surgery was further down the road nearly opposite the local library. By this time, a chemist had also opened in premises next door to the new surgery.

Sectarian violence erupted all over the city as crowds attending the unionist Vanguard Association mass rally at Stormont dispersed. The rally had been organised to protest against the end of local government and the imposition of 'direct rule' from Westminster. It was Tuesday 28 March, the second day of a general strike organised by Vanguard. "At 8.30 p.m. empty buildings were set on fire and the blaze spread to a doctor's surgery and a chemist's shop. A mob stoned police and firemen who went to assist a youth struck by an army vehicle which was arriving at the scene. Firemen withdrew returning later under strong army protection. The blaze was brought under control but at least four buildings were destroyed and another was damaged." This was how the *News Letter* newspaper reported the torching of the surgery and chemist's in their edition the following morning. Dad believed the former was targeted purely due to the fact that he and Dr O'Gorman were Catholic doctors. Their practice included many Protestant patients and it saddened him greatly that a number of them whom he had brought into the world were among the arsonists.

The *Belfast Telegraph* newspaper had earlier in the evening reported on the wounding of two Protestant men by a gunman which had led to the setting up of barricades. The Catholic Our Lady of Mercy School in Ballysillan was attacked by a mob resulting in a revenge stoning of windows at the nearby Protestant St Gabriel's Boys' School on the Crumlin Road. The front page of the *Irish News* newspaper two days later carried a photo of Sister Carmel, whom I presume was the principal of Our Lady of Mercy, going through the wreckage of the assembly hall which had been desecrated after a mob had torn down the front railings of the school to gain access.

The violence was not confined to Belfast. Two civilians died when a massive IRA bomb exploded in a hijacked van outside Limavady RUC Police Station and 35 shots were fired at the army at the Brandywell and from Derry's nearby famous walls.

The *News Letter* also carried a report at the time of Portadown reaching the All Ireland Women's Senior Hockey Final after their 3-0 victory over Munster's Old Ursulines. Rugby and boxing are two further examples of sports that have always been the flag-bearers for sports with a dimension extending across the island, and which aim to break down barriers between the two communities in the north.

A short time after the arson attack, Dad was gratified by a letter from a reader of a local newspaper which I reproduce below:

"Burning – way of saying thanks to doctor"

Sir, may I express my sympathy, together with hundreds of grateful patients, to Dr Murray of Oldpark Road, Belfast, whose surgery and contents were destroyed by fire on Tuesday, March 28th.

When Dr Murray was imprisoned by the Japs in the last war, he saved the lives of many wounded soldiers in the POW camp. It did not matter then if he was a Catholic; nor did it matter later when he was honoured by Queen Elizabeth.

Perhaps burning his surgery and contests [contents] was only the Belfast Protestant way of saying "Thank you."

Yours etc., A GRATEFUL PATIENT. Belfast, 14.

Dr O'Gorman and Dad set up a temporary practice near our home but

Dad was upset and saddened to receive an anonymous letter from a local who objected to the presence of working class patients in an area they considered to be middle class.

The Loyalist Workers' Council called a general strike in May 1974 to protest against the Sunningdale Agreement which was designed to introduce power-sharing for the first time between the two communities. There were shortages of fresh food in the shops. The key support for the strike of electricity workers at Ballylumford Power Station led to intermittent power access for consumers. Everyone did essential clothes' washing based on the daily timetable of cuts. Fortunately, we had a gas cooker. Battery-operated radios were the only reliable way of finding out what was going on as the strike dragged on for two weeks. I well remember the feeling of fear and intimidation as my sister and I drove home one afternoon across town from Queen's University wondering if we would be stopped and searched by the paramilitary UDA (Ulster Defence Association) who had mounted checkpoints all over the city. Without intervention from the army or the police, it was not surprising that the strikers succeeded and power-sharing was temporarily confined to the bin.

The following year, at the age of 62, Dad had had enough. He and Mum sold the family home for a paltry four figure sum in an area which by then had come to be known as 'murder mile' and retired to a small bungalow they had bought in the seaside resort of Newcastle, Co. Down. One by one my siblings and I joined the thousands of others who chose a more tolerant and decidedly safer existence across the Irish Sea in England and, in the case of my eldest sister Villana, Canada. Our parents were hugely relieved as, indeed, were we to know that their lives would now revolve around a more integrated society in a quiet town at the foot of the Mourne Mountains. It did nothing, however, to lessen the abject and guilty sadness we all experienced at the end of our staggered visits home when we had to bid farewell to them and return to our own lives.

CHAPTER 12
"LOUGH DERG"

"A journey to a holy place for religious reasons/ A journey to a place that is connected with someone or something that you admire or respect"

Oxford Learner's Dictionary definition of 'pilgrimage'

The remaining 18 years of Dad's life were spent with Mum in the idyllic surroundings of Newcastle. Unlike Mum who dreamt of travel to far-flung corners of the globe, Dad was content tending to his small, immaculately manicured garden at the front of the bungalow and the fertile sandy soil at the rear where he grew lettuces, scallions, parsley, raspberries, strawberries and blackcurrants. Former patients visiting the seaside town as day-trippers or staying at the many caravan parks would often engage him in conversation as they stopped to chat on the footpath beyond the low walled front lawn and flower bed. He even exchanged words once with the controversial English politician and Ulster Unionist Party MP for South Down, Enoch Powell, who came canvassing for votes past the bungalow with the assistance of a loudspeaker atop his poster-bedecked support vehicle. I watched the two of them from the front room. Carl has told me that they discussed their respective military services during the war. Dad told him that he had taken part in the Malayan campaign. Powell replied "I missed that one" to which Dad responded "You didn't miss much." As an aside, Dad would definitely not have shared Powell's racist views but it was typical of him that he would always find time to engage anyone in conversation.

One by-product of myself and my four siblings taking up residence across the sea/ocean was the regular correspondence by post that Mum and Dad kept up with us. Our replies were probably not as copious as we preferred the convenience of ringing and, in my case, sending postcards from different parts of Britain and northern Spain where Jan and I would holiday with our young son Andrew. Mum's letters related mostly to updates on family, friends and golf, her great sporting passion. At one award presentation in Bundoran Co. Donegal, she received a trophy recognising her achievement as Ireland's oldest ladies' golf captain. This dated back to 1939 at Omagh Golf Club. Dad was so proud of this particular recognition being bestowed on her. Incredibly, she was still playing the game when well into her 80s.

As well as being full of news and liberally sprinkled with his biting wit, our dad's missives occasionally struck a more reflective tone. Indeed the following paragraph, written shortly before Christmas 1980, borders on the morbid though in a hilarious fashion: "And now yesterday is no more and today another one almost gone and will be duly ticked off the calendar. And life is like that only now 'Father Time' gallops – he has abandoned his scythe and his coat-tails are flying he is in such a hurry!" (I do like his overlapping metaphors!) He was only 68 at the time but was obviously feeling his age.

It was only in the final few months of his life that the horrors of his incarceration, relived during his day spent with Mitchell in Sussex in 1983, brutally returned with a vengeance. One Friday night the year he died in 1993, I phoned him from a pub at Gloucester docks after the unwinding delights of another week 'at the chalk face' were fully indulged in five-a-side staff football. At one point in the conversation, he uttered the words I will never forget: "Paul, you know the war is nearly over". I tried not to show how upset I was by this totally unexpected interjection but could not hide my tears as I returned to the welcome embrace of my colleagues.

After he was admitted to the Downe Hospital in Downpatrick, Mum was alarmed to notice bruises on his wrists. The staff explained that his mind had regressed to the war years and he was attempting to escape from the ward which he was convinced was one of the prison camps. The whole episode really upset her. She tried as best she could to reassure him that he was not under any threat.

All four of our grand-parents as well as one brother and one sister of Dad's are buried in Milltown Cemetery on the Falls Road in Belfast. He was adamant that this was not to be his final resting place as he confirmed during Carl's interview: "I don't want to go up the Falls again, alive or dead." We naturally respected his wishes when the time came for old 'Father Time' to really come knocking. It was 25 September 1993, Carl's 38th birthday.

As the symbolic first sods of earth were gently showered upon his coffin in the peaceful country churchyard at Bryansford with its stunning backdrop of Slieves Donard and Commedagh, BBC cameraman Ingo Prosser[1], my cousin Fionnuala's husband, turned to me and said that the world needed to know Dad's story. Many people have said the same to my family in the more than a quarter of a century it has taken Carl and me to share it.

The second of the Oxford Learner's Dictionary's above definition of 'pilgrimage' definitely applied to me as, five years later, I prepared my rucksack in readiness for my 500-mile trek from the French border, over the Pyrenees, along the Meseta, and on to the sacred shrine of Santiago de Compostela, the religious capital of Spain. I wanted to experience something, albeit at a tiny level, of what Dad had endured during his long period of captivity when he called upon every human and divine resource to survive. The long five-week school holiday in the UK is periodically extended to six and just such a year was 1998. I calculated it was going to take me around five weeks to walk the route, giving me one further week to recover before the return to lessons in early September. How right this proved to be!

What had happened in the interim? Carl had certainly been busy. In correspondence with Clarence House in London, he had asked if the Queen Mother would be willing to present our mum with Dad's military MBE. Confirmation duly arrived through the post and in May 1995 Mum flew over to London to join Carl in an unforgettable day.

Mum and Dad's reasons for going on pilgrimage to Lough Derg were different from mine in that they went solely for religious reasons. There are as many as 11 references to their visits to the shrine in their letters. Dad went six times and Mum five. The lake itself is situated inland in south-east Donegal at the opposite extremity from Ranafast on the Atlantic north-west coast where they first found love. Similar to its more famous neighbour, Lough Erne, across the border in Co. Fermanagh in Northern Ireland, there are many islands on the lake – 46 in all – of which Station Island is one. St Patrick's Purgatory on the island is described in a beautifully illustrated book by Ian Bradley[2] as "undoubtedly the most penitential [pilgrimage] of any in Europe." The link with Ireland's revered national saint comes from a cave on the island revealed by God to him as a passage into the underworld.

I have no doubt that Mum and Dad would have strictly adhered to fasting from the midnight prior to the day of their arrival. There is an option to do a one-day pilgrimage but the majority of penitents who attend go for three days. On reflection, I suppose the latter equates to their status as 'genuine' pilgrims in much the same way as pilgrims on the Camino de Santiago in Spain are viewed by some as only being 'authentic' if they carry their own rucksacks all the way to Santiago and stay in pilgrim hostels as opposed to hotels and guest houses. My own view that has shifted over the years is that the elderly and infirm who journey by coach as well as walking pilgrims who choose a luggage transportation service deserve to be considered as pilgrims just as much as those of us who walk the entire route with our rucksacks on our backs.

The removing of socks and shoes for the duration of one's stay on Station Island in addition to the fasting which restricts the penitent to dry toast and tea or coffee alone are not, according to the Irish novelist and contemporary of mine, Colm Tóibín[3], the most physically demanding aspects of the Lough Derg pilgrimage. Nor is the repetitive incanting of 'Our Fathers', 'Hail Marys' and 'Creeds' as the nine times-repeated 'Stations of the Cross' are walked and knelt in front of in precisely the same ritualistic order. Pilgrims go there to pray, after all. (As an aside I should say that as a family we used to recite the five decades of the Rosary on our knees each evening. As a young boy, I found the constant repetition of the same prayers lacked all meaning.) According to Tóibín it is rather the sleep deprivation of the first night's vigil that pilgrims find the most arduous. In the same vein, the most difficult thing about sharing a crowded pilgrim dormitory on the Camino is the presence of snorers though their unwelcome intrusions can be reduced by the insertion of earplugs. However, I could not imagine staying up all night even if this only occurs on the first night at Lough Derg. Once again I am sure that our parents would not have eaten a proper meal until after midnight on their third day, by which time pilgrims traditionally are back home. By contrast, on his third day at midday, Tóibín has no hesitation in tucking into a hearty lunch back on dry land at the Railway Hotel in Enniskillen[4].

Two Irish poets who capture in verse their own strong emotional experiences on Lough Derg are the 1995 Nobel Prize Winner for Literature, Seamus Heaney, and Patrick Kavanagh. Outside Ireland, Kavanagh is probably most famous for penning the poem 'On Raglan Road' which Luke Kelly of the traditional folk group, The Dubliners, adapted to a hauntingly melodious 19th century tune. The more prosaic tone of Kavanagh's poem 'Lough Derg' is easier to unpick than the imagery of Heaney's 'Station Island', though a reading of the latter is no less rewarding. There are lots of references in Kavanagh's poem to pilgrims praying out loud for special intentions such as a good harvest, a cure for a friend's or loved one's illness or the passing of an exam. I can remember Mum frequently saying to us as children "Offer it up for the intentions of the holy souls" when we were facing something unpleasant. She attended Mass daily throughout her life. I have a bizarre association of the physical manifestation of this encouragement to pray for God's help in moving those souls from the half-way house of Purgatory to Heaven. It used to occur every Saturday evening in the UK National Lottery television programme *In It To Win It* in which the host Dale Winton asked contestants quiz questions to move them out of the red area into the white area so they could remain in the contest. If successful, they would stand up and walk towards the white segment of the studio otherwise they faced elimination. Kavanagh's lament of his sin of pride goes back to a time of greater orthodoxy and adherence to the sacraments in the Catholic Church when Confession, now appropriately renamed Reconciliation, was the weekly channel in front of a priest for asking God's forgiveness of sins.

Dad's tone in a letter to Mum from Malaya dated Halloween '41 is endearingly boastful. It comes a matter of months since their engagement: "I have trained myself in a hard school and it began when I went to Lough Derg as a boy with my father and Una [Dad's sister]! I can now endure any discomfort or hardship and live under any condition, and still it would not cost me a thought." Perhaps the spartan conditions of the pilgrimage to the island in the days of a "cold wooden church" before a basilica was built prepared him better than the five weeks of army training he had at Crookham Camp in Fleet, Hampshire which he began on Sunday 3 December '39. It was the eve of his 27th birthday.

Mum pledged to make nine pilgrimages to Lough Derg. This figure is possibly explained by the Catholic tradition of devotional praying repeated for nine successive days or weeks in the formalised setting of a church. She faithfully attended these 'novenas' as a young woman at her local church in Belfast – Clonard Monastery. Dad also organised and led a weekly 'novena' in the improvised chapel which I think was the assembly hall in Muroran Camp. This began in October '44, though there was opposition from the men who complained that the Thursdays he chose coincided with bath days.

Coincidentally, Mum's third 'Lough Derg' comes in August '42, two months after Patrick Kavanagh's. She goes again the following year with 10 other girls and notes there are some 600 pilgrims on the island. Tóibín, in fact, remarks that the majority of the penitents were women. Her fifth and final one takes place in 1944 with her brother Hugh.

Our parents never did go to Lough Derg together despite their promises to each other to do so during the war years. Rearing a young family probably put paid to that. I have, however, come across an attestation of pilgrimage certificate made out to Dr Murray and signed by, among others, the mayor of Jerusalem, Teddy Kollek, in 1979. Such documents seem to have been issued en masse to pilgrims to the Holy City and Dad's marked his visit with Mum and a group of parishioners from their church in Newcastle to the Holy Land that year. On their return home, I remember him lamenting the conditions of the Palestinians. Such an impression mirrored his championing throughout his life of the underdog.

NOTES

1. *BBC cameraman Ingo Prosser filmed events in Tiananmen Square, Beijing and the collapse of the Berlin Wall in 1989.*

2. ***Pilgrimage A Spiritual and Cultural Journey*** *by Ian Bradley, Lion 2009, p.131.*

3. *Chapter 3 'Dark Night of the Soul' from **Bad Blood: A Walk Along the Irish Border** by Colm Tóibín, Picador 2001.*

4. *As above, see p.44.*

Pilgrims at Pettigo Station, Co. Donegal, 1946, returning from Lough Derg.

Coláiste Bhríde, Ranafast, Co. Donegal.

SW HOKKAIDO, JAPAN

- Akabira
- Utashinai
- Raijo
- Nishi Ashibetsu
- Bibai
- Sapporo
- Chitose
- Muroran
- Yakumo
- Hakodate

*Propaganda photo of two British POWs at
Muroran POW Camp.*

Pte Raymond Suttle

Cpl Mitsuo Umeki on roof of Raijo POW Camp. Photo taken Aug. or Sep. 1945. Note PW rather than POW sign to guide American air drops.

Lt Kaichi Hirate at Yokohama War Crime Trial, April 1946.

Lt Col Shigeo Emoto & wife.

Frank Murray & David Marshall, Singapore, Dec. 1977.

Frank Murray & Keith Mitchell, Shoreham, Aug. 1983.

Refugio Gaucelmo Pilgrim Hostel, Rabanal del Camino, Spain.

Three Caminos, Spain

Oviedo

Santiago   *Primitivo*   St Jean Pied de Port

Camino Sanabrés   *Camino Francés*

Burgos

Zamora

Salamanca

Vía de la Plata

Seville

*View of eastern side Inishkeel Island, Co. Donegal &
its two ruined churches.*

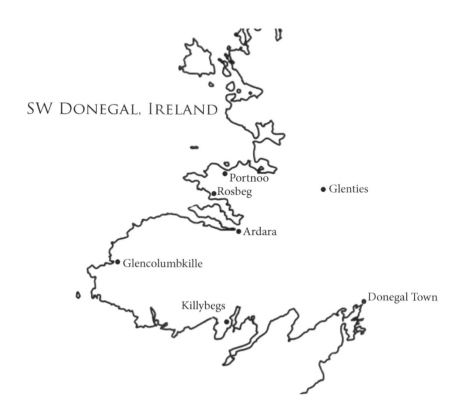

SW DONEGAL, IRELAND

Portnoo
Rosbeg
Glenties

Ardara

Glencolumbkille

Killybegs

Donegal Town

Pilgrimage to Inishkeel Island from Narin Beach, 1 July 2018.

Gallagher sisters examine St Conall's bell & shrine, Dolmen Centre, Kilclooney, 13 July 2015. L.to R. Kathleen, Rose, Mary (at back) & Nellie (far right).

Ruins of O'Boyle's Castle on Kiltoorish Lake, Rosbeg where some of Santa Ana crew took refuge. Trá Mór Beach & Loughros Mór Bay beyond.

Belgian diver, Robert Sténuit, examines cannon beside O'Boyle's Castle in 1968.

Portrait of Alonso Martínez de Leyva by El Greco

Castle housing Spanish National Archives, Simancas, Valladolid.

Gold ring recovered from Girona wreck. Carries inscription 'No tengo más que darte.'

Cross of Knight of Santiago probably belonging to de Leyva & recovered from Girona.

Extract from letter dated Jan. 1589 of two Spanish sailors' second-hand account of sinking of Santa Ana & Girona.

Jonathan Marshall, Villana Murray & author preparing to re-enact walk into captivity from St Andrew's Anglican Cathedral, Singapore to Changi, 7 Oct. 2017.

Graves of Suttle, Angell & Durrant side by side, Commonwealth War Cemetery, Yokohama, Japan.

*Interpreter Chris Holmes &
author, bridge over Ashibetsu River
downstream from Raijo POW Camp.*

*L. to R. Yoshikazu Yamamoto, guide Taeko
Sasamoto & Satoshi Motono examine
Singapore Straits' Times newspaper
& documents near site of Muroran POW
Camp.*

*Eizenji Temple, Hakodate. Originally
hospital building & located at Hakodate
Main POW Camp. L. to R. NHK TV
camerawoman, interviewer Nobuyuki
Hanaoka & Hakodate Shimbun newspaper
journalist Daisuke Nakagawa.*

*Eileen & Frank Murray, Newcastle Beach, Co. Down.
Slieve Donard in background.*

CHAPTER 13

"PILGRIMAGE 1, CAMINO FRANCÉS, 1998"

"I made my second meal in four weeks – mushroom soup from a packet but too watery. Iñaki, a Basque monocycle rider now resident in middle of Majorca, arrived without food so we all offered to share what we had – he couldn't believe it and commented later that he hadn't met kindness like this since Burgos. Turns out he runs circus classes for children and specialises in clown acts."

Diary entry, day 28, Sunday 16 August.

The miraculous discovery of the body of St James, one of Christ's 12 apostles, early in the ninth century was the reason for pilgrims making the journey to Santiago de Compostela to venerate his remains. The seizure of the Holy Sepulchre in Jerusalem by the Turks in 1078 which rendered any pilgrimage there impossible was viewed as an opportunity to divert pilgrims to another important Christian place of worship. The 11th and 12th centuries saw over half a million pilgrims make the journey each year. In 1998 there were only 90,000. The incredible popularity in the pilgrimage is borne out by the most recent statistics for 2019 from the pilgrim office in Santiago which recorded over a third of a million pilgrims registering to collect their *compostelas* (pilgrim certificates). These figures must be viewed in the context of the minimum walking distance required for the issue of a '*compostela*' as being 100 kilometres. There is no doubt that there are many more pilgrims nowadays who are ticking off the pilgrimage from a bucket list and beginning at Sarria, just over 100 km from Santiago. However, there has also been a noticeable drop in pilgrim numbers over the last two years east of Sarria and back along the Camino Francés, the most popular of the many routes through Spain. I have first-hand experience of this in the lower numbers of pilgrims staying in the donations' hostel I help to run, 10 days on foot from Santiago. This is confirmed in chatting to our neighbours in the village where the dramatic drop in foot-fall, particularly in the summer months, is beginning to affect their livelihoods.

I chose the summer of 1998 as it marked the end of my year as temporary head of modern languages at St Peter's Catholic High School in

Gloucester. One minute I was in my classroom on a Friday afternoon and by the Monday morning I was embarking on my adventure starting on the French side of the Pyrenees. My fear of the unknown involved in walking 800 km through largely unfamiliar terrain was lessened by the company of our neighbour Keith who had asked if he could join me a matter of weeks before.

Medieval pilgrims would have made preparations before their departures in the event of them not returning. Pilgrimages in those days were fraught with danger whether from bandits, wolves or poisoned water given to horses. They lasted for months with the additional challenge of covering twice the modern distance in order to return home. My planning was confined to arranging for Jan to pay our monthly household bills and shifting full responsibility onto her shoulders for looking after Andrew whilst juggling running our home with her part-time job. Dad, by contrast, had already left home. Whilst on leave from Crookham in England, he returned to Belfast to say his proper goodbyes, fully expecting to be back within a year.

Like him, I was determined to keep a daily diary to record my thoughts. Carrying a ridiculously heavy rucksack up and over the Pyrenees, even if it was via one of its lower cols, was a lesson I would soon come to learn. The diary itself was A5 size and hard-backed when something smaller would have sufficed. I packed a pair of trainers in case my feet did not adapt to boots and I even supplemented my metal water carrier with a glass bottle, thus adding unnecessarily to the 14 kilos registered at baggage check-in at Heathrow Airport.

Our first experience of basic pilgrim-style accommodation was 55 Rue de la Citadelle in Saint Jean Pied de Port on the French side of the Pyrenees. Today it is the municipal hostel with its distinctive red door and shutters but 23 years ago it was a tiny, private one with a very dark interior, no kitchen and only six beds. However, the thing that most filled me with foreboding was the sight of the horribly blistered feet of Andrés, a 60-year-old Spanish grandfather from Toledo. My intentions were to use sheep wool carefully positioned between my toes but I was now very fearful at the prospect of my poor feet ending up like his. I had also heard stories of tar melting on the roads in periods of high temperatures. I must confess to feeling sceptical at the time at his assertion that Santiago Apóstol would get me to journey's end.

Keith and I had earlier trotted up the hill on the short walk from the town's railway station to the pilgrim office on the Sunday, the eve of our departure. We were in search of our first pilgrim stamp in our *credencial* (pilgrim passport) which is used as proof of making the pilgrimage to Santiago. We were invited to sit as we received our stamps and were treated to a glass of diabolo menthe (mint cordial) by the office volunteers. I protested and said that we had not actually begun our pilgrimage yet but this was swept aside in this first gesture of hospitality. That small but significant welcome to this charming little town remains with me to this day.

Eager to be on the road early on our 28 km crossing of the mountains into Spain, Keith and I aimed to set off at 5.30 the following morning. Naively, in view of it being the month of August, I had not expected it to be still dark at that hour and insisted we not begin until 6 when the crescent moon finally began to wane. Through the arch of the Porte d'Espagne, across the River Nive and up the Rue d'Espagne we went. Our adventure had finally begun. Visibility was good so we followed the quieter and more beautiful Route Napoléon but oh how incredibly steep it was! The gentle breeze back down the hill at St Jean gave way to gales on the higher slopes and it took all our concentration and energy to strike a path up the middle of a narrow minor road to avoid being blown beyond either side of the uneven camber and down the steep verges.

Four kilometres from the border at Vierge d'Orisson, a Frenchman appeared out of the blue with bottled water for us to drink. It was yet another act of kindness. I nicknamed him 'Monsieur Ange' (Mr Angel). Perched on a boulder at the side of the path was a statue of the Virgin Mary, now instantly recognisable as one of the places where Emilio Estévez, as the deceased son Daniel, appears to Tom, his father the actor Martin Sheen, in the 2010 film *The Way*. It is a fictitious story but is my favourite of all the many films and documentaries on the Camino and has led to a massive increase in the numbers of American pilgrims who now form the third largest foreign nationality behind the Italians and the Germans.

Following a steep descent through a forest and down into Spain, our beds for the night were in the large dormitory of the Augustinian Monastery at Roncesvalles. Mass in the collegiate church that evening was concelebrated by five priests. At the end they invited all the pilgrims to come forward to receive a blessing. Curiously for me, they asked us to pray for them when we got to Santiago. The extra responsibility thrust on our shoulders increased my sense of purpose in that the pilgrimage would not be just about remembering Dad. At that stage, however, I was not really one who said daily prayers.

I only found out recently that day two of our pilgrimage, 21 July, marked the day in which the POW camps' interpreter, Lt Oswald Wynd, passed away. At 35 km, it proved to be our longest. (My subsequent experiences of 30 km-plus days I always compare to the 'death zone' at high altitude on Everest in that literally every muscle in the body hurts.) We covered it in 10 hours as far as Trinidad de Arre and our convent lodging for the night, a short walk from the city of Pamplona. We were hot and tired and our shoulders ached from the weight of our rucksacks. As we had walked 13 km more than what turned out to be our average day, it was not surprising that there were few pilgrims we recognised from the previous night in the 20-bed dormitory.

The Camino is no discriminator of social class and we were to share the route, like the POWs, with people from every walk of life. Just because the open road stretched out for 800 kilometres towards the west with its heady intoxication of space, natural beauty and, in total contrast with the POWs' situation, the freedom to wander at will, it did not mean that we had nothing in common with those brave men. Getting on with people who are complete strangers and whom we came to respect through a shared goal is a thread that runs through both experiences. This would frequently involve looking out for each other, a quality made easier as technological advances this century make contact with one another so much more accessible. Texts and phone calls giving advice from pilgrims ahead were reciprocated and became a daily feature of my subsequent pilgrimages when I was equally thankful for the help given to me over terrain with which I was totally unfamiliar. An unexpected message or a sympathetic ear can often brighten one's outlook and many of the prisoners certainly had this caring quality in abundance.

This is not to say that often cramped dormitories do not produce the occasional outburst of bad temper. Early morning departures are a case-in-point particularly if they involve the rustling of plastic bags. Snorers are especially intrusive when everyone is desperate for a sound sleep after the intense physical exertions of a day's walking. Looking back, I still find it hard to recognise my behaviour when being sorely tempted to throttle one particularly loud Spanish snorer as I stood over him and berated him one night in a hostel at Molinaseca. A number of pilgrims had opted to sleep outside on that warm evening although, on reflection, they may have recognised the man after their sleep patterns were disturbed in previous hostels.

The Spanish word '*peregrino*' is derived from the Latin '*peregrinus*' which, Ian Bradley points out, literally means '*per ager*' or 'through the land'. The idea of movement and always in one direction (in the case of the Camino Francés east to west with the sun on one's back every morning) is one which he expands by calling pilgrimage "a provisional, transitory state."[1] Many consider it to be a metaphor for life's journey as we progress from birth, through childhood and adolescence, to adulthood, and ultimately death. The literal parallel is the enthusiasm and energy for the path ahead in the climb up and over the Pyrenees, the challenges half-way posed by the seemingly endless, flat horizon of the Meseta, and the life-affirming arrival in Santiago. In our modest case, after a difficult descent over treacherously unsteady stones below the Alto del Perdón Ridge beyond Pamplona, Keith and I faced the equally daunting task of negotiating our ascents into triple tier bunks and the even scarier prospect of alighting from them in the dark when nature called! This was the accommodation in the parochial hostel in Puente la Reina on day 3.

In the same hostel, a young Spanish pilgrim was very upset at having to end his journey early due to leg problems. As his friends tried to console him, I couldn't help thinking about the analogy of those who 'stay the course' and live to a good age and those who die prematurely. None of us knows when our time is up and it took the distressing prospect of this inconsolable young pilgrim to make me reflect on my own mortality as well as the thousands of Allied POWs who never made it home.

By day 4 and convinced of the unsuitability of Compeed gel plasters on the worst of my toe blisters, I took Keith's advice as a marathon runner to dispense with sheep wool in favour of liberally spread Vaseline on the hotspots of my feet. We had reached the pretty Navarrese town of Estella and waited patiently along with lots of other fellow pilgrims sitting on the footpath and propped up against our rucksacks for the large hostel to open its doors. A shabbily dressed man in a short white tunic and carrying a half-torn plastic bag breezed past us loudly proclaiming that he would be back at 6 that evening to treat leg strains and blisters. No-one reacted and I suspect most dismissed him as a crackpot.

My perception the next day to Los Arcos was that we had made steady headway thanks to the lower temperatures afforded by cloud cover. Keith was to shatter my optimism by commenting that he had slowed down to take account of my slower pace. Another blister had erupted but worse was the pain from my right ankle which we suspected was tendonitis due to the weight of my rucksack. My feeling of invincibility garnered through a lifetime reaching mountain summits meant that I had foolishly ignored the sensible precaution that the weight of a rucksack during a period of weeks of long-distance walking should be limited to a tenth of one's body weight. In my case, 7.5 kilos was way under what was actually on my back. The Camino was teaching me yet another lesson. Surrounding yourself with material goods, none of which you can take with you when the time comes to depart this life, is a waste of time if it prevents you from reaching your ultimate goal. A less materialistic life beckoned post-Camino. In practical terms I donated my favourite sweat shirt and silky smooth royal blue tracksuit bottoms to the hostel in Logroño and further on, from Castrojeriz, posted my trainers and sleeping bag on to the poste restante facility in Santiago. In total, Keith and I divested ourselves of nearly six kilos. What a difference this was to make both to my physical and mental states!

Aware that lightening my rucksack was not going to be sufficient, I knew that I was going to need treatment for my swollen ankle. Reports began to circulate round the hostel at Los Arcos from pilgrims who had received help with their leg problems from a man the previous evening back at Estella. It just had to be the guy who had passed us in the street boasting of his miracle cures. My mind was made up and, after nearly a week on foot, it felt very strange travelling by bus and totally counter-intuitive to be heading back towards the Pyrenees.

Sitting patiently on his own in a room off the hostel's main entrance as I hobbled in was Jesús. What other name could he possibly have had! From his same grubby plastic bag, he extracted a dark brown-coloured poultice with bits of seed interspersed which he proceeded to wrap inside a bandage and strap to my ankle. Dad had never spoken about the merits or otherwise of alternative medicine and, before Jesús got me to stand, I was convinced that my reverse trip back along the Camino road was a complete waste of time. How wrong I was. The anti-inflammatory effect of what I subsequently learnt to have probably been extract from the camphor plant was immediate. He would not accept any payment and, so grateful for my instant relief from pain, I thanked him profusely. His response was "¡Vaya con Dios!" (God go with you!). It reminded me of the commonly uttered goodbye in Ireland, "God bless", as frequent among Christians as among those with no particular faith except that for me it really was redolent of God's blessing. I needn't have worried about him not turning up at the hostel as he told me he had been coming every evening for five years. Free of pain, I trotted back to fetch the bus, not in the slightest self-conscious of the bulky weight attached to my foot.

The whole experience taught me to be less judgmental, a theme visited by Ian Bradley in the introduction to his book[2] in which he too mentions snorers and also a pilgrim he initially found to be "brash and superficial". We are all guilty of this in life but moments of high emotion brought on by physical and mental duress accentuate our frailties and sometimes distort our regard for our fellow man. My desire to help others on the Camino certainly increased after encounters with the 'Jesuses' of this world who ask for no financial recompense. I left instructions to volunteers at a pilgrim hostel on the final steep climb up the mountain to O Cebreiro and the last autonomy on the route, Galicia, to look out for a pilgrim who had misplaced his stick and could they please recycle any ones left behind by previous pilgrims. In the dormitory of a basic hostel in Frómista, I tried to identify the owners of two over-heavy rucksacks. This was something completely out of character for me as I listened to myself loudly addressing the occupants of the dormitory. I know that Dad actively put into practice the lessons he learnt in the camps which he summarises so eloquently in his most reflective entry of all, dated Friday 11 August 1944, and which I have reproduced in full in the epilogue. Suffice it to say for the moment that the reflection, dedicated to his fellow man and not specifically to Mum, opens with the lines "I THOUGHT TODAY that all men should spend part of their lives as prisoners of war."

The Camino does, however, have a habit of bringing the pilgrim back down to the real world with a bump especially during the most difficult times in the day when the sun is at its hottest and the distance covered is great. I found these were periods when I felt disinclined to chat to Keith and my thoughts would turn to a refreshing shower, the wonderful prospect of boots removed and sandaled feet or, alternatively, to the by now daily prayers offered up to relatives and friends, past and present. Fatigue and ethereal thoughts inevitably came crashing back to earth with a speeding car coming suddenly round a corner, the fierce barking of a dog or an unwary step on an unseen stone threatening to twist an ankle. Just such a moment occurred as I walked beyond the arch at the ancient Hospital San Antón, three km from Castrojeriz in the middle of the Meseta. This time I was hit by a different pain, sudden and sharp and lower down my left leg.

A 20-minute massage that evening at another basic but very welcoming hostel by Inés, a volunteer masseuse, provided much relief. I did offer payment but expected it to be rejected and once again I felt humbled. The next day it took only the first few steps to realise that what Inés suspected was a muscle contraction was not going to go away. I was especially grateful for Keith's company as we moved slowly up the hill, all the time discussing our future plans. I managed a smile near the summit as I posed for a photo on what I fully expected to be the 13th and last day of my pilgrimage. Chilly mornings on the Meseta at whatever time of year are not conducive to walking slowly and I knew Keith was finding it difficult to walk at such a slow pace. We resolved to split for the day and meet at a hostel at the next main town, Frómista.

Aware that I would need transport and in the days before mobile phones, I scanned the horizon from the top of the Mostelares Hill with its iconic 360-degree view of golden wheat-fields rippling in the gentle early August breeze. Beyond the shadow of its west-facing slope, I made out a straight thin line of greenery which I took to be the River Pisuerga. According to my guide book, this meant that the ancient hermitage of San Nicolás, converted into a pilgrim hostel by an Italian pilgrim association, lay somewhere along that line. All the pilgrims who had spent the previous night in Castrojeriz had long since passed us as I set off down the slope for what I knew would be a solitary couple of hours before eventually being passed by fast-walking pilgrims further back along the route.

Much to my amazement Keith was finishing off his second breakfast of the day at the hostel when I eventually hobbled in. It is famous for the ritualistic washing of the pilgrims' feet in a gesture that mirrors Jesus' humility in doing likewise to his apostles after the Last Supper. The 2018 BBC 2 television series *Pilgrimage: the Road to Santiago* contains a scene in which seven celebrity pilgrims visit the hermitage. They include Heather Small, the lead singer from the soul group M People. She is irate when she tells the others outside as they prepare to leave that she was racially abused inside. Unfortunately this is not filmed. I have no reason to doubt her conviction but misunderstandings in a foreign language can lead to the most horrendous outcomes and I have encountered, some of them when dealing with young people on foreign language exchanges.

Empathy and tonal inflection in addition to linguistic skills are essential in attempting to smooth over troubled waters. The role of an interpreter is so vital in accurately conveying the gist of a conversation to both parties and carries huge responsibility. Chris and Taeko in Japan were indispensable to me in the same way that Oswald Wynd's translating meant there was at least some communication between guards and captives.

The volunteer *hospitaleros* in the charming old stone hermitage managed to rustle up a late breakfast for me also. San Nicolás is also known as a hospital which dates back to the days when pilgrim accommodation was synonymous with physical care for sick pilgrims. This must be the derivation of the word hospitality, so much a feature of the very best hostels on the Camino as well as what strangers are so generously offered in Muslim countries. I was to find people particularly welcoming everywhere I went in Japan. In the middle of the 2019 Rugby World Cup in the country, the media was full of stories of foreign fans being overwhelmed by the sincerity of Japanese hospitality. It has taken sport to finally begin to break down some of the barriers between the Allied countries and Japan, albeit in the minds of a younger generation.

I got a lift from one of the young Italian *hospitaleros* in their minibus to Frómista, some 15 km away. This broke all my self-imposed rules of walking every step of the 800 km on foot but, as I was resigned to the possibility of giving up my Camino, I knew that I could restart at the hermitage one day in the future. Arriving at the town mid-morning that Saturday meant I had time to visit a local clinic for treatment. I did not expect to receive a massage from the doctor particularly in view of the large number of patients in the waiting room-but she had ulterior motives as she explained during the pummelling of my leg and the extensive bandaging she applied. Ireland was her next holiday destination and she asked for as many recommendations as I could manage! Almost in passing, she reassured me at the end of a procedure she had obviously administered to pilgrims many times before that I should from now on walk for three days and rest for one.

My next port of call was the chemist's where the doctor had told me to buy some arnica – tiny sugary homeopathy pain killers which are placed underneath the tongue to dissolve for maximum effect. They are so small that the hardest part of the process is to extract each one into the palm of your hand before it falls on the ground. Armed with a train timetable to plan my reunion with Jan, Andrew, and Keith's wife and two daughters at Santander in their hire car, I sat down outside at, ironically, the most basic hostel we had encountered on the Camino to await Keith's arrival. The showers were cold and bare wires were protruding from the light switch in the bathroom. Nowadays, most pilgrims would give such hostels a miss and it is true that they are now very much in the minority but it is ultimately spiritually rewarding to subscribe to the Spanish adage '*El peregrino agradece; el turista exige*' (The pilgrim is grateful; the tourist demands). A recent addition to pilgrim vocabulary is the word '*turigrino*' which conveys the idea of pilgrims who enjoy their creature comforts by pre-booking hotel accommodation and using a transportation service for their cases or rucksacks. They can readily be identified on the Camino as they carry a small day pack. Again, my view is that they should still be considered pilgrims. Some are, in fact, physically incapable of carrying a heavy rucksack.

Keith and I had established a routine of eating our meal each evening after the day's walk which meant we would reach most hostels by 2 p.m. at the latest. I felt like an over-protective parent in the hours until he finally showed up at 5 but I recognize now that my anxiety was being fuelled by my vulnerable emotional state. Montse, the leader of a group of 16-year-olds whom she was preparing for the sacrament of Confirmation by walking the Camino, had meantime offered to ring a bar back down the road at Boadilla to see if Keith had been sighted. The bar owner confirmed that there had been a raucous group of nine pilgrims who had not long left after enjoying a late lunch and some drinks. His description of them matched Keith and the other pilgrims I had expected to arrive earlier at the hostel. The whole experience at least left me relieved in the knowledge that he was making new friends and had by then acquired enough survival Spanish to get by for the remainder of his pilgrimage.

Olga, a young pilgrim in our dormitory, had earlier beckoned me to come downstairs. Her older sister, Pilar, one of the *hospitaleras* at Castrojeriz, had arrived to see how her pilgrimage was progressing but was also enquiring about my leg. I was so appreciative of her concern and she assured me that the important thing was the journey and not the arrival at Santiago. I thanked her and replied that I was not dejected at preparing to give up but had found an inner peace from everything the Camino had taught me over the fortnight. Mum's favourite biblical quotation was "let not my will but Thine be done"[3]. Josette recently told me that during the war Mum used to deliver this resignation to God's will in a more hushed tone in the fervent hope that Dad would return safely. Dad himself adhered to the same philosophy but his was more secular in tone, his version being "Whatever will be will be."

During our rest day as prescribed by the doctor, I made two phone calls to relate my newly laid plans to walk the 19 km to Carrión de los Condes and give up if my leg did not allow me to continue. Jan was fantastic in her support and said to see how I got on, take it one day at a time, and return on a different flight to them if I got delayed or had to abandon. I then rang mum in Ireland and convinced her of my belief that a pilgrimage could be done anywhere and not necessarily the Camino de Santiago. I could, for example, walk from Belfast to Dublin and pray in a few churches along the way. Mind you, I would certainly have missed the company of my fellow pilgrims! She immediately understood.

My diary for Monday 3 August includes this entry: "And so to judgement day – from a car you miss a lot, from a bike you see more, at a four km per hour walking pace you take in a lot more but it is amazing how much you absorb the sights and sounds at a steady two-km-per-hour!!. Everyone so concerned as they overtook us…" Once again I persuaded Keith to continue on his own and we would make the split permanent at Carrión. I was going so slowly that giant ants were easy to spot in front of me on the dusty terrain. A shepherd even halted his flock of sheep so I didn't have to break my stride. Gradually, more and more pilgrims passed me that I had never seen before and the realisation slowly dawned that future friendships would be fleeting and of one day's duration if I continued at my snail's pace. My state of mind was in complete contrast to the superiority I had experienced in the early days over the Pyrenees and its foothills as we blasted past every pilgrim in sight. I felt humbled. That evening we discussed the remainder of the route and divided up our maps.

There was plenty of time for solitary contemplation on the long 15 km walk to the village of Calzadilla de la Cueza, in those days the most isolated stretch of the Camino with no facilities whatsoever. The adobe-walled hostel was reported in my guidebook as being dirty and infested with mice but there was a lovely atmosphere as I arrived with the *hospitalero* Fernando from Málaga tending to pilgrims' blisters out in the street. No hot water again but large plastic bottles filled with water and arranged on the patio in the sun provided a welcome hair wash. That night I fell asleep not to the scurrying of tiny feet but to the flamenco guitar playing accompanied by the hauntingly beautiful voice of Fernando. Divested of my sleeping-bag, I did forgive him for forgetting to provide me with a blanket as insulation against the chills of a Meseta night.

I gradually picked up my pace again, ever mindful of the words from T'Pau's song 'China in Your Hands' – "Don't push too hard" – ringing in my ears. A fortnight later, I caught up with some pilgrims I hadn't seen since Frómista and it mattered not a jot that they admitted to having slowed down to enjoy some late evenings and shorter walking days. I still felt elated as I wrote "It did my confidence and self-belief the world of good!"

My worst day on the Camino coincided with the final steep climb up to O Cebreiro and into the final autonomy on the route. It was Saturday 15 August and I had enough knowledge of Gallego, the language now spoken widely in Galicia, to get the gist on my basic radio of news of the Real IRA car bomb back home in Omagh. A violent storm the night before had severed electricity supplies and land-line phones but a Spanish pilgrim lent me his primitive mobile. I spoke to Mum in Newcastle who said there was no news of my sister Edmée who had a work placement at the time in a psychiatric hospital in the town. The bomb came at a time of great optimism following the Good Friday Agreement and the target was, inexplicably, a mainly nationalist town. It was to claim the lives of 29 people. Poignantly for me, these included one young Spanish and three Irish exchange students along with a 23-year-old Spanish teacher. It was not until power was restored the next day in the valley at the bottom of the mountain that I rang again when Mum gave me the news that Edmée had been shopping in Belfast on her day off. Twenty years ago, public telephone queues and the lack of privacy for those speaking were the norm and patience was required in abundance. How different must it have been for the POWs desperate to impart and receive news from their loved-ones. At least my inner torment had only lasted 12 hours.

The closer I got to Santiago, the more I realised that I would now be able to fulfil my dream. The uncertainty and doubt I had experienced back down the Camino had now gone and I could even contemplate an approximate date for my arrival. It must have been a deliriously happy moment when the prisoners could finally give full rein to the prospect of being reunited with their families again after 42 months when many would have despaired at ever returning home.

My happiest memories in '98 were not of the stunning landscapes of the mountain cols, the colourful fields of sunflowers in Navarre, the vineyards of the Rioja, the never-ending, mind-blowing horizons of the Meseta, or the verdant landscapes of Galicia, but rather the joy of companionship with shared experiences. A flavour of this can be communicated to those who have not done the pilgrimage but 'talking the talk' is not the same as 'walking the walk' and it is only by embarking on the pilgrimage with its incumbent vicissitudes of pain and elation that you can fully appreciate what it involves. Reliving moments with fellow pilgrims in years to come creates joyful memories in contrast to the POWs in the past in their isolation and their frequent inability to share their distressing thoughts with anyone.

As in life, friendship groups are created, sometimes staying together, sometimes separating and occasionally re-forming. The tendency in a group can be to remain comfortably insular and not interact, particularly with individuals who may be experiencing loneliness (though this should not be confused with those who prefer their own company). Inclusivity and making others feel wanted and good about themselves should be a human trait we all aspire to. Five days from Santiago at Puertomarín on the banks of the River Miño, I found myself in just such a group with five others. Else from Austria, Eugen from Germany, Anne from Liverpool, Paul and Richard also from England, and I formed an inseparable group. We literally shared everything as we walked together – animated conversation and anecdotes, anti-inflammatories, octopus cooked from a van in the street at Palas de Rei, and spaghetti bolognaise ingredients bought at Melide and carried the 12 km to the quiet, idyllic setting of the hostel at Ribadiso to be cooked and savoured that night for dinner. I wasn't so happy about the almond tarta de Santiago (Santiago cake) which had to swing in a plastic bag from my rucksack so as not to be crushed and upset my balance as I walked. Some of us had made a secret diversion to a local cake shop but it was worth it to celebrate Richard's birthday with this delicious traditional Galician dessert.

A month of being in the embracing cocoon of the Camino bubble needed an escape and I found it at a barber's in Sarria where I waited for over an hour for the most amazing haircut delivered by a hairdresser who evidently took great pride in his profession. This brief but significant activity prepared me for my reinsertion back into the real world as well as sparing Jan from the sight of her scruffy husband at Santiago. It reminded me of Dad being billeted on the family in Vancouver for a few days before the final legs of his journey home. Apart from the improvement to his diet, it must have afforded some relief from almost six years' constant immersion in a military environment.

One hears stories of banners and bunting in the streets of towns and cities welcoming home the men from the war. Dad's was a more private embrace with Mum at Larne though he was impressed by the terrific reception for HMS *Glory* at the harbour at Victoria in Canada on 26 October '45. "All the ships' sirens sounded their welcome and the crowds cheered and waved for hours on end. I saw several glad reunions and it brought tears to my eyes to see wives and children greet their dear ones on the dock." For days I had tried to imagine my reunion with Jan and Andrew in the Praza do Obradoiro in front of the cathedral in Santiago. Our gang of six had split before I entered the old walls of the city at the Porta do Camiño. Ironically I was facing the prospect of getting my longed-for first sight of them in the square in the company of an '*ex-hospitalero*' walking the Camino who, a week before, had berated noisy pilgrims, me included, for getting up at 5 a.m. to leave a hostel. I dallied by the north door of the cathedral to give him time to proceed on his own. Then it was through the arch, past the ever-present Galician bag pipe player and out into the square to see Andrew racing towards me and the prospect of a gigantic hug. Jan held back to make sure she got the picture before joining us. I had missed them so very much. We had never before spent so long apart.

The square, thankfully now restricted to traffic, is the most incredible place from early morning as weary but happy pilgrims gather to embrace and have their photos taken with the magnificent backdrop of the towering part-Romanesque, part-Baroque cathedral. I knew I would have to forego the midday Pilgrim Mass but Andrew and I joined the line of mainly tourists in the Pórtico de la Gloria porch queuing to place our hand in the five indentations at the foot of the Tree of Jesse. My prayers of thanksgiving were dominated by my intentions for a close friend of Jan's fighting cancer. I had felt Dad's watchful presence every step of the way.

Molly Malone's Irish pub was the venue for celebrations that evening when I was so happy for Jan and Andrew to meet my five special pilgrim friends. Anne was eagerly looking forward to the champagne welcome at her parents' home back on the Wirral and her brother's wedding the following week-end. Nineteen-year-old Eugen chatted enthusiastically about his forthcoming entry to a seminary in Germany to train as a priest. A bout of food poisoning from the night before had left him weak and I had flagged down a motorist who offered to take him the final 10 km into the city. The poor lad had begun his pilgrimage 165 km further east of us at Somport and had walked almost 1,000 km! He had been asking for me at the pilgrim office where I had gone to collect my '*compostela*' and I was ushered into a back room to find him prostrate on a couch grinning enormously from ear to ear. Nothing would have kept him from joining us that night even if it meant catching a lift on the final lap of his journey and not walking all the way.

My mind was in overdrive that night in our hotel near the airport where we met up with Keith and his family. He had arrived a full five days before me. Some of my clothes had served as a pillow for me for almost five weeks and it was too soon to adapt to the comfort of a fluffy one, a soft mattress and freshly washed and ironed sheets. Instead, I sat on the toilet seat for an hour writing postcards. I too had lost weight, at least half a stone though not nearly as much as our dad.

Back in England I had a voracious appetite and for days snacked constantly between meals. With only two sets of polo shirts and shorts for so long, it was strange familiarising myself again with a seemingly vast array of clothes in my wardrobe and I felt almost ostentatious when I ventured out of doors for the first few days. I thought of my companion Eugen beginning a new chapter in his life as he began his training for the priesthood. What could I put into practice from my pilgrimage? The experience itself proved to be very far from the anti-climax some pilgrims feel when they reach Santiago. At school, I was looking forward to a new academic year without the responsibilities of running the department. One completely unexpected by-product was the confidence in public-speaking that I acquired from my first slide presentation of my pilgrimage to the whole school staff. Sharing my message from my first Camino was infectious. Since then, I have continued my talks to many groups of prospective walkers and people interested in pilgrimage in addition to my students learning Spanish and, in retirement, to new cohorts of A level students at St Peter's as well as other local schools. Five years after Dad's passing, I had felt incredibly close to him throughout. The experience of pilgrimage, however, is all about what you carry forward from it. For me that was mainly about looking out for others, finding the time to be reflective, and also finding the time to pray.

NOTES

1. **Pilgrimage a Spiritual and Cultural Journey** *by Ian Bradley, Lion 2009, p.21.*

2. *As above p.18.*

3. *Based on the New Testament, chapter 22 verse 42 "Father, if You are willing, take this cup from me; yet not my will, but Yours be done."*

CHAPTER 14
"RECONCILIATION, 2006"

"The Camino had offered me an unexpected setting in which to seek rec-
onciliation, one which I had never foreseen until I heard about the family
in the village. A visit to Japan, however, was something I had not yet envis-
aged. It was to take a further ten years for those early seeds to germinate."

Keith and I had joined the Confraternity of Saint James[1] shortly before
our Camino. They are a charity who actively promote the pilgrimage in
all its manifold aspects – historical, architectural, cultural, and religious
to name but a few. Their practical pilgrim days, held in venues all around
the UK in the months before the main pilgrim season begins at Easter,
give great practical advice to those about to embark for the first time.

The CSJ now runs two pilgrim hostels in Spain, one in the village of
Rabanal del Camino in the Montes de León on the Camino Francés, and
the other in the hamlet of Miraz in Galicia on the Camino del Norte, the
northern route. After I returned home, I was motivated by a strong desire
to give something back and to use my Spanish in a practical and useful
way. I attended training in London to be a *hospitalero* in Rabanal for a
fortnight in the summer of 2004 and volunteered again two years later.
Completing a Camino is a pre-requisite for working as a volunteer.

The following is an article I wrote in the *Bulletin*, their biannual magazine, in June 2012.

"RECONCILIATION ON THE CAMINO" by Paul Murray

My story dates back to the night after the feast of Saint James in
2006 when I was coming to the end of my second stint as a warden
in the CSJ's Refugio Gaucelmo in Rabanal. I shared my *hospitalero*
duties that summer with Gilbert from Belgium and we had managed
to keep the barn open for most of the two weeks to cope with the
high numbers of pilgrims. A sudden drop in numbers on this particular day meant pilgrims only in the main dormitory and Gilbert
and I eagerly looked forward to a slightly more relaxing evening.

I had heard from Angela at the Tesín Refugio lower down the

Calle Real that she had welcomed three generations of a Japanese family. They were a most unusual combination of a grandmother, a mother and her two young sons both aged under 10. Angela had explained that they had planned to attend vespers and compline in the church. It struck me that here was the opportunity for me to bury once and for all my demons which had stretched back to my youth. My late father's love for his fellow man had never extended to the Japanese following his three and a half years' incarceration firstly in Changi in Singapore and then in six more prisoner of war camps on Japan's main northern island of Hokkaido. My attitude to the Japanese until that summer evening in the Montes de León, whilst never remotely hostile, could best be described as indifferent and I vividly recalled shunning groups of their teachers when they visited the school where I worked, ironically as a modern languages' teacher, for 25 years.

The idea had been growing in my head that, at the very least, I could show them some hospitality by inviting them to view our *refugio*. Sure enough, they emerged from the pilgrim blessing at vespers to chat with the monks outside their retreat house and readily accepted our invitation for a short tour of the wonderful sanctuary which is the *refugio*. The mother was the only English speaker and dutifully translated into Japanese for her off spring and her mother as we toured first the welcoming reception area, then the cosy barn with the bunks neatly arrayed for the next pilgrim arrivals and finally the *huerta* (orchard) where the two young boys no longer had to endure tales of '1073 and all that' when Alfonso VI granted a charter to the hermit Gaucelmo to build a refuge up the mountain at Foncebadón. They screamed in sheer delight as they ran round the fruit trees and played catch by the pilgrim benches.

All too quickly, the guided tour came to an end and I resolved that I would unburden to the mother the shame of my 52 years of indifference towards her nation. As the little group stood on the cobble stones in the street at Gaucelmo's entrance, I told her that my father had been a POW. I shall never forget the initial look of terror that came over her face and I remain convinced to this day that she thought I was going to enact some physical retribution on her. I quickly moved to reassure her, kissing her on both cheeks, bowing and saying *sionara* (goodbye). She must have explained what I had said to her mother but the incredible emotion of these cathartic moments blurs any memories of this. Gilbert, who had observed the whole scene unfold, immediately encouraged me to watch the little group as they approached the corner of the street to return down the hill to Tesín's and, sure enough, they turned back to wave goodbye and respond to my waves.

I had thought that the family might have called the next morning as they walked up the Calle Real (Rabanal's main street) on their journey to the Cruz de Ferro [2] but the raw emotions of the events of the night before probably made that very unlikely.

Gilbert, meantime, turned to preparing the kitchen for breakfast while I sobbed inconsolably at the door of the '*refugio*'. He then, in his usual sensitive way, judged that the time was right to give me the pilgrim nationalities and stats to fill in.

After turning in for the night, I tried to listen to KISS FM for company on my radio headset but my tears persisted until the wee small hours – tears of sadness thinking of my deceased father, tears of shame at my years of indifference towards the Japanese and the initial anguish I had caused one particular family a few hours before, and finally tears of relief that I could now get on with the rest of my life and treat these people with the respect that all nationalities deserve on this earth.

And a final footnote, I just knew from the first words of Padre Javier's sermon at Sunday Mass in the tiny Santa María Church opposite our hostel a few days later that the theme for his homily was going to be reconciliation.

NOTES

1. *The CSJ website is www.caminopilgrim.org*

2. *The Cruz de Ferro at 1,504 metres marks the highest point on the Camino Francés. Pilgrims traditionally leave a stone that symbolises a weight being lifted from their lives at the foot of a tall wooden pole with an iron cross on the top.*

CHAPTER 15

"PILGRIMAGE 2, CAMINO PRIMITIVO, 2009"

"I dripped sweat all over the marble reception desk but they took my €43 and never was a shower so sweet, with my socks and underpants getting extra soaping under my feet."

Diary entry day 1, Sunday 19 July, at Hotel Palper, Grado.

Feeling close to Dad was an undeniable attraction for my second pilgrimage but Mum's diagnosis of cancer had a more urgent bearing in my choice of the summer of 2009. The high five she gave me prior to my departure will always be a special memory. That year also marked the end of my full-time teaching career with the appealing prospect of two part-time years ahead before early retirement at the age of 57. A presenter from BBC Radio Gloucestershire, Faye Hatcher, came to interview me at school. She had walked part of the Francés and I felt particularly relaxed chatting about my new pilgrimage with a fellow pilgrim. I also welcomed the opportunity to give publicity to the three charities for whom I was collecting money namely NASS (1), HCPT (2), and my choir Philomusica. I chose the second of these because of the tremendous work that sixth formers in St Peter's used to do in accompanying disabled youngsters from St Rose's Special School in Stroud on their annual pilgrimage to Lourdes in the French Alps. Each and every one of them whom I taught returned to lessons after the Easter holidays with a newfound empathy for those less fortunate in our society. This they extended, in turn, to those around them.

Secure in the conviction that you are never on your own on the Camino even if you have no walking partner, I set off from Oviedo, the capital of Spain's northern autonomous principality of Asturias, to walk the 300 km Camino Primitivo. It gets its name 'Primitivo' from the Asturian monarch, King Alfonso II 'El Casto' (The Chaste) who, tradition has it, was the first pilgrim to make the journey to Santiago to venerate the bones of the saint in the ninth century.

The San Salvador (Holy Saviour) Cathedral on a hill in the city centre is the traditional starting point for the pilgrimage. I sought out the beautiful polychrome statue of Christ the Redeemer, humbly positioned not within the precinct of the altar railings but symbolically beyond it in the main body of the church where He is closer to his flock. He holds a globe in one hand and raises the two index fingers of His right hand as He blesses mankind. It was 18 July, the 73rd anniversary of the outbreak of the Spanish Civil War. I prayed for the victims of that terrible conflict, for Mum in her final battle, and thought of 113-year-old Henry Allingham, the oldest living man ever recorded from the UK and the last survivor of the First World War, who had died that same day. My diary entry that evening read: "The Saviour held him longer than most in the palm of his outstretched left hand."

After the Saturday evening vigil Mass where the celebrant, as per usual in 'high churches' in Spain, made no reference to any pilgrims present, I pursued the priest into the sacristy for the first stamp in my *credencial*. The first steps in one's pilgrimage are enormously symbolic. Not one to draw attention to myself, I stood behind the enormous door of the private hostel the next morning at 7 o'clock, listening for a quiet moment in between the noisy Saturday night revellers and the refuse lorries doing their rounds, before launching myself on my latest Camino. So many questions flashed through my mind. How long would it take me? Would I have leg problems? Would I reach Santiago? Who would be the pilgrims I would meet and with whom I would forge a special bond? Would I have to curtail my pilgrimage if Mum passed away? At least my mobile phone meant I could now keep in touch more easily with my loved ones but feelings of vulnerability still persisted as I embarked once again into the great unknown.

All pilgrims dread negotiating their way through large cities and this was especially true of setting off from one when my mind was not yet accustomed to the ritual of route-mapping. Helpful brass scallop shells (3) embedded in the paving stones near the cathedral soon gave way to the strategically placed blue and yellow ceramic tiles or the ubiquitous yellow arrows painted on street corners. Fortunately, I reached the outskirts relatively quickly and soon began to enjoy the beautiful green rolling landscape, and the pink hydrangeas and wild flowers growing everywhere in great profusion. The Primitivo does not attract the same numbers of pilgrims as the Francés but the tranquillity and the joys of nature heighten one's feelings of spirituality. The distant striking of church bells at midday prompted my singing of the Bells of the Angelus, always shyly delivered out of the earshot of any passing locals.

Although I enjoyed the solitude of the walking and the absorption of all the details of the landscape, I did look forward to the interaction with other pilgrims each afternoon and evening in the hostels. One such perfect setting was the hamlet of Bodenaya. It is approached as you climb out of a valley with huge concrete pillars supporting the twin carriageways of the N634 and the thunder of passing traffic high above your head. An ugly quarry and its enveloping clouds of dust added to my feelings of discomfort but I was so glad I made the decision to stop and not push on to the top of the pass. Alejandro, the *hospitalero,* is a former taxi driver from Madrid who made the decision to get out of the rat race and renovate an old building as a donations' pilgrim hostel. The entire *albergue* (hostel) is open-plan and a shrine to the Camino with mementos, photos of smiling pilgrims, and *compostelas* adorning its humble walls. A communal meal was planned for the evening at which I got to know two Spanish pilgrims, Mario and Chule. Something unheard of on any Camino in my experience was a consensus requested by the *hospitaleros* for everyone to get up at the same time the following morning so as not to disturb one another. Impressed by this sensitivity as well as the prospect of a hearty breakfast on offer, I was only too happy to comply and didn't hit the road the following morning until 8.25. I kept well behind my two new pilgrim friends as they walked faster than me but caught them up as they took longer rests.

Three days later lay the steep climb up the Ruta de los Hospitales, at 1,120 metres the highest section of the pilgrimage. Campiello was the last village before the mountain col in which to eat and stock up with provisions. The Bar Tienda Herminia reminded me very much of rural Ireland in the '70s and early '80s when you could have a drink in a bar but also purchase groceries on display behind the counter. The owner, Herminia, gave us a beaming welcome, called each of us *cariño* (darling) and served a delicious meal with free coffee thrown in, again unusual for Spain as they usually make a charge. In spite of it being a busy lunch-time, she also took the time to write a comment in our *credenciales* next to her pilgrim stamp. Mine read *"Hoy has venido por aquí...mis deseos que la mano de Dios te proteja, su palabra te hable y sus ojos te miren."* (Today you have come here...my wish is that the hand of God will protect you, His word may speak to you and His eyes look at you.) What a wonderfully personal invocation to God. I felt truly humbled by the sentiments of this special lady and true friend of the pilgrims.

Before leaving, I spotted four young Slovak pilgrims having lunch. We had met them for the first time the previous day in the former health centre at Tineo, now called the Mater Cristi Pilgrim Hostel. Their interest in the pilgrimage had led them to drive 3,000 km from their home. Each day they committed to all walking together and would then take it in turns for one to return by bus at the end of the day back to their starting point to pick up their car. Boris and Martin were priests and Katka and Martina teachers. The guys would ask local priests along the route if they could celebrate Mass in their churches.

Martina explained that *primitivo* in Slovak means easy. We both concurred that this was definitely not the case as I was to discover the following day when Mario, Chule and I set off together from the basic hostel at Borres to tackle the high mountain Ruta de los Hospitales. The 2006 edition of the CSJ guide gave the following warning: "This mountain route should only be attempted in good weather, by well-equipped and experienced hill walkers, in groups of not less than two, i.e. no solitary walkers." We had difficulty locating the fountain in the village of La Mortera but it was essential that we drank and replenished our bottles before the 17 km traverse. I marvelled at the long since dilapidated *hospitales*, now used for sheltering livestock, and thought of the thousands who had made this isolated and perilous crossing in times gone by. I also thought of those who cared for the pilgrims and treated them with herbal remedies right up until the 19th century. My mind then jumped forward to the duty of care that Dad and the other medical staff so selflessly displayed in the camps.

Earlier, as Mario tenderly massaged his companion's right knee back down by the fountain, he told me the story of his four months in Limerick in Ireland where he was exploited by an inscrutable landlord offering the most basic accommodation. His father had become paralysed in an accident at work and was subsequently confined to a wheelchair. He struck me as a remarkably resilient young man.

My knee hurt and I got progressively slower as we climbed. Both my new friends would push on, stop every so often to allow me to catch up, and to enquire as to how I was feeling. They kept encouraging me to keep going. We passed the eerie skeleton of a horse which Mario identified by a few tufts from its mane, then a small lagoon with some horses and their young foals drinking and grazing in this most idyllic of spots. I had slowed to two km per hour walking pace so the time had come for us to split. We exchanged mobile phone numbers though they would have been useless in an emergency as there was no coverage. The cloudless golden sunrise was a distant memory in the midst of what was now a howling gale but at least the visibility was good. I knew they would be looking out for me at the village of Berducedo lower down off the peaks and cols.

It was a long, very steep and painful drop down off the mountains but the views inspired me. I could not have managed without my trusty Leki walking poles and managed to reach some buildings at Montefurado, perched precariously astride a lower col. Martina texted me a few days later to say that they had stopped there earlier for the men to celebrate Mass in the open air and had included Mum in their intentions. They probably didn't know it but this was a throw-back to penal times in rural Ireland when the practice of the Catholic faith was prohibited. Finally, after 11 hours, I reached our pre-arranged hostel at Berducedo at 6 o'clock. I paid my €3 and unrolled my sleeping-bag only to be told by some other pilgrims that Mario and Chule were staying in a private hostel in another part of the village. I didn't hesitate, repacked my rucksack and, with the aid of a cyclist who offered to carry it, set off to join them. Mabe, the *hospitalera*, had made up a bed in the unused dining room where she assured me I could enjoy a quiet night's sleep to recover from the trials of a long day. By then reconciled to the prospects of my spending two nights in the village, the three of us set out to look for somewhere to eat and to share a last meal together. A sweet elderly lady who owned a bar apologised and said she had stopped serving the evening menu but could rustle up a couple of fried eggs and some rustic bread for each of us which we washed down with the famous acidic Asturian cider. We took it in turns to pour it into the traditional wide-brimmed glass from above our heads so as to stimulate its fizz and refreshing taste. It was just as well we set about this in the street as some of us more than others wasted lots of the glistening golden liquid on the pavement!

We were joined in an adjacent bar for a couple of drinks by Robert from Ireland and his Spanish wife Teresa from Ciudad Real. I had met them on my second day and greatly enjoyed their company. Tere suggested that I post some of the contents of my over-heavy rucksack to her parents. I was so annoyed with myself that I was repeating the same mistake of my first pilgrimage. Its contents weighed in at 11 kilos and this, together with the recent climbs and descents, had contributed to my knee problem.

Knowing that there was no post office in the vicinity, I resolved to donate a polo shirt, multi-purpose knife, map, and magnifying glass to Mabe for the use of other pilgrims.

The next morning I rose early to say goodbye to the two lads. They looked weary and texted me a few days later to say they had been forced to give up their pilgrimage. Sadly Mario added that, in addition to the blisters, aches and sun-burn, the experience had not brought with it the fulfilment for which he had longed.

I spent a relaxing but very lonely morning in the hostel, well aware that there would be no new pilgrim arrivals on the long trek over the mountains until later that afternoon. I missed Mario and Chule's stimulating company which mirrored Dad's accounts of many evenings spent with George Reuneker and Krish Nair when he felt he had at last found two genuine friends. By midday, my desire to move on and not spend a second day recovering was overwhelming. Armed with some cheese, crisps, fruit and chocolate which ironically weighed more than the items I had chosen to remove from my rucksack, my goal was the tiny hamlet of La Mesa. It was only a short 4.4 km away and I took it slowly so as not to aggravate any tweaks to my knee. The lyrics "Don't push too hard..." from my first Camino filled my head as I spent an immensely satisfying two and a half hours walking west with not another living soul for company.

I was rewarded with the sight of the most spectacularly situated cluster of houses on the Primitivo. La Mesa (literally 'the table') sits astride another mountain col with plunging views down into deep valleys on either side. Incredibly, in such an isolated spot, it had its own church and I was fortunate in that the priest only celebrates one service there per month. It was 25 July, the Feast of St James. I felt so privileged to be able to attend Mass along with some 30 other locals, all of us squeezed in like sardines and sitting precariously on narrow sloping benches. The priest delivered a homily about an incident from Santiago's life. He may have had little success at the time in converting the people of Iberia to Christianity but his legacy and the devotion of so many nowadays to the cult of St James more than make up for it.

The enriching, spiritual experience of the service was not matched by the run-down 14-bedded hostel which had extensive mould round the window frames. These types of basic hostels do not enjoy the luxury of a permanent *hospitalero*. I was entrusted by the other pilgrims with the key for locking and unlocking the building. On the surprisingly extensive village green, I joined one of them at sunset on a picnic table for my frugal meal. He was a huge hulk of a man who ate his bean stew out of its original tin by using the razor-sharp peeled back lid as a spoon. He was a man of few words but I exchanged enough with him to know that he was very focused on completing his pilgrimage.

In the gathering gloom I found a spot above the hamlet with better phone coverage so I could ring Jan. Encouraged by her support, I set off the next morning up and round the side of Buspol Mountain, past the ubiquitous wind park and braced myself for the 300-metre drop down through the spectacular cloud line and a further 800 below it to the Salime Reservoir. Ironically there was no access to any water on what was a very warm day. As I prepared myself for the long slog on an asphalt road up and out of the dam precincts, two young Spanish pilgrims blasted past me at a metronomic pace. When I bumped into them again at the next small town, I sensed that Javi and his wife Bea would become my new walking friends. Although I could not match their pace especially in those early tentative recovery days, we did the usual and arranged to meet each evening at a pre-selected hostel. In many ways, this is the ideal pilgrim scenario, a day's solitary reflective walking followed by an enjoyable and frequently animated exchange of experiences each evening along the lines of "I saw this..." and "Did you see that?" They now live in Burgos and have two young sons. He is a teacher and she a doctor in the local hospital. We had a great tenth anniversary reunion in the city two years ago. My affectionate nickname for them is '*Corre Caminos*' (Road Runners) after the speedy children's cartoon character.

A chance read of a local newspaper at a bar six days from Santiago led me to tear up my walking schedule to the city. If I could get there in five, I would fulfil a life-long ambition to see Bruce Springsteen performing live in concert in, of all places, Monte del Gozo (Mount Joy). This hill was traditionally where pilgrims got their first glimpse of the twin towers of the cathedral. A huge pilgrim hostel with capacity for 500, monuments to mark Pope John Paul II's visit in 1989, and an amphitheatre constructed for him to celebrate Mass, now extend over much of the hill-side. The latter was the venue for the concert. A phone call to Andrew, who had beaten me to it by seeing the 'Boss' at Glastonbury earlier that summer, was successful in getting me a ticket though I had to make him promise he would destroy my credit card details after the transaction was processed!

The longer five stages to Monte del Gozo meant diverting off the Primitivo towards the north and joining the Camino del Norte for four stages. These included an overnight stay in the Cistercian monastery of Sobrado dos Monxes. It was a wonderfully tranquil, welcoming setting, and a building that, unusually, also included tourist accommodation. The monks strictly adhered to their pilgrim house rule of lights out at 10 which left us scuttling around in the pitch black for mobile phones and torches. The community then consisted of 17 monks. Putting these numbers in perspective, I learnt that in medieval times they catered for up to 8,000 pilgrims a night!

The last night of my two-week pilgrimage was no different from all the others in that, concert or no concert, I was still going to wear flip-flops to let my feet recover. This meant standing at the very back of the amphitheatre so as not to get them trampled. My judicious feet placements and frequent hand-offs of innocent spectators made me feel guilty. I felt sad for those poor fans with tickets who were refused entry after many ticketless ones were admitted thanks to a chaotic manning of the entrances. There were 40,000 spectators. I sang myself hoarse for over three hours to tracks from Bruce and the E Street Band such as the appropriately named 'Long Walk Home' and 'Working on a Dream'. Singing to keep my spirits up had become a big part of this Camino as it did for our dad in the camps when he would sing through his repertoire of Irish songs. One song, however, stood out. In my diary I wrote "The most memorable delivery was without a doubt 'The Rising' as the protagonist rises through the mayhem of the Twin Towers – I cried tears of sadness at this fantastically emotional song and thoughts inevitably turned to Dad as someone who also entered the pain zone…and ultimately survived."

Sitting on my flimsy bed roll with the uncomfortable sensation of prickly grass coming through, I had earlier in the day phoned Mum, now living in Reading in England and in the loving care of my sister Edmée, with the news of my arrival. I didn't expect her to say much as she was now suffering from the cruel ravages of dementia but I knew she would be listening to every word. I was conscious that each required slow and deliberate enunciation. Edmée then took the handset and said how happy they were for me and how Mum had prayed every evening for a successful outcome to my pilgrimage. She passed away the following month at the grand old age of 96. She had outlived Dad by 16 years and is now permanently reunited with him.

I did enjoy the leisurely final four km stroll down into the city the next morning. Before entering the square, my excitement and reverie were suddenly punctured by a 10-year-old boy coming in the opposite direction who was verbally abusing and gesticulating obscenely at his mother after she had confiscated his mobile phone. I slowed my gait as in '98, reluctant to carry such a discordant image to my appointment with Santiago and his 'Master'.

As the pilgrim enters the square he or she is faced with the statue of Santiago Matamoros (St James the *Moor-Slayer*) on his white steed high on top of the Palacio Rajoy opposite the cathedral. This is a reminder of the ambivalent nature of the saint who is depicted in many churches in a blood-thirsty pose severing Moorish heads. I have always thought that it was the height of insensitivity for the Spanish Army to bear the motif of the blood red-coloured Cross of St James, a mixture of the fleur-de-lis and a sword, on their uniforms. Fortunately most pilgrim gazes are drawn to the benevolent statue of the pilgrim saint with staff and gourd atop the soaring cathedral opposite.

I had imagined that nothing would top Bruce's memorable concert but, as I returned to the square later, I was aware of a scrum of paparazzi at the foot of the cathedral steps. I texted Andrew after I heard the name Sheen mentioned. He replied that the celebrity of interest might be the English actor Michael Sheen. There then followed a second text excitedly asking if it was the American film actor and star of *The West Wing*, Martin Sheen. This was indeed confirmed at the midday pilgrim Mass by the welcome that the dean of the cathedral gave him on the occasion of his 69th birthday. As for me, I felt incredibly proud when, having received my *compostela* a mere 90 minutes before at the pilgrim office, my pilgrimage was announced over the tannoy as "*Uno de Irlanda que salió de Oviedo*" (One from Ireland who left from Oviedo). The nationality and starting place of each pilgrim is traditionally read out at the Mass but I had not expected such a fast turnaround.

After the service in which there was a mention of Martin Sheen's pilgrimage, I spoke briefly to his son, Emilio Estévez, to enquire as to their departure point. To my surprise, he replied that they had not yet begun but they were planning to start at St Jean Pied de Port. I wished him the customary "*¡Buen Camino!*" and thought how lovely it was for him to walk with his dad. It was only when I read an in-depth interview with his father in the local newspaper, *La Voz de Galicia*, the next day that I realised Emilio was directing him in a film called *The Way* which they were planning to shoot at various stages along the Camino Francés. Despite the antics of some zany, barely credible characters, it is a wonderful story of a unique bond between a father and his dead son as the former spreads his ashes along the route.

NOTES

1. *NASS stands for National Axial Spondyloarthritis Society. Their website is www.nass.co.uk*

2. *HCPT stands for Hosanna House and Children's Pilgrimage Trust. Their website is www.hcpt.org.uk*

3. *The scallop shell is the iconic image pilgrims associate with the many Caminos that converge on Santiago. The shell itself was used as a bowl to hold food and drink. There are many theories as to its origin but the symbolism of the shape of a hand is one that greatly appeals to me.*

CHAPTER 16

"PILGRIMAGE 3, VÍA DE LA PLATA PART 1, 2012"

"Walked through miles and miles of orange groves, past olive trees and a few yards onto a private estate drive-way with a lethal barbed wire fence which dramatically recoils as you unhook it."

Diary entry day 2, Friday 5 October, on the path to
Castilblanco de los Arroyos.

Retirement in 2011 gave me the opportunity to accept an invitation made years earlier from the recently deceased and inspirational leading light of the CSJ, Marion Marples, to join the committee that run the Gaucelmo Pilgrim Hostel in Rabanal del Camino. This mirrors the desire of many pilgrims to give something back which I was already doing as a regular volunteer *hospitalero*. Caring for up to 40 pilgrims a night in the idyllic surroundings of the former parish priest's house in the village is exhausting but, nevertheless, one of the most rewarding experiences of my life. I admit that altruistic tendencies were also tempered by an interest in tackling another pilgrim route and seeing what other lessons the experience of long-distance walking towards a holy place might bring. I was intrigued by the prospect of walking the 1,000 km Vía de la Plata beginning in Seville in the far south of the country, an area I had only once visited before as an undergraduate during my year abroad teaching English conversation classes in A Coruña in 1975. However, six weeks away from Jan was too long apart from the fact that, approaching my 60th year, the physical challenge would be too great so I divided the pilgrimage into two with the first half ending at Salamanca.

The Vía de la Plata is the longest of the pilgrim routes in Spain, is impossible to walk in the summer months due to the brutally high temperatures in Andalucía and Extremadura, necessitates careful planning so as not to run out of water, and, due to its isolation, lacks the pilgrim infrastructure of many of the other routes. Walking on my own once again, there was going to be ample time for reflection and prayer. Thoughts of Mum and Dad were uppermost as were those directed towards my best friend, Kiko. A photo of the two of us walking down the Calle San Andrés in A Coruña in 1975 adorned the front of my small diary and on the inside cover I stuck a trimmed photocopy of a dedication he had written to me in 1990. When I first knew him, he was an illegal Cuban immigrant and was exploited by his two uncles in his job as a barman in A Coruña. Despite his low income, none of the students from Asturias or myself living in the *pensión* (guest-house) two floors above the bar ever forgot his generosity towards us or, for that matter, his engaging smile. He used to frequently buy us a drink or alter the pin-ball machine in the bar so we could play for free. I had gone to visit him and his family shortly after my Primitivo when he was in poor health. It was a terrible shock to receive an email from one of his daughters three months later to say her father had died later that same month.

The late night coach journey to Gatwick Airport took me right past the church in Cheltenham where the funeral of Paul Gleadell's daughter, Virginia, had taken place four years earlier. It felt good that Dad's link to India and a family that meant so much to him was forming a part, albeit a small one, of my latest pilgrimage.

I was fascinated by my visit to the enchanting Moorish fortress of the Alcázar in Seville and its highly informative audio guide. During Mass on the eve of my departure at the church of El Salvador, the second largest in the city after the cathedral, my gaze wandered away from the celebrant at the high altar to one particular statue in a side aisle. It depicts Christ in a very human pose of fatigue with his chin resting on his left hand and his right reposing on his knee. It reminded me of another sculpture, a real favourite of mine, of the Virgin and Child in the cathedral at Toledo where the latter is tickling his mother's chin as she holds him in her arms. These are the human depictions of the Holy Family with which we can perhaps better identify than with more traditional iconography. At the end of Mass, following the priest's final blessing – "The Mass is ended. Go forth in peace." – Dad would always give the "Thanks be to God" response from the congregation a wickedly irreverent twist in a relieved tone of voice. Two further images stayed with me throughout my pilgrimage before I left the city. They were the 17th century paintings of a handsome, youthful Santiago in the Museo de Bellas Artes by Francisco Polanco and José de Ribera and were a refreshing contrast from the older, bearded saint who figures prominently in the statues in the many churches named after him in Spain.

The Poor Clare Convent in a quieter part of Seville was my choice of accommodation. I was given a simple white-washed room behind a wrought iron gate with its own small patio and array of potted plants, the perfect setting for the start of my latest pilgrimage. It was 4 October which appropriately coincided with the feast of St Francis of Assisi, one of the earliest pilgrims to Santiago. Attendance at 8 o'clock Mass in the simple adjacent church meant a late 9.15 start on the road. The traditional first steps outside the cathedral back in the city centre were not for me which made the early toot of recognition from a driver and a cheery "*¡Buen Camino!*" as he rolled down his window all the more special. A cyclist deliberately dismounted on the confusing northern ring road to direct me across the Guadalquivir River as I headed due north. Pilgrims on this route south to north are very aware of the sun in the morning, not on our backs to the east but on our right-hand side, hence the need to cream up those particular exposed areas of skin. The Spanish have a curious expression for 'losing one's way', both in a literal and a metaphorical sense. It is '*perder el norte*', literally 'to lose the north'. This was highly appropriate for me given where I was heading for the next 1,000 km!

My destination on day 1 was the town of Guillena. As its white buildings emerged in a horizontal line beyond a low ridge, I met a goat herder coming in the opposite direction. He had no dog and instead perfectly controlled his flock by throwing a stone if they wandered too far off the track. I marvelled at the accuracy of his aim.

Apart from Guillena's sports' centre which doubled as a pilgrim hostel and represented an average walking day for me of 23 km, I had another important reason for staying in the town. My year teaching in A Coruña coincided with the final months of the Franco dictatorship. The Spanish Civil War from 1936 to 1939, the almost 40 years of repression of all opposition to his regime, and the transition to democracy have always held a special fascination with me. I had come across a Spanish historical website[1] with the story of 17 women from the town who were arrested in 1937 for no other crime than that they were related to men who were fighting for the left wing Republic. After their heads were shaved, they were paraded through the town before being executed and buried in a mass unmarked grave in a cemetery at the nearby town of Gerena. They became known as 'Las 17 Rosas'. Early in 2012, the bodies were exhumed and identified by various personal items. A lady at the local tourist office pointed me in the direction of Guillena's cemetery where I knew there was a Republican memorial to the disappeared from the war and its aftermath. She echoed my hope that the bodies be soon returned to their own home town. I waited patiently at the cemetery gates while mourners at a burial slowly filed out. The distinctive tricoloured Republican flag drew me to the memorial and I carefully placed an artificial red rose I had brought from my father-in-law's grave back in England among the faded pink posies. A 2010 Spanish film, *Las 13 Rosas*, tells another poignant story based on historically true events surrounding 13 young women in Madrid, mostly under the age of 23, who were executed after the Civil War ended in 1939. One of the shots in the extra scenes of the DVD shows a young actress in tears being comforted by other cast members at the end of a particularly harrowing scene involving separation from her companions in the film. As I prayed in front of the memorial at the end of the first day of my pilgrimage, my mind was drawn to the 13 who died on Dad's watch in yet another sphere of man's inhumanity to man. The Spanish Civil War, like all wars, brought atrocities on both sides. Dresden, Hiroshima and Nagasaki should move us to tears just as much as Coventry and Guernica. Two months after I passed through Guillena, the bones of the '17 Roses' were finally returned for a proper burial in a specially constructed pantheon at the cemetery.

As I set out the next day for the shorter walk to Castilblanco with thoughts of the striking colours of the solitary red rose and the myriad of pink ones still in my mind, I looked down at the two wristbands on my right hand. One was green with the word Camino and the arrow in yellow. The other was orange and represented the NASS charity for whom I had collected on the Primitivo. Completely unintentionally on my part, the colours now became symbolic of the two Irelands. I promised myself that they would remain on my wrist at all times until the end of my pilgrimage as a constant reminder of a divided island.

Day 3 to Almadén de la Plata remains to this day the most arduous stage of all my three pilgrimages. A long strength-sapping and blister-inducing 16 km on asphalt beside a main road is followed by the mercifully peaceful 11 km through a provincial nature reserve. Near its entrance, I found some limited shelter from the sun by a gate post and devoured my lunch of two bananas and a packet of nuts. The unseasonably high October temperatures which climbed to around 33 degrees by each mid-afternoon in my first two weeks of walking were an unwelcome addition to my walk. I had finally learnt the lesson of reducing the weight of my rucksack to under 10 kilos but there were to be nine stages to Salamanca where I had to carry two litres of water. I evenly distributed two half-litre bottles in the side pockets of my trousers. This led to embarrassingly sagging attire in the first half of each day but at least did not add weight to my backpack and my shoulders. Alas, there is no topping-up at the wells and fountains in southern Spain as the water is non-drinkable.

I emptied the last of my bottles at the foot of the aptly named and viciously steep Cerro del Calvario (Calvary Hill) before its two km climb and descent down the hazardously stone gully track to the pretty village of Almadén. All I could think of was removing my boots to expose my hot aching feet, long since devoid of lubricating Vaseline. Disinclined to seek out the pilgrim hostel at the upper end of the village, I opted for a private *pensión* near the pretty clock tower in the centre. The owners were in London on holiday and had left the guest house in the hands of their son Jesús and the family bull terrier Tara. The entrance passageway was narrow as well as dark and my Reactolite glasses made me miss the small step down into the bedroom. As I stumbled and, still with my rucksack on my back, the young man laughed. It was not a judicious start to my stay. I was to be the only guest there that night but met Michael from Ireland and Daniela from Germany for dinner in a bar that evening. I had shared a dormitory in both pilgrim hostels with them on the previous two nights.

Michael and I set off together shortly after dawn but I was never going to match the pace of a seasoned third-time pilgrim on the Vía de la Plata. He did, however, draw my attention to my first sighting of black pigs, famous for the popular *jamón ibérico* (Iberian ham). Sixteen km later at El Real de la Jara, a painful blister forced me to call a halt for the day. As I waited for Rocío, the owner of the immaculately maintained pilgrim hostel, to arrive with the keys, Daniela passed me in the street. As with life, friendships evolve – some continue while others do not. As we hugged, I suspected that our paths would not cross again. Rocío could not have been more helpful in making me feel at home and providing me with the wherewithal to treat a blister.

As I had walked a relatively short distance, I feared I was to be the only pilgrim in the hostel that evening. I rang Jan's mum back in England to wish her a happy 95th birthday and wondered if she would eventually surpass our own mum's 96 years. She had become a second mum to me now in the three years that had elapsed since Mum's passing. A restless, lonely night ended with me going up another flight of stairs from the first floor dormitory to emerge on the open terrace before dawn to be greeted with the most wonderful starlit sky, made special by the virtual absence of light pollution. Thoughts and prayers turned very much to departed loved ones in the stillness of some magical moments from the superb vantage point overlooking the small town.

Remembering to pop the keys through Rocío's letter-box next door, I set off back down the hill past the bar where, due to the intense heat the night before, I had by half-time given up watching the first '*el clásico*' of the football season between Real Madrid and Barcelona. Just before the outskirts below a ruined castle, I did a double take before the penny dropped and I worked out a local's response to my question about the final score. His reply "doh a doh" with the usual letter "s" missing in the heavily accented Andalusian accent told me the result was a 2-2 draw!

Padre Miguel Angel, the parish priest in the first town of Monesterio in the next autonomy of Extremadura, has transformed the parochial house into a pilgrim hostel. As I entered the open door of the first floor building on the main street, my gaze alighted on a welcoming bowl of fresh fruit prominently displayed on a table. Sacri (an abbreviation for Sacramento), the *hospitalera* on duty, appeared later to sign me in and pointed me in the direction of the local clinic. A nurse treated me for a toe infection and carefully bandaged it only to step on it moments later! She apologised for her clumsiness and admitted this was one of her traits! I quickly reassured her that no harm was done and that I was very grateful for her help.

The prospect of two days' rest in the town no longer frustrated me the way enforced halts had done in my previous two pilgrimages. Some other pilgrim friends had warned the young priest to look out for me and I felt a special connection with him when he walked up the aisle, put a hand on my shoulder, and uttered my name as I waited for Mass that evening in the local church. A homily is not normally preached on a week day but Miguel Angel was different. His theme was from the gospel message "Who is my neighbour?" It seemed perfectly appropriate at the sign of peace when, instead of the expected handshake, the worshippers, who were mostly women, all kissed each other.

For a second successive night I was on my own. This homely building I expected to normally resound with the animated chatter of walking and cycling pilgrims. I missed their company and thought how successive pilgrimages had changed me from a shy individual to someone who actually enjoyed others' company. I recalled one such occasion as a hos*pitalero* in Rabanal. On the morning of my departure after my two week volunteering stint, I asked some pilgrims if I could join them at breakfast in our kitchen rather than sit on my own at a separate table. In a similar vein, Dad wrote to Mum from Malaya on Monday 1 September '41: "I, the very self-conscious young student of former days, am now as brazen as brass!! I have warned you of the terrible person I now am and how much I have changed!" I should think she would have been intrigued when she read this particular entry.

A visit to the recently opened modern Museo de Jamón (Ham Museum) on my full recovery day gave me the opportunity to email Jan on their PC, update her on my slowed progress, and thank her for all her support. I felt it churlish to decline the receptionist's invitation for me to view what turned out to be an impressive though rather distasteful audio-visual experience of the traditional slaughter of a pig. Armed with a silicone toe-cap from a chemist's to replace the bandages, my next port of call was the only shoe shop in the town. Padre Miguel Angel had insisted I pay it a visit. The shop owner was expecting me and, neatly arranged on a counter, was a selection of white 'dri-fit' socks with a red R and L to denote which foot to put them on. I bought three pairs and returned to the hostel overwhelmed by the support I had received from the people of Monesterio. To say I was delighted to find 11 pilgrims already in residence is an understatement. We all patiently took it in turns to cook. One of them was walking in the opposite direction north to south. This made sense in that he was heading from the lower autumn temperatures further north towards the warmth of the south but inevitably meant that it was a lonely existence rarely spending successive days with the same pilgrims. Perhaps that is an attraction for certain pilgrims but, as for myself, I was happy to be walking north in the direction of the main flow.

Among my companions on that second night was Pierre, a French pilgrim in his late 60s. I didn't know it at the time but we were to spend the next two and a half weeks in each other's company. He always left before me and had a ritual each morning of stopping for a rest slightly off the path and always on the right-hand side. As I passed unaware of his presence, he would sing a little tune. We would laugh and I would swear that I would spot him the next day but I never did. On he would go at his incredibly steady pace and we would catch up at a pre-arranged hostel each afternoon. We shared a meal in the evenings and my rusty French improved no end. His Spanish was very basic but, despite having a good sense of direction for locating lodgings for the night, he would always question the locals for help. It was his way of connecting with people and inspired me to take every opportunity, when I returned to the pilgrimage two years later, to greet and engage the local inhabitants in conversation. (This was to mean that I was always the last to arrive and led to much leg-pulling about my slow gait.) Pierre's favourite drink after a day's walking was a fizzy mineral water and I have now adopted the same penchant for a very reviving drink on a hot day. Jan and I had the immense pleasure of staying with him and his wife for a night in their home in the beautiful Béarn area of south-west France. He has produced a giant mural of a medieval pilgrim on an outside wall and with some friends has renovated an old mill on his property. He had talked during our pilgrimage of his regular midnight strolls in the woods near his home and painted such a vivid image of them that I joined him that evening as we walked and recalled old times and special moments together. Would that our dad had enjoyed a similar reunion with George or Krish…

Five km beyond the historical town of Zafra, I came over the brow of a hill in the chilly light of dawn to see the village of Los Santos de Maimona on the plain below me. Alison Raju, a good friend and writing guru on many Caminos both in Spain and beyond, describes the so-called 'saints' as important local citizens in her guide-book to the Vía de la Plata[2]. They sounded as if they were too full of their own self-worth. I searched unsuccessfully for the yellow arrows out of the village and approached a mother and her two young daughters for help. To my surprise, she responded in perfect English and then proceeded to invite me for breakfast to her aunt's house round the corner. I had only had yoghurt and fruit back in Zafra and was soon savouring the taste of cake washed down by restoratively warm *café con leche*. I thanked Elizabeth for her kindness and grabbed my lucky mascot and veteran of two pilgrimages, Santi the bull, whose head was always deliberately peeping out of the side pocket of my rucksack. Little Ursula was the beaming recipient of my gift. I had spent the most delightful 40 minutes in the company of four ladies who straddled three generations of a family. I then had to work out how I was going to explain to Jan that I, in turn, had given away what had been her gift to me! I left the village knowing that it would now be a quiet walking day with my fellow pilgrims well ahead of me. Thoughts of Dad's gift of Jennifer, the toy dog, to little Virginia filled my head.

In an effort to reduce the weight of my rucksack, I was only carrying the CSJ's basic version of Alison's guidebook. Without a GPS tracker on my phone, I paid for my mistake by getting lost three times on my pilgrimage to Salamanca. Instead of walking north out of the Roman town of Mérida, I missed the yellow arrows and was soon aware I was going due east in the direction of the dazzling sunrise. Later that morning I found myself saying *"Eres un ángel"* (You are an angel) to a motorist who had stopped to point me in the right direction. On another occasion, I misread a diversion sign away from building work on the high-speed AVE train line and ended up with my boots clagged in mud and no alternative but to cross a local railway line into the village of Cañaveral where an elderly couple kindly gave me water. A land dispute on the path between the village of Grimaldo and the walled town of Galisteo – still ongoing according to what I have read on social media – led me again to follow the wrong path. Half an hour later I stood contemplating whether to climb a high fence with a large flock of sheep on the other side or to retrace my steps back to where I knew I had made the mistake. Where there are sheep in Spain there also lurks a fierce dog so I phoned Pierre in desperation. He interrupted a taxi driver who was having his Sunday lunch in a bar and the latter managed to locate me based on my description of my surroundings. The metaphorical path we take in life when faced with two alternatives was not lost on me. Admittedly choosing the wrong way was not life-changing but my angst at facing the unknown on my own, albeit for only a few hours, was highly thought-provoking.

Two other days stand out for me but for entirely different reasons. A religious community in the small town of Alcuéscar look after some 80 disabled men and have set aside part of the main building next door for pilgrims. When Pierre and I slipped into the back of their church, we quickly realised that a funeral Mass was about to take place. As with weddings in Spain, no objections are raised to outsiders attending. We learnt that the deceased's name was Francisco, yet another link to my pilgrimage. In the long, dimly-lit corridor outside the chapel following the service, there came a terrible cry of anguish which we later learnt from Ángel, the volunteer *hospitalero*, was from the dead man's mother. He told us that she had relied on a weekly taxi ride to visit her son whereas his other relatives were only now putting in an appearance at his funeral. We returned to the church later to receive our own special pilgrim blessing from Padre Luis. That night, Ángel served us a delicious communal meal of soup, salad and potatoes in scrambled egg down in one of the cellars of the building. As we washed the dishes, we reflected on what a privilege it had been to share for a few hours the life of this special community.

I have no doubt in naming my favourite day as 23 October. Pierre and I had been the only occupants of the charmingly rustic hostel at Oliva de Plasencia. I set off feeling really good after some calf-stretching exercises recommended by Jan over the phone following pain at the back of my legs the day before. To reach Oliva had necessitated a six km detour on an unforgiving tarmac road but that was quickly forgotten as I opened a gate leading into the huge farmland estate of Los Baldíos. There was no wind and the glorious early morning sun from a cloudless sky soon dissipated the autumn chill. Cows grazed peacefully and I even disturbed a wild boar at its watering hole behind a fence. Off it took squealing over the fields. I called this a 'Mrs Boyle's morning', a reference to the farmer's wife in the house we used to occupy with her and the rest of her family in Co. Donegal each July. As she and Dad chatted outside the house one beautiful morning, her words to him were "Isn't it great to be alive on such a day!"

Throughout Extremadura on the Vía de la Plata, a large metal square serves as a waymark but also provides a useful seat for tired pilgrims. A motif of an arch engraved on each denotes the Roman city of Cáparra. As I left the estate and re-joined the route, there it loomed in the middle of nowhere. It really was the perfect setting especially so early in the morning before the arrival of tourists at the visitors' centre which gives access to the city's ruins. For the first time on my pilgrimage, there was Pierre waiting patiently for me under the arch so we could share the moment together. As I boasted to him of my fleeting encounter with the wild boar, he told me he had spotted an eagle! The arch itself has four broad pillars and is symmetrically designed in that the height is exactly twice the width. It was built by a grateful son in the first century BC as a tribute to his parents. The gardener offered to take our photo and bade us a cheery farewell and a "*¡Buen Camino!*" as we set off again through the arch. Symbolically, the route is signposted through this iconic, historical monument of filial love.

There was a healthy turn-out of parishioners that evening at San Servando Church for the feast-day Mass of this Spanish saint in the pretty village of Aldeanueva del Camino. The gospel reading was the Beatitudes, based on the wonderfully succinct but evocative Blessings on the Mount[3]. As the priest uttered the words "Blessed are they that mourn; for they shall be comforted", I realised it had been a week since we had witnessed the mother's pain. As I write, I think it more appropriate to quote the words in German rather than Spanish as my mind is currently full of the same two opening lines from Brahms' magnificent Requiem which my choir Philomusica sang in a packed Tewkesbury Abbey two nights ago: "*Selig sind, die da Leid tragen, denn si sollen getröstet werden.*"[4] (We were thrilled on the night to welcome our vice-president, Roderick Williams, the renowned baritone, as one of our soloists.) Singing with the choir and undertaking walking pilgrimages rank as two of the greatest privileges in my life.

Pierre and I had calculated four more days to Salamanca and I was reluctantly anticipating the moment when I would have to say good-bye to my special pilgrim friend. Brutally hot days in the south three weeks before had been replaced by cold nights and early mornings as we steadily climbed into the sierras of the third autonomy on the route and Spain's largest – Castilla y León. We had a great welcome at the Alba Soraya Pilgrim Hostel in the village of Calzada de Béjar which lovely *hospitalera* Manuela had named after her two daughters. The warm fire was especially appreciated and she washed our clothes, made us a superb evening meal, and returned the following morning at 6.30 from her home next door to prepare breakfast for Pierre and me who had been joined by four other pilgrims. The few euros she charged could never match the hospitality she had shown us and was in the finest tradition of that given by locals from every corner of the country to pilgrims for hundreds of years. Before I left, I was moved by some of the quotations of Mother Teresa of Calcutta in large lettering on the walls in the living-room. She was revered by Mum and Dad who had told me that her work with the poor had brought her to conflict zones throughout the world but that she had never experienced hatred such as what she had encountered between the two communities in Northern Ireland.

Two days before Salamanca, I knew that Pierre was having difficulty walking. A painful left foot slowed his pace to a point where I was actually walking faster than him. He feared that his pilgrim 'fix' would in future be confined to a bicycle and this has proved to be the case. The temperature had plunged to one degree Celsius as we posed for a photo in the city's famous Plaza Mayor. With his bright red jacket, bearded countenance, and long wooden staff that nearly reached his shoulders, he gave the impression of being a medieval pilgrim. I was always amused when he used the staff to dry any wet washing when he used to wedge it between bunk beds. In the concluding page of my diary and in the same vein as Dad singing the praises of George Reuneker and Krish Nair, I described him as someone "who has taught me to appreciate nature better in all its glory, to converse with any stranger and to grow as a person even if his short chat is in stilted Spanish, to see the face of Christ in all our fellow men, and to always view the glass as half full. Angels come in many guises. We are life-long learners not just in the field of adult education but in the walk of life."

We shared a fine meal together that night in a restaurant in the city before we tearfully embraced and I caught the bus to León and then on to Rabanal to assist in the myriad of tasks involved in closing the hostel before its winter slumber. My thoughts were initially filled with Pierre, by then safely back in France with his family, and then with those pilgrims we had encountered before Salamanca and who would now be battling with the wind and the freezing rain on their pilgrimage north to Santiago. I was already wondering when I would return.

NOTES

1. *The Spanish website of the Asociación para la Recuperación de la Memoria Histórica is www.memoriahistorica.org.es*

2. *See* **The Way of St James: Vía de la Plata, Seville to Santiago** *by Alison Raju, Cicerone 2001, p.58. Alison sadly passed away in November 2020.*

3. *Matthew's Gospel, Chapter 5, verses 3-12.*

4. *Brahms' **Ein Deutsches Requiem**, Edition Peters, p.3.*

CHAPTER 17

"PILGRIMAGE 3, VÍA DE LA PLATA PART 2, 2014"

"Down into the gully then forced back up again with more flooding and difficult to balance with nine kilo rucksack dragging me uncontrollably this way and that through the scrub. Forty-five minutes after we left the bridge, we finally summited all the undergrowth to emerge on the cliff top with fabulous views south to where the dam becomes a river again."

Diary entry day 7, Sunday 6 April, wrong decision to turn left after the bridge crossing the Esla Reservoir… just about worth it for the panoramic view!

Three senior members of staff and valued ex-colleagues from school died within four months of each other at the start of 2013. The third was Lawrence Montagu, affectionately known to everyone as 'Larry'. I had joined St Peter's in 1986, two years after his appointment as head teacher. He was an inspirational leader and had an incredible memory for names and faces, seemingly of every one of some 1,500 young people as well as office-staff, dinner-ladies, caretakers, and cleaners. Despite his heavy work schedule which included serving on local and national education committees, the door to his office was always open if any of us had a problem or needed advice. He had unbelievable energy and was passionate about creating an environment where our students could benefit from the best possible teaching methodology. He was also a superb orator and effective communicator and his down-to-earth Liverpudlian humour and infectious chuckle, allied to the finger he had on the pulse of everything going on in the school, helped to ensure that his message never fell on deaf ears. My dad never met him but they shared a love for their fellow man that was grounded in their innate Christian beliefs. Both were, above all, leaders who inspired loyalty in the many lives that they touched.

Larry passed away on the evening of 5 April. When my successor as head of modern languages, Jo Beamish, rang me at midnight with the sad news, I later reflected that it was around the time my choir had been rehearsing the life-affirming song 'Rhythm of Life' from the musical Sweet Charity. The lyrics "Go, go, go. Tell them everything you know." aptly summed up Larry's philosophy of encouraging young people to express themselves and stand up for what they believed in. An estimated 3,000 mourners attended his funeral in the only venue big enough in the city to host it – Gloucester Cathedral. Over the centuries there have been very few Catholic funerals in this magnificent Anglican edifice, an indication of the high esteem in which Larry was held. When our staff and student choir emerged from the chapter house at the back of the cathedral, we were awestruck by the size of the crowd of mourners through whom we had to weave our way to reach our seats by the altar. At the end of a service hugely symbolic in ecumenism, the cathedral resounded to the strains of 'Sing it in the Valleys', a hymn everyone at St Peter's associates to this day with the final minutes of school Masses when Larry used to deliver a trademark sway of the hips to accompany its joyous beat and singalong lyrics.

Later that year Lynn Helliker, the bridesmaid at our wedding and Jan's best friend, also passed away. (Coincidentally, Seamus Heaney died the same year.) It seemed fitting that I should return to the theme of a sponsored pilgrimage when I flew to Spain to continue my walk to Santiago in March 2014. Although neither Larry nor Lynn had used Maggie's[1] in their battle with cancer, my ex-colleague, Jo Beamish, was receiving incredible support from this charity following her recent diagnosis with the disease. Their homely centre at Cheltenham for friends and family as well as sufferers is situated, like their other 19 centres throughout the country, near the hospital's oncology unit. Her description of the centre and the staff who offered her a place in which to relax at the time of her treatment at Cheltenham General Hospital reminded me of our pilgrim hostel in Rabanal in terms of the practical support we offer in addition to the sympathetic ear for those who like to talk about their motivation for doing their Camino. A further change from my second pilgrimage in 2009 was to use the services of social media via the website, Just Giving, in order for family and friends to donate to Maggie's. I decided to dedicate my pilgrimage to the memory of Larry and Lynn.

The demands of the spring working party in Rabanal meant I had my duties to attend to at the end of March before my return to Salamanca. We were a cohesive team of seven and, as I cleaned the grouting in the shower units and trimmed the ivy in the lane outside, I kept wondering which pilgrims and locals would make my forthcoming journey special. On the way to our annual general meeting with the local pilgrim association across the mountains in Ponferrada, my mobile suddenly rang. It was our son Andrew speaking from a street in the centre of Barcelona with the news that his interview in his job as a football magazine journalist with one of the world's greatest players, Lionel Messi, had gone well. Mum and Dad had always encouraged our love of sports. Larry too would have been proud of the heights achieved by yet another ex-pupil of St Peter's.

Heavy snow enveloped the village later that week. The idea of a sponsored pilgrimage is not a concept with which the Spanish are familiar. Here in the UK, friends usually ask "Who are you walking with?" and are surprised by my answer "No-one". The locals in Rabanal still appeared puzzled when I declined their suggestion to stay in the local family run hotel to await the thaw after the working party concluded and the hostel opened for pilgrims on 1 April. Undeterred, I took a taxi to Astorga, the nearest town, and a bus to Salamanca. It was bitterly cold as I walked due north the next morning out of the 'Pierreless' Plaza Mayor for part 2. The bull ring and football stadium made the tedious outskirts more interesting until I finally reached the open rolling countryside where I came across a farmer in bright green overalls busily scattering minerals by hand over his wheat field. Mindful of the example set by Pierre, I stopped to chat to Antonio who made me promise to pray for him in Santiago. It was nice to be acknowledged as a pilgrim, an unusual occurrence on the Vía de la Plata.

I was entrusted with the key at the basic €5 municipal hostel on day one at Calzada de Valdunciel. Only four of us slept inside the building but incredibly, given the low temperatures, a multi-lingual Brazilian called Luis pitched his tent in the outside yard and slept beside his faithful dog Gugu. I had forgotten that this was standard practice for pilgrims walking with their dogs. He politely knocked on the door the next day to ask if I could fill his water bottle and I immediately ushered him in. I gave him a bar of chocolate and, as he left, he was most insistent that I lock the yard door behind him. I was so impressed by his conscientious attitude and felt humbled by his gratitude for the little I had done for him.

A private hostel at El Cubo de la Tierra del Vino was my lodgings for day 2. The chatty proprietor moaned about vagrant pilgrims so the last person I expected to see there that night was Luis. The adage 'never judge a book by its cover' applied perfectly to the owner who ensured that master and dog had both dinner and breakfast. We are sometimes too quick to dismiss others by what they say. I left before dawn knowing that the owner had offered Luis true pilgrim hospitality. I met Luis again as I passed a bar in the same village where one of the waiters had supplied him with an extra plastic sheet. It was to be another two weeks before our paths crossed again, this time by a stream many kilometres to the north on a beautiful spring morning. There, he reiterated the fact that penniless pilgrims and their dogs are viewed with suspicion in cities and so he always ensures that they walk through them when looking for somewhere to spend the night. I recently listened to a video blog on a Camino social media forum[2] where a pilgrim in conversation with a nun recalls the latter's belief that the Camino is a microcosm of God's dream about how we should be with each other. The physical demands of the pilgrimage and its inner spiritual path convey a powerful message of tolerance which we hopefully take back to our lives. As a footnote to my stay in El Cubo, after I left the *salón* (lounge) at half-time in the Champions' League quarter final between Barça and Atlético Madrid to nip to the loo, I returned to find the television switched off and the room and hostel plunged into darkness. It was a salutary reminder to me of the needs of those who care for pilgrims as well as pilgrim themselves to have a good night's rest!

There are only two cities on this largely rural second half of the Vía de la Plata and, now in my 60th year, I was quite happy to confine my walking on day 3 to the 13 km stretch to the village of Villanueva de Campeán rather than to push on a further 19 km to the bustling metropolis of Zamora. An unexpected bonus that afternoon was a visit to the ruins of the Franciscan Monastery of Nuestra Señora del Soto. As I trampled over the warm, wet, overgrown grass in my recovering sandaled feet, its soothing effect added to my feelings of inner peace. This was helped by the fact that I was completely on my own. It put me in mind of a favourite photograph sent as a postcard by Dad to Mum from India's North West Frontier and dated 27 July '41. It had the following dedication written on the reverse: "*This snap was taken in Indian Territory…The river is the Kabul as it flows down from Afghanistan. Do you like my bare feet? Love, Frank.*" I managed to find a reversible photo frame so that Mum could always view it on both sides.

As for the monastery itself, the façade of the building is in remarkably good condition with its coat of arms of San Francisco de Asís clearly visible. It seemed appropriate that I was there in the year commemorating the 800th anniversary of the saint's pilgrimage to Santiago as well as the second year of Pope Francis' pontificate, the latter being the widely admired first Spanish-speaking pope. Ian Bradley devotes a chapter to Assisi and the ever-popular saint in his aforementioned book and draws attention to his message of a simple way of living and of peace, both as relevant now as they were in the 13th century. I hadn't forgotten the symbolism of my departure on the saint's feast day from Seville some 18 months before.

Zamora beckoned the next day. Although the scallop shells and yellow arrows facilitate directions for those, like me at the time, without a smart phone, I knew for this pilgrimage that I needed the help of Alison's more detailed guide-book[3]. Jan had rightly chided me for not taking this with me from Seville and she came up with the idea of photocopying the relevant pages and reducing them to a more manageable A5 size. Each evening I performed the ritual of disposing of the page or pages that described the day's stage. It seems incredulous to say that the removal of each small sheet made my rucksack feel lighter. Perhaps it was a psychological moment of relief as I performed the daily ritual marking the end of another day of my pilgrimage whilst looking forward to the start of a new one.

With the city still a distance away across the flat plains, I unexpectedly came across three 20 foot high monoliths. I sat down to read what I am calling a 'ring of promises'. They were erected by the Fundación Ramos de Castro and I was struck by the earnest tone of their pleas to passing pilgrims to actively seek to promote a more peaceful world. One concludes thus:

"DEJA AQUÍ PEREGRINO LA PROMESA
"PILGRIM, MAKE YOUR PROMISE HERE
Y, SEA CUAL SEA TU ANDADURA,
AND, WHATEVER YOUR PACE MAY BE,
HABRÁS HECHO CAMINO
YOU WILL HAVE MADE YOUR CAMINO
ANTES DE LLEGAR..."
BEFORE REACHING YOUR DESTINATION..."

I loved the inclusivity of the carved symbols above the written exhortations, not just confined to Christianity but also to the Arabic and Jewish faiths. It had been amazing to see original *'miliarios'* (ancient Roman stone pillars) measuring out mile distances further south. New concrete replicas now also carry Arabic wording on this part of the route which is known as the *'Senda para la Paz'* (Route for Peace).

My photocopies were no help in negotiating the northern outskirts of Zamora the next day thanks to the diversions caused by the building of the high speed Ave train line. Once again, I found myself crossing what, this time, was, a busier track. As I looked back in horror afterwards to see a modern train thunder past, I realised that the path ahead of me was taking me in the direction of the nearby Portuguese border! By the time I re-joined the proper route at the village of Roales de Pan, I had added an extra three km to my day and roundly cursed the Ave. I missed the only bar in the village and knew that there were no communities for the next 12 km so I stopped a lady carrying her shopping and asked if she lived nearby and could I have some water. Transi proceeded to lead me into the old people's home where she worked, insisted I sit down while she made me a warm cup of coffee, and then scolded me for not putting sugar in it to boost my energy levels. Before I knew it, I was back out in the street, water bottles replenished and, morale boosted, ready for the second half of an eventful morning.

Saturday 5 April was an overcast day. The low cloud was in keeping with my reflective mood at the first anniversary of Larry's death. A slight detour off the busy main road provided welcome relief as I approached the imposing turreted remains of Castrotorafe Castle. It was formerly the seat of the Knights of the Order of Santiago. Set back outside the walls within which there was a town until the 18th century, I spotted two more peace monoliths. These contained specific references to world leaders such as Nelson Mandela and Pope Francis. One inscription in particular caught my eye in its laudable plea to remember the guilty as well as the victims:

"A LOS QUE POR VIVIR LOS VALORES

"TO THOSE WHO, THROUGH ABIDING BY THEIR PRINCIPLES,

DIERON AQUÍ SU VIDA **GAVE THEIR LIVES HERE,**

NUESTRO RECUERDO ETERNO.

WE REMEMBER YOU FOREVER.

A LOS QUE POR VIVIR SUS VALORES

TO THOSE WHO, THROUGH ABIDING BY THEIR PRINCIPLES,

QUITABAN AQUÍ LAS VIDAS

HERE TOOK THE LIVES OF OTHERS,

NUESTRO OLVIDO Y PERDÓN."

WE FORGET YOU AND FORGIVE YOU."

I have yet to establish if the allusion to killings on that spot is related to the atrocities of the Spanish Civil War but will follow this up in the same way my discovery of the story of the '17 Rosas' in Guillena aroused my fascination.

A day's diversion off the route to spend an evening with an old friend and now retired teacher from previous school Spanish exchanges curiously provided me with a welcome respite from all things pilgrimage. Dad had no such options. We talked of old times in the bar Manolo frequented in the village of Villarrín de Campos where he grew up. It was a bitterly cold night and I was grateful for the heavy-duty curtain covering the exit which helped to keep my sandaled feet warm. We were still at a height of over 700 metres on the Meseta. He joined me for a couple of days on the route and enjoyed the experience of walking and adapting to staying in a pilgrim hostel. I introduced him to my five favourite companions, all of whom had been walking from Seville. Paco was Spanish, Jolanda came from Holland, and Lisa, Sebastian and Heiko were three 'young 'uns' who hailed from Germany.

As with my previous pilgrimages, it took about a week before some part of my body started to give problems. Again the offending limb was my second toe. Jan had pointed out the obvious in that it was the same length as my big toe, hence the discomfort as it rubbed against the front of my boot. Free treatment at a local clinic in Mombuey thanks to my European health card and status as a pilgrim was gratefully received and this time I was prescribed anti-inflammatories. There was no need to go in search of a chemist as I always keep a supply for my ankylosing spondylitis. This condition, which causes inflammation of the joints, strangely never manifests itself on my pilgrimages despite the huge pressure all pilgrims exert on our limbs for days on end carrying a rucksack. Suffice for the moment to state that daily exercise is the best anti-dote for the condition.

I had earlier stopped at a hotel before the village where I had thought it wise to take a day off. Ironically, it was the only time on the entire route when I was met with a distinct lack of hospitality as the receptionist refused to put my rucksack aside while I visited the clinic. I pleaded with him that I fully intended to return and spend the night there but he would have none of it. I stormed out, incredulous at his dismissive stance. As I waited at a café for my medication to kick in, I pondered at the sadness of not seeing my new-found walking companions again. By mid-morning, I decided to give it a go. I could always turn back to Mombuey if my toe proved too painful. My limp had magically disappeared and I literally walked on air as I flew the 17 km to the sports' centre which doubles as a hostel at Asturianos. There, set against the backdrop of the snow-covered mountains awaiting two days hence, I had a long chat with Jolanda who told me of her battle with cancer back in 1998, the year of my first Camino. Now free of the disease, she relishes walking and has an incredibly positive outlook on life. We have remained friends ever since.

I relished the prospect of the climb up a further 600 metres to the mountain pass at Padornelo though another wrong turn had meant I was rather too close for comfort to the barrier separating me from the busy N525 road. The uneven ground fell away at times and forced me to vault the barrier onto the hard shoulder. When I managed to catch up with my 'favourite five' pilgrims two days later at Lubián, we were joined by a Spanish mother and daughter who had been dropped off by car. They were first-time pilgrims and were aiming to reach Santiago for Easter Sunday. We were all incredulous when the mum produced a hair-dryer the next morning, definitely not an item packed in the average pilgrim's rucksack! I waited until my companions had departed before giving the new arrivals a few tips on what to expect on their first day. It was muddy underfoot that day and, when they arrived at the next hostel with their trainers looking pristine, one of our group churlishly commented that they had never walked all the way. I thought back to the treatment I had received for tendinitis from Jesús back in '98. It was not our place to be judgmental, a trait Dad was also to learn in the camps.

Apart from the shared experience of that final week into Santiago and the knowledge, like the POWs, that the longed-for goal was firmly in sight, my abiding memory was the arrival of spring. My companions had all experienced the higher February temperatures encouraging the surge of blossom on the trees and the burst of colourful wild flowers back in Andalucía. Now it was my turn. Walking for some seven hours a day heightened my joyful sensation coinciding with the warmth of the spring sunshine on my back in a way I have never experienced before. Every sense was stimulated in this wonderful outdoor panacea. The men's 20 months at Muroran included two bitterly cold winters when they must have longed for the soothing balm of spring to envelop their emaciated bodies.

The thrilling traverse on Palm Sunday of a series of hilltops above the ugly town of A Gudiña opened up vistas of the Embalse das Portas Reservoir far below. At 34 km, the day was my longest but the most satisfying. Lisa was not walking with her two friends who had decided to camp out on the hills overnight and, wary of a giant Leonese mastiff sheep-dog ahead, she asked if we could walk together in order to give it a wide berth. I had often come across them in Rabanal and, reassuring her of their basically docile nature when away from their sheep-minding duties, I suggested we each carry one of my walking sticks but in a vertical pose in front of us instead of a threatening one. I had a sudden vision of the two of us as acolytes walking up a church aisle carefully carrying lighted candles. Perhaps I had lately been in too many churches! Carl and I had briefly been altar boys in our early teens.

I was now back in Galicia for the first time in the five years since Mum's passing. Each of the four settlements on the hill-tops begins with the Gallego word 'Venda' (in Spanish venta) which means an inn. They were normally run by a strong-willed woman and, among others, would have provided accommodation for Galician farm labourers planting seed in the spring for cereal crops in the fields of the sparsely-populated kingdom of Castile to the south. They would duly return in the autumn to harvest the crops and invariably paid a visit to the Virgen de la Tuiza Church as part of their devotion to the Virgin. I had passed the shrine a few days earlier only to find it closed like so many of Spain's churches. I am the first to admit that my awareness of the history of such communities on the Vía de la Plata is increased by my knowledge of Spanish and the buzz it gives me when I engage with the locals. However, no linguistic skills are necessary on this day's isolated walk when the pilgrim begins the inevitable descent and reaches the delightful hamlet of As Eiras. By the side of the route there is what has become a frequent sight on many Caminos nowadays – a stall offering fruit, cereal bars, water, and even a flask of coffee with a donations' box. This *punto de apoyo* (support station), however, was unmanned. I am sure the provider's generosity was not abused.

Back up into the hills the next day, Jolanda, Paco, and I stopped for an early morning drink at the Bar Rincón del Peregrino (Pilgrim Corner Bar) in the village of Alberguería. Its owner, Luis, has mounted several thousand scallop shells on every conceivable wall and ceiling space. Each is dated, signed and displays its own message written with a felt-tip pen which he gives passing pilgrims who pop in for some refreshment. The idea is a brilliant one, a living testimony to those who have endured this most demanding of all Spain's pilgrim routes. I wonder what he will do when he eventually runs out of space though it must be borne in mind that under 3 per cent of pilgrims choose this route so perhaps he need not be concerned just yet!

A sudden frisson gripped me when I rested by a fountain in the middle of the hamlet of Bobadela. Almost 40 years after the death of Spain's fascist dictator, General Franco, the last thing I had expected to see was the Falangist symbol of the *yugo y flechas* (yoke and arrows) but there it was staring right in front of me on a stone engraving above the water spout. My regression to the sinister 1975 public symbols of the regime throughout A Coruña was fortunately short-lived as, to my amusement, a strategically placed stone bench in the square carried the message on its backboard in three languages – *Buen Viaje, Bon Voyage*, and Have a God Trip! The divine dimension to the pilgrimage was certainly in evidence in these parts.

Ourense is the final city on the route but the route out goes up a steep and brutally sustained climb of almost 300 metres in the space of only 3 km. The long incline led to me tweaking an Achilles tendon. One hour into the ascent, a local approached me as I sat on a bench to rest. Yet again I was meeting a Francisco. He engaged me in some light-hearted banter which I always enjoy and informed me that it was he who had installed the seat. He pointed out that it would cost me €1,000 to sit on it! I pleaded that I was only a poor pilgrim but the really bitter pill to swallow came with his next utterance: any pilgrim sitting on said bench would not reach Santiago as it was a poor show for anyone to be resting at such an early time of the day! I politely begged to differ but, mindful of the forfeit and curse he administered to me that Holy Thursday morning, I did not tarry long!

The high-vaulted ancient hall lined with bunk beds in the Cistercian monastery at Oseira was my chilly lodging for the night. To be honest, the cool temperature provided some relief from a hot and tiring 30 km day. I slept fitfully, aware of an upcoming live interview on BBC Radio Gloucestershire's breakfast show. I chose a quiet spot with a seat under a tree to await the call to my mobile phone. The signal was good but the loud chirping of the birds made for a noisy backdrop. I had spoken to the interviewer some years before direct from the hostel in Rabanal and this time ensured that he got the message that walking pilgrims carry their own rucksacks, in my case weighing nine kilos, and that we walk for days on end as opposed to a one day hike. The delayed phone call meant all my fellow-pilgrims had long since departed. I chatted to a relaxed Padre Luis, the monk who not only co-ordinates the allocation of the pilgrim bunk-beds but also serves in the monastery shop. I felt immensely proud when he shared his conviction that the pilgrims of today are like the Christians of old. I took this to mean that, regardless of whether we carry an overtly Christian message, our example of depriving ourselves for a period of time of our creature comforts is one that emulates that of our forebears. And, of course, the way we, in theory at least, interact with people on our return to our homes is hopefully a powerful force for encouraging tolerance and understanding.

We were all delighted to meet up with a smartly dressed Luis and his faithful Gugu in our final week. He had been given some work and new clothing by a local man who wanted repairs done to the roof of his home back in Alberguería, the 'shell' village. The N525 fell largely silent on Good Friday afternoon, that most holiest of times in the Christian calendar. My thoughts wandered back to the long church services in the Belfast of my youth and the image of the crucified Christ.

Newly arrived Spanish pilgrims had now joined the route in order to be in Santiago by Easter Sunday in preparation for going back to work the following day. I had no such deadline though I had fallen a day behind the schedule I had circulated to friends back home before I left. On that quiet Easter Sunday morning, a full day before I had planned to reach the city, I received congratulatory texts from four special friends. These were so welcome and in the peaceful solitude I sat down by the side of the path to reply to each. I subsequently learnt that the donations to Maggie's had reached £2,400 and felt humbled by everyone's generosity. Suddenly, across the rolling countryside and on a traffic-free country road, I could hear the distant music of the 'Ave María'. Was this call to the Angelus some figment of my celestial imagination? I had sung it daily for three weeks in Mum's memory and as close to midday as possible, mirroring the lunch-time prayer over the school tannoy delivered by Larry for so many years. (I had always thought the school loudspeaker system unique until I watched *Clockwork*, the film in which the British actor and comedian John Cleese plays a head-teacher.) The pre-recorded tune was, in fact, emanating from the small church at Dornelas and, hastily depositing my rucksack at the back, I joined a small group of parishioners to celebrate the Mass on this special '*Día de la Resurección*'. I prayed for the recovery from cancer of a young girl in Donegal whose family are good friends. I had been carrying this special intention from Salamanca.

Thankfully, this brave little girl has now overcome it.

A very different 'Ave' greeted me on my final day into the city. I had been dreading passing over the fateful railway line at Angrois where the distracted train driver of Alvía 151 from Chamartín Railway Station in Madrid to Santiago crashed his train on 24 July 2013, the eve of the feast of St James. As it approached the bend before the local station, it was travelling at 179 km/h. Automatic emergency braking had not been installed and tragically 80 people needlessly lost their lives. I had not passed a single pilgrim all day and in the eerie silence realised that I would not see the line until the last minute. The bridge to this day is festooned with pilgrim mementoes as well as tributes from the families of the victims. I carefully attached the first of two tiny crosses I had been carrying, with a dedication to the deceased, to the metal grilling and said a quiet prayer. Many more were offered years before in Muroran POW Camp for the souls of Angell and Durrant, two other victims of another totally needless train accident.

It was a further four km through the cloying Easter Monday drizzle to the city's Sar district. One final hill and I went under the arch of the Porta de Mazarelos, the only surviving medieval gateway through the city walls. When I reached the square in front of the cathedral, it was a shock to join many other pilgrims who had completed their Camino Francés. A lovely phone call to Jan to confirm my safe arrival was followed by a text from Andrew to say he was back in Barcelona interviewing and training with Spain's winning goal-scorer from the 2010 World Cup Final – Andrés Iniesta. What a day it was proving to be! Inevitably, given my solitary final day's walk, I didn't recognise a single other pilgrim as I queued with the eagerly chatting throngs for my *compostela* at the pilgrim office. This was remedied that evening when I rendezvoused with Jolanda and Paco for wine and tapas.

The feeling of superiority on reaching Santiago whereby one 'owns' the city for those few hours is one with which I never feel totally comfortable. However, reality most definitely dawns the next day as the mind prepares to reluctantly adjust to the routine and conformities which dictate so much of our lives. Three events were to make the transition more tolerable.

Firstly and quite unexpectedly, I bumped into Luis and Gugu as they were setting out east just like the pilgrims of old walking back to their homes. This particular master and dog couple, however, do not have the luxury of a home. I made Luis promise to spend a night in the CSJ hostel in Rabanal where they were subsequently given a special welcome by a mother and daughter *hospitalera* team. As usual, he asked for nothing but I thought giving him money rather than chocolate would be more practical. In the emotional moment of our farewell embrace, I forgot to tell him that, of our little group of pilgrims, his was the only mention at the midday pilgrim Mass in the cathedral. (Gugu received no such acknowledgement!) The words of two of the Beatitudes apply perfectly to this gentle soul: "Blessed are the poor in spirit for theirs is the Kingdom of Heaven…Blessed are the meek for they will inherit the Earth."

Secondly, I joined the 4 o'clock tour of the cathedral roof. Health and safety restrictions would prohibit such a tour in the UK due to the darkness of the steep, narrow staircases and the lack of a handrail on the roof's more exposed areas. The view of the city's ancient streets and distant countryside was thrilling as I gazed down on pilgrim clusters meandering their sometimes animated and, at others, contemplative way across the main square.

Finally, as my second evening approached, I waited patiently at the bottom of the cathedral steps in anticipation of one final shared meal with the three German youngsters. They had pre-arranged to walk towards me from three corners of the huge square: Lisa to my right from the Parador de los Reyes Católicos (the Catholic Monarchs' Parador), Sebastian directly opposite from the Rajoy Palace, and Heiko from the left. Still filled with thoughts of the Camino, this unique convergence reminded me of the fan-shaped ridges of the scallop shell. On my recommendation, we headed for my favourite outdoor restaurant which I had also confirmed was showing the Champions' League decider between Atleti and Chelsea. Their youthful exuberance was infectious and I envied their energy when, after more than six weeks walking from Seville, they were planning to continue out to the Atlantic and 'the end of the world' at Finisterre.

Before I left Spain, I had one more task. My second tiny cross was destined for Kiko's grave in the village of Coristanco in the north of Galicia. His widow, Cuqui, drove me to the cemetery on a beautiful sunny day with only the odd high wispy cloud. I think I caught his spirit as I stood by the family grave of my best friend. As is the custom in Spain, it was built into one of the cemetery walls but, alas, his was beyond my reach. The cross now resides in Cuqui's flat in A Coruña. It was the final act in the most memorable of all my pilgrimages where the intentions of so many family members and friends had accompanied me on every step from one end of the country to the other.

NOTES

1. *Maggie's is a cancer-care charity inspired by the ideas of Maggie Keswick Jencks. Its first centre opened in Edinburgh in 1996. Its website is www.mag-gies.org*

2. *www.caminosantiago.me/community is a forum for pilgrims to post questions, observations and advice on all the Caminos.*

3. ***Vía de la Plata: The Way of Saint James, Seville to Santiago*** *by Alison Raju, Cicerone 2001.*

CHAPTER 18

"INISHKEEL ISLAND, CO. DONEGAL"

"Inishkeel is the most loved place of all....On first setting foot in the island, one is conscious of an atmosphere of sanctity and peace. It is treeless, and the effect of dazzling light on sand and sea, the strong colours and soft Atlantic air is entrancing."[1]

Our parents' affinity to Donegal drew them back in the late '50s but not to Ranafast. Narin and Portnoo further south along the coast were the only places myself and my four siblings ever wanted to holiday in every summer for a decade. Admittedly, those were the days before package holidays and second homes abroad but I think our parents would not have been attracted to them even if they had been available. The seven of us would set off on 1 July each year in the family Austin Cambridge for the four-hour journey from Belfast. It was always a special moment when we passed the border post at Strabane and crossed into Lifford in the Irish Republic. There was something exciting about entering what many to this day still like to call the 'Free State'. I did not view the name in political terms but rather in the sense of four weeks of freedom from the restrictions of school routines and life in a large city. All five of us looked forward to the prospect of having our dad to ourselves and not having to share him with his patients.

We were so busy playing golf in the mornings – a family ticket on the local links for the entire month cost only five punts or about £4 – swimming in the waters off the two-mile long Narin Strand in the afternoons, and playing tennis on the grass court off the first fairway during the endless summer evenings that we rarely gave a thought to Inishkeel Island. It lies in the bay opposite the twin communities and is exposed at low tide in the summer months. Our parents were wary of the danger of being stranded on the island due to the incoming tide but, on one particular day, they decided that we should go on an adventure, cross the sandbar and head inland to explore. Unfortunately, we were to encounter the unwanted attention of the resident bulls! I remember Mum panicking as we were forced to turn and dash back across the fields in the direction of the mainland. By now, the tide was well on the turn. With Carl on her shoulders, she waded through the sea leaving Dad to ward off the bulls with the aid of some items of red clothing. By now, the girls and I had the water well above our waists. Dad finally joined us and we reached the safety of dry land in a wet, bedraggled state. The whole experience left Mum shaken and as a family we never went back.

Nowadays, Jan and I love to stroll across the sand-bar at low tide but always go armed with the tide timetable. She will invariably linger on the shoreline and her favourite rock to observe the moment when the first shallow waves meet each other denoting that the tide is once again on the turn. I, on the other hand, make a right turn, cross a small, sheltered beach and head for the two ruined churches and the cemetery beyond. The view back to the mainland from the peaceful graveyard on a sunny day is unrivalled. The eye is drawn to the three distant mountain summits of Errigal, Snacht and Muckish while a climb to the top wall of the cemetery is rewarded with the views of gentle Crohy Head, the next peninsula to the north, and Arranmore Island – the county's largest inhabited island – peeping out beyond.

Inishkeel has long been a place of pilgrimage and I am indebted to Lochlann McGill for his meticulously researched book, *In Conall's Footsteps*, which gives great insights into the archaeology, history and folklore of this part of Donegal. St Conall's is the first church. To the right of the door but outside the church is an ancient recumbent flagstone depicting the figure of Christ on the cross. Curiously, his head is not tilted but upright suggesting that he is still alive. It is such a poignant image and I always make a point of bringing Dad's garden shears to trim the grass which frequently overgrows the flagstone. Lochlann states that St Conall's was traditionally known as 'the church' and St Mary's, the second church, as 'the monastery'. This is because there was a monastic community on the island from the time of St Conall in the sixth century.

It would have amused Dad greatly to learn that, as a young man, Conall Caol 'was no saint'. In fact he committed patricide! His penance for striking his father dead with a hammer was to be banished to an island long enough for birds to nest and rear their young in the palm of his hand[2]. His seventh year on Inishkeel coincided with a very good summer. It is not known for how long he fell asleep one day but, when he did wake, a nest and hatching chicks in his hand was the sight that met his gaze. Knowing that he had at last completed his penance, he proceeded to do a *turas* round the island. *An turas* in Irish literally means 'the journey' as Christian pilgrims would have visited various 'stations' (as with the link to Station Island on Lough Derg) to say prescribed prayers at places such as holy wells and Christian-decorated cross-slab stones. These pilgrimages were enacted out on the island until recently and Lochlann describes in detail how a local woman and devotee, Beatrice McHugh, instructs him on how to go about this[3]. The ritual reminded me of what is expected of pilgrims at Lough Derg and, although I have used Lochlann's book to follow the trail of holy places on Inishkeel, I baulk at the idea of ever reciting endless 'Our Fathers', 'Hail Marys' and 'Glorias' as I reach three hugely symbolic piles of penitential stones. The ritual includes circulating the mounds three times in a clockwise direction and visiting St Conall's Well which is also on the north side of the island. Jan and I did, however, enjoy the communal experience of joining a sizeable crowd consisting of the local parish priest, Fr Daly, his parishioners, and holiday-makers on the annual pilgrimage to the island in July 2018. The weather was not the best and neither were the tides generous in terms of the time we were afforded on the island but I was struck by the sincerity and faith of those around us as we sang hymns and recited some short prayers for our own intentions as well as in honour of St Conall and St Dallan, the other saint associated with the island. A photograph of Beatrice lying on her back on an indented large boulder in the cemetery adorns the front cover of Lochlann's book. St Joseph's Bed reputedly has healing powers for those with back problems and always forms part of my own visit to the island. Its hardness gives me no relief but staring up at the firmament wonderfully relaxes the mind.

I now come to the story that most resonates with the locals and frequent visitors and to which Lochlann devotes chapter 5 in his book – the bell and shrine. Pilgrims used to leave votive offerings at the symbolic sites on the island. These might have taken the form of Rosary beads, a holy image, or simply a ribbon to remember a deceased loved one or to ask for a cure for an ailment or some disease. Pilgrims on the Camino Francés will be familiar with this as the Cruz de Ferro is festooned with such mementoes. On a smaller scale on the Vía de la Plata is the Pico de la Dueña, two days' walk before Salamanca, which commands superb views across the plains of Castilla y León to the east. Prior to the 1850 banning of the Inishkeel *turas* by the Catholic clergy due to their grave concern over a not infrequent "carnivalesque atmosphere involving music, revelry, heavy drinking, sexual licentiousness, and even serious violence"[4], a bell thought to have belonged to St Conall formed an integral part of the pilgrimage. It is only about seven inches high and was in the keeping of the O'Breslin family. An additional embellishment in the form of an elaborate bell-shrine was added in the 15th century. This is the more eye-catching of the two ornaments[5]. Pilgrims to the island would have queued in front of the elder O'Breslin to kiss the bell-shrine which hung around his neck from a chain. Lochlann quotes local tradition as hearing him say *"Pinginn domhsa agus póg don Bheárnáin"*. (A penny to me and you can kiss the Beárnán.)[6] On a more contemporary note, even though the Camino Francés has become similarly commercialised, it is my firm belief that, with the possible exception of the final 100 km from Sarria, the 21st century pilgrim continues to enjoy a strong spiritual experience untainted by the demands of consumerism.

The bell and shrine were subsequently sold to a Major Nesbitt in nearby Ardara, stolen from his house on the night he died in 1845, and eventually ended up in the British Museum in London where they have remained ever since. Occasionally the more ornate shrine is loaned out to museums round the world. For one summer only in 2015, the Donegal County Museum in Letterkenny became the temporary home of both bell and shrine. The 13th July was a very special day indeed when they returned, accompanied by security guards, to the Dolmen Centre in Kilclooney, not far from the island. Over a thousand people queued to see the artefacts and these included Jan and me, as well as Carl and my sister-in-law. We were never going to miss such a wonderfully symbolic occasion. 'Think you are from Portnoo' on Facebook provides a great selection of photos on a day which will live for ever in the minds of the locals and the many others who know the history of the island. The sadness comes from the knowledge that this was probably a one off though a replica bell is now on display in the centre.

Before leaving the island to move to another part of the county, I wish to share a story that an Irish pilgrim passing through Rabanal during the March 2019 working party told me. I had escaped my cleaning duties to pop over to the Mesón del Refugio small family-run hotel across the square for a morning coffee. A pilgrim came in seeking accommodation. Hearing his weak grasp of Spanish, I interpreted on his behalf with Cristina who runs the busy establishment along with her brother, Antonio. He was interested to hear about Gaucelmo though disappointed that we had not yet opened for the season. I could see that he wanted to tell me his story and the reason for his pilgrimage. He recounted how his journey had been up to this point. It included boot problems but he was now

happy with a second pair which he had broken in. Then, totally unexpectedly, he told me that, the year before, his son had committed suicide
by hanging himself. My duties would have to wait a little longer. Before
he, the father, had discarded his old boots, he had removed the laces and
these he was planning to attach to the giant cross at the top of the mountain the following day as a votive offering. Of all the stories I have had the
privilege of sharing with pilgrims on the Camino, this was perhaps the
most tragic and all the more poignant coming from a fellow Irishman.

NOTES

1. Isabel Crozier, **Donegal Annual: Journal of the Donegal Historical Society
   1957**, p.67.

2. **In Conall's Footsteps** by Lochlann McGill, Brandon/Mount Eagle Publica-
   tions Ltd., p.47.

3. As above, pp. 76-77.

4. This description comes from the leaflet distributed to pilgrims going to Inishkeel Island, 1 July 2018.

5. The bell and shrine featured in the BBC programme **Ireland's Treasures
   Uncovered** presented by Professor Alice Roberts and Dr Gavin Hughes and
   first broadcast in February 2016.

6. See note 2, p.81.

CHAPTER 19

"DON ALONSO MARTÍNEZ DE LEYVA, SECOND-IN-COMMAND OF THE SPANISH ARMADA"

"He saieth that Don Alonso, for his stature, was tawle and slender, of a whitly complexion, of a flaxen and smothe heare, of behaviour mylde and temperate, of speeche good and deliberate, greatly reverencid not only of his owne men, but generally of all the whole companie." [1]

Statement given by James Machary of Co. Tipperary before the Lord Deputy of Ireland, Sir William Fitzwilliam, on 29 December 1588 about the commander of the *Santa Ana* Armada ship.

No visitor to the Portnoo area of south-west Donegal can fail to notice the initial signage pointing the way round the circular driving route known as 'Bealach Santa Ana' (Santa Ana Drive). Unlike the new information board out on Inishkeel Island next to the two ruined churches, there is nothing currently on the route to indicate the specific landmarks related to the grounding of the *Duquesa Santa Ana*, a 900-ton hulk from the Andalusian squadron of the Spanish Armada. The ship was one of at least 26 which were shipwrecked off the north and west coasts of Ireland on their circuitous return route to Spain via the north of Scotland following their defeat at the hands of Queen Elizabeth's fleet in the English Channel.

Machary's description of the character of Don Alonso Martínez de Leyva, appointed by King Felipe II as the second-in-command of the Armada, reminds me greatly of our dad. He too was a mild-mannered person, he too was greatly admired by the British POWs whom he commanded and for whom he patiently cared in the camps as their MO. The following is a description of a reception in Lisbon prior to the departure of the Spanish fleet and given by de Leyva on board the *Rata Santa María Encoronada* in honour of the Duke of Medina Sidonia, the Commander of the Armada: "Sixty sons and nephews of the most noble families in Spain surrounded him [de Leyva], eager for battle and glory. They had deemed it a point of honour to serve under no-one but him. No wonder the grandees of the kingdom would have entrusted their heirs, the

157

hopes of their families, to none other than Don Alonzo."[2] Of course the men in Japan didn't choose their CO but the giant scroll presented to our dad at Raijo in September 1945 is testimony to similar feelings to those expressed by de Leyva's young admirers.

The *Rata* was the first of the three ships under Don Alonso's command to be shipwrecked. This was in Blacksod Bay in Co. Mayo in September 1588. He and his crew then transferred to the *Duquesa Santa Ana* which, following repairs, headed back north in the direction of Scotland. This was explained by the fact that the country was viewed as sympathetic to the Spanish cause. On 28/29 September, she ran aground in mountainous seas on rocks at the head of Loughros Mór Bay in Co. Donegal. As children on holiday in Portnoo, we had all heard of the *Santa Ana* shipwreck off-shore at the nearby townland of Rosbeg (from the Irish *rós beag* meaning small peninsula). We all knew there was an Armada cannon beside the ruined O'Boyle's Castle on a small island on Kiltoorish Lake but never thought to ask ourselves how on earth it got there.

In May 1968, a television programme was broadcast about the discovery of the wreck of a Spanish galleass off the north Antrim coast by the Belgian diver Robert Sténuit and his team of four. Our three sisters were all boarders at a convent secondary school in nearby Ballycastle and, on a designated Sunday each month, Mum and Dad would drive up with Carl and me from Belfast to take the girls out for the day. On one particular visit we went for lunch at a hotel in Portballintrae and a bracing beach walk afterwards. The thought of possible sunken treasures from a Spanish Armada vessel really fired our imaginations though it was years later that I learnt that de Leyva was the commander of what, indeed, turned out to be the *Girona*. It was to be third time unlucky for him. One month after the grounding of the *Santa Ana* at Rosbeg, he perished along with 1,300 sailors, soldiers and the cream of Spain's young nobility when the *Girona* smashed into rocks off Lacada Point near the Giant's Causeway.

In Sténuit's concluding chapter to his engrossing book, *Treasures of the Armada*, he calculates that over the course of three summers his crew spent 6,000 hours trawling the sea bed to uncover the *Girona's* cargo. "We found 47 gold jewels, eight chains, 1,256 coins, two insignia of knighthood, and any amount of gold table plate and silver, proof that there must have been many rich men aboard."[3] The extensive inventory also included 61 iron cannon balls and 127 stone balls. I was asked by Paula Harvey of the incredibly active Donegal GAP Heritage and History Group to give a talk on de Leyva at their annual Warp and Weft of Heritage Weekend in October 2018. When I told a friend of the invite, the man, who has a holiday home in the area, told me that in the late 60s he had a summer job in a hotel near the diving site. He then proceeded to say that, as a gesture of thanks, the divers had given him one of the stone cannon balls! I didn't hesitate to ask him if I could borrow it for my talk. It was such a special few days to be the keeper of an artefact, however humble, dating back over 400 years. It weighed nearly four kilos. But what of the treasure itself? What most brought it to the attention of the media was the opening of the Girona Exhibition on 22 June 1972 in the Ulster Museum, Belfast. This priceless collection has been on permanent display ever since and is a source of great pride to the people of Northern Ireland.

I began studying Spanish in my fourth year of secondary school in 1968 and made sure I was an early visitor to the new exhibition. One particular ring features a tiny hand holding a heart and an open belt clasp. It has an inscription which reads *"No tengo más que darte."* (I have nothing else to give you.) One can only surmise as to the identity of the young nobleman who received it as a parting gift from his beloved. He must have been so proud to wear it as he set sail with the others from A Coruña on 21 July 1588 knowing that there was someone special longing for him to make a safe return. As soon as Mum had chosen her three-stone, diamond engagement ring, she ensured that she had a photo taken of her proudly displaying it outside the family home in Belfast's Springfield Road, and promptly posted it to Dad. She now had something tangible to remember him by were he not to return from the war. For his part, he would have an image to inspire him, strengthen his resolve to survive his imprisonment, and hopefully achieve a safe return home.

One of the two insignias of knighthood recovered by the divers was a cross of a Knight of the Order of Alcántara. By a remarkable coincidence, I had spent a night in a pilgrim hostel with Pierre in 2012 overlooking the vast Alcántara Reservoir north of the historic town of Cáceres. De Leyva himself held two distinguished titles. One was Commander of Alcuéscar. This was the small town where we had chanced upon Francisco's funeral service three days before we reached the reservoir. However, what was even more intriguing was that de Leyva was also a Knight of the Order of Santiago. Essential conditions of membership included purity of blood and submission to the Order's rigid code of discipline. Its original military objectives in Spain were achieved in 1492 with the *Reconquista*

(Reconquest) from the Moors whereupon it turned its attention to the New World. Each member was the recipient of a cross in the form of the lily-sword of St James. There, in one of the exhibition cabinets in the Ulster Museum, lies de Leyva's beautiful cross mounted in an oval ring with a suspension-loop at the top where he would have hung it from a chain round his neck. I had no knowledge or interest in de Leyva on that first visit as a teenager but what a thrill to come across it on a recent return to the museum. An armament was another must-see exhibit. The *Santa Ana* cannon from O'Boyle's Island on Kiltoorish Lake is now on display by a large window in the special gallery which houses the *Girona* treasures. In 1969 it had been removed illegally from the island, reportedly by someone from Northern Ireland. Niall Fallon, who has written the most authoritative book on the Armada in Ireland, describes the theft as "shabby and unforgiveable treatment of a priceless and hitherto unique relic of the Armada"[4]. Happily restored by the museum, it now takes its place alongside the treasures recovered from de Leyva's final command. However, one does have to ask the question why the cannon is not on display at the Dolmen Centre at Kilclooney as it is so near to where the *Santa Ana* ran aground. A spot next to the other historical displays in this fine community centre would be a far more fitting repository for an artefact that had lain undisturbed down the road at Rosbeg for some 430 years.

Lochlann's book and especially chapter 9, 'Kiltoorish and the Armada', had inspired me to find out more about Alonso Martínez de Leyva. An on-line search produced some interesting details in Spanish on the background to his life from a Cuban-based website[5]. He was born in 1554 and his father had been viceroy of Naples. In a link with my first Camino, the family name de Leyva meaning "from Leyva" derives from a village north of Santo Domingo de la Calzada on the Camino Francés in the wine-producing region of La Rioja. Intriguingly, the village has had a castle on the same site since 1335. This is certainly a trail to pursue for the future. Every on-line search of de Leyva that I have come across throws up a strikingly handsome portrait painted by the artist El Greco in 1580. I have always thought that de Leyva bears a close resemblance to the English comedian and impressionist, Alistair McGowan.

Returning to the area where the *Santa Ana* ran aground, Loughros Mór Bay is the bigger of two bays. To the south lies the smaller Loughros Beg Bay and, in a link with the story of St Conall centuries before, Lochlann tells the tale of the saint being pursued by his enemies across the bay after an ecclesiastical visit to Glencolumbkille further to the south. (The latter is another area endowed with a great concentration of pilgrimage sites and was a place our dad and my recently deceased Uncle Fergus loved to frequent and not just because of the warm waters of the nearby 'Silver Strand'.) Exhausted, the saint falls asleep on the sand and, as the tide comes in, the sand rises up to form a small island. "No matter how big a tide there is, this island is never covered by the incoming water, in honour of the time that St Conall lay on it."[6]

As well as describing de Leyva, Machary's testimony is a first-hand account of the grounding of the *Santa Ana*. The ship:

"made saile for Spain, in which course by a contrarie wynd they were driven back upon mc Swine ny does Countrie to a place called Longherris, where falling to Anckor, there fell a greate storme which brake in sonder all theire cables, and stroke them upon grounde, whereby Don Alonso and all his companie were enforced to go on shoare taking all theire goodes, and armor w[i]th them, and there by the ship side incamped them selves for the space of 8 or 9 daies."[7]

It must have been bewildering, if at times overwhelming, for the isolated community of Rosbeg to witness a sudden influx of some 900 foreigners in encampments scattered around the area. A second-hand account mentions an Irishman who was able to communicate with some of the crew in Latin. The strand immediately to the south of the wreck is called the Trá Mór, literally the Big Beach. It is aptly named and is very exposed to the elements even on a calm day. As children, we regularly built rock pools by the promontory close to the site of the shipwreck. Mum and Dad restricted our swimming to paddling on the foreshore due to its unpredictable tides. Still today, only strong swimmers venture deeper.

Fearful of an attack by English forces who were wary of the possibility of the locals allying themselves with the armed crew of an Armada ship, the nobles on board sought the extra protection afforded by O'Boyle's Castle on the nearby island in the lake. First of all, however, they had to deal with their commander's immobility which Machary describes thus:

"Don Alonso before he came to Lande was hurt in the legge by the Capestele [capstan] of the ship in such sorte as he was nether hable to goe nor ride, nether duering the 9 daies of his incampinge, nor upon his remove, but was carried from that place..."[8].

161

I will return to another second-hand account of the *Santa Ana* wreck but was keen to see for myself at close quarters the remains of the castle where he was carried and to take a photograph from the spot where the cannon had lain for centuries. In a chat with a local man whose wife was a good friend of our parents, he confirmed rumours that I had heard from at least three other sources relating to a second cannon which had ended up somewhere in the silt of the lake. What I had not expected to hear, however, was that a quantity of what he called "white gold" recovered from the wreck had been handed down from one generation to another of families in the area. In order to prevent it falling into the hands of the Black and Tans during the Irish War of Independence between 1919 and 1921, it had been hidden somewhere in the lake. I was highly amused when he proceeded to compare the fruitless search for the treasure after the war to "trying to find holy water in an Orange hall." ('Orange' is associated with Protestants and 'holy water' with Catholics.) Sadly this simile continues to be most apt given the divisions between the two communities in Northern Ireland.

The opportunity to visit O'Boyle's Castle presented itself in the summer of 2017. Two local men agreed to row me over to the island but, due to the rotten wood which caused one of the oars to snap, we were reduced to using the other as a punt. This was not difficult as the water was under a metre deep following a dry spell though early on the short traverse we had to extricate ourselves from a rock on which the small boat had grounded. Comparisons to the fate of the *Santa Ana* abounded! On reaching the island, we scrambled up the bank and approached the ruins of the castle. The tower was originally about 15 metres high. There was some evidence of mounds which denoted the outer wall. These extended in a semi-circle to about 50 metres inland. I enjoyed taking in the panoramic view across the twin Loughros bays, fully aware that it was a sight I had never before experienced from that particular angle. Unfortunately, the gathering evening gloom curtailed our visit and we returned to our respective spouses to relate the story of our hilarious crossing.

One document in relation to the *Santa Ana* that is frequently acknowledged in both Lochlann McGill's and Niall Fallon's books is kept in the Archivo General de Simancas. This is a veritable treasure-trove of vast numbers of documents spanning five hundred years and going back to the early 15th century. They are housed in a medieval castle in the small town of Simancas which lies a short distance south of the historic Spanish city of Valladolid. It was the 'Armada king', Felipe II, who is most associated with establishing it as one of the country's national archive repositories. Incidentally, the king once spent the night during a hunting expedition at a large house called the 'Casa de las Cuatro Esquinas' (the Four-Cornered House) in the middle of the pilgrim village of Rabanal. Felipe was assiduous in maintaining contact with all his commanders during the whole period of the Armada and their correspondence is frequently annotated by him in the margins of their letters. I find his writing for the most part illegible but, nevertheless, I gained a special sense of history as I examined six documents relating to de Leyva on my first visit to the castle's reading room in 2016. The staff were wonderfully accommodating and keen to help me with my research. They subsequently forwarded me on-line the letters I requested. I was most impressed by their proficiency not to mention the negligible cost of the documents, and promised to return.

To continue de Leyva's story and that of the crew of the *Santa Ana*, they receive word that there are three Spanish ships at the harbour at Killybegs some 30 km to the south. After nine days, they move out en masse for the trek along the Trá Mór Beach, through the sandy terrain of what is now the Sheskinmore Nature Reserve, past the huge sand dunes of Ballinreavy Strand and round the bay to Ardara. They then follow the pass through the hills to reach Killybegs, still today one of Ireland's largest fishing ports. (In addition to hosting the Warp and Weft of Heritage Weekend in 2018, the GAP Heritage and History Group organised a re-enactment walk along the route to commemorate the 430th anniversary of the *Santa Ana*'s crew's march.) The still incapacitated de Leyva is carried by four of his servants on a sedan-type chair. (Our guide on a day trip to Bath a few years ago described how servants used to carry their masters on these chairs to the baths to partake of the waters. The story immediately resonated with me.) On a set Sunday each July, Dad would drive us along that same road through the hills to the port where the seven of us would board one of the many trawlers to sail out to the mouth of Donegal Bay. There the ceremony of the Blessing of the Fleet was enacted by the local bishop.

The news was bad when the men reached Killybegs. In fact only the galleass, the *Girona*, was anchored in the harbour. Machary states that repairs to the vessel took nearly a fortnight. To accommodate the extra 1,000 men, many of the ship's bronze cannons had to be jettisoned. In a newspaper article by a local historian, Pat Conaghan, he speculates that many of them lie deep in the mud "and are now buried for ever underneath the pier works".[9] Niall Fallon paints a moving picture of the heavily overladen *Girona* with 1,300 on board sailing out of Killybegs at dawn on 26 October[10]. Some 200 other foreign nationals were left behind as priority would have been given to Spaniards. The former would have included Machary, originally a conscript, who had embarked on de Leyva's first ship, the *Rata*, in Lisbon. In the castle in Simancas, I discovered a letter to the king from Mattias van der Locht begging him for financial assistance. He was Flemish and numbered among de Leyva's 36 servants. His foreign nationality undoubtedly saved him from being allowed to board the *Girona*. As Jan, her brother, her sister-in-law, and I sat on the grass in a farmer's field at the mouth of Donegal Bay in June 2015 to watch the departure of the cruise ship *Oriana*, I thought of the *Girona*'s same course out into the open sea to ultimately meet her fate two days later on 28 October. There were only nine survivors. One of these was a Greek sailor called Jorge de Nicolo de Zante. In another pleading letter to the king which I came across, he claimed to be the helmsman of the *Girona*. Presumably his key job ensured that he was allowed to board the ship.

The main reason for my return to Simancas in 2019 was to discover the letter that Felipe II had written to the Duke of Medina Sidonia appointing de Leyva as commander of the Armada. (A further link between the duke and the *Duquesa Santa Ana* was the naming of the ship after his wife whom he had married when she was only 10 years of age.) It was only to be opened in the event of Medina Sidonia's death. I had searched for it without success three years before but under the heading of letters from the king to de Leyva. Unsurprisingly, I had received very short shrift in the interim when I wrote an email to the librarian staff saying that I should have been searching under correspondence with Medina Sidonia and could they investigate! The king's correspondence with all his commanders was extensive. I felt such a fool. One stunningly beautiful image which they had sent me was a 1596 coloured map produced for a possible subsequent invasion of Ireland by the Spanish. It showed Killybegs and the whole inlet where the *Girona* would have sailed as she made her way out to the open sea. I enjoyed renewing acquaintances with the staff including Isabel who at the time was still in charge of the references' department. I felt like an old hand as I went through the routine of placing my things in a locker and taking only a pencil and small sheets of paper into the magnificent wood-panelled library. The requested files are brought out a few at a time by staff wearing long white coats. The covers are always cold as they are stored at a very low temperature somewhere in the castle vaults. The tactile sensation of the historical parchment paper once again filled me with a privileged sense of history. The sense of anticipation was again quite overwhelming.

After two days, my search for the king's letter to his trusted and much admired commander proved elusive. I approached Francisco, the staff member in the reading room who is available to help with research. Bemoaning my lack of success, I then vaguely remembered the names of two Spanish sailors mentioned by Niall Fallon in relation to the *Santa Ana*. He scribbled them down and promised to search for them on his computer. The next day, my last one in Valladolid, I only had a few hours to spare in the castle but was thrilled when Francisco gave me the appropriate reference numbers. He confirmed their names were Francisco de Borja and Juan de Nova. As the white-coated assistant brought the folder, I dreaded the scribe's hand-writing being semi-illegible but instead I found myself staring at a neat, flowery script. It was prefaced in French as the sailors gave their statement at a French Channel port on or around 6 January 1589. Francisco explained that the French took a great interest in what had transpired in the waters north of their sphere of influence. I only had time for a cursory look at the seven-page document but had seen enough to know that it would provide me with more details on the wrecking of the *Santa Ana* and its aftermath. Whilst admitting that Fallon's description is copious[11], it was still a very special moment for me to read the two sailors' account in its original Spanish.

Back in England, it took a few days for my international money transfer to be processed though longer for Francisco to email me the correct documents after an initial error. As with the documents I had requested in 2016 and had included in my conference talk, I was surprised at how much of the 16th century Spanish I could understand. They contained the usual problems which included the interchanging of upper and lower case initial letters in places where I least expected them, disparate words being joined together, a confusing lack of punctuation and accents, and a rambling sentence style. However, the more I studied them, the more they made sense. It was like unscrambling a giant word puzzle as I second-guessed more and more illegible words from the existing context. Finally they began to form coherent sentences. Paula was keen to use my translation which she planned to read out during the 2019 re-enactment walk on 3 August. As luck would have it, a Spanish tourist on holiday in the area noticed a poster advertising the walk and offered to fill in the gaps in my translation. Emilio has a strong marine background. In an email exchange I learnt that he too has walked the Camino Francés and stayed in Rabanal!

The disadvantage in the two sailors' testimony lies in the fact that it is a second-hand account of the sinking of the *Santa Ana* based on what they heard from one of the nine survivors of the Girona. How reliable it is, therefore, is open to question but there is certainly far more detail than in Machary's account particularly in the matter of the crew's attempt to secure the vessel :

"con un ferro por no llevar otro y con la gran corriente se le quebro y con una barca hecharon cavo atierra atandole en una peña y la corriente en callo la nave y viéndose deesta manera salto en tierra toda la gente sacando el poco bastimento que tenian y algunas municiones y una pieza de cam-paña..."[12] ("dropped one anchor as they didn't have another and with the strong current it broke away and using a boat they tied a rope to a rock and the current forced the ship to run aground and upon seeing this the people jumped ashore taking with them the few provisions they had and some armaments and a cannon...")

There is no description of their stay at Rosbeg but there is a passing reference to the unfortunate de Leyva as *"...llevando a Don Alonso de Leyva en una silla por estar malo..."* ("...carrying Don Alonso de Leyva in a chair as he was injured..."). This is in the context of subsequently heading for the *Girona* which the witness describes vaguely as being *"mas arriva"* ("further up") as opposed to what we know as Killybegs lying to the south. It has to be borne in mind that Spanish navigation maps of the time were quite basic and did not show, for example, the north-western bulge of Co. Mayo which would have explained some of the previous problems facing the ships returning to Spain. The sailors' account ends with an understated summary of the terrible loss of life of the galleass. One salient detail is their description of the position of the rock which the vessel hit at Lacada Point on the north Antrim coast:

"...dando con una peña queestava a un tiro de Arcabuz metida en la mar donde se hizo pedazos la Galeaza ahogandose mas de 1300 hombres queyvan enella dequesolos se salvaron 9 marineros..." ("...striking a rock standing only a musket shot off-shore where the galleass broke into pieces drowning more than 1,300 men of whom only 9 sailors survived...").

This terrible loss of life is mirrored further south in Co. Sligo. Of the crew of 1,100 on three ships wrecked on Streedagh Strand the month before, some 800 drowned or died from exhaustion and exposure. There is now a permanent exhibition on the Armada wrecks in Ireland in the nearby village of Grange. The Grange Armada Development Association annually commemorates the loss of life of the Armada ships. The Donegal GAP Heritage and History Group posted a video on their Facebook page of the 2019 ceremony in Killybegs attended by members of the crew of the Spanish navy patrol ship, the *Centinela*. It vividly captures the strong emotional bonds between the two countries. The victims are thus never forgotten. One sailor who did survive the Sligo wrecks and who wrote a fascinating account of his hazardous journey through counties Sligo and Leitrim to ultimately return safely home to Spain was Capt. Francisco de Cuéllar. The well-signed de Cuéllar Trail round both counties is worth following and is a fine example of exploring living history.

Before returning to the main theme of my book, there is one final remarkable coincidence that links the castle at Simancas with Donegal. Red Hugh O'Donnell, the Earl of Tyrconnell, fled Ireland with his father-in-law Hugh O'Neill, the Earl of Tyrone, after their defeat along with a Spanish force at the hands of the English at the Battle of Kinsale in 1602. He was a swashbuckling figure, the subject of the 1966 Walt Disney film *The Fighting Prince of Donegal*. I must confess that I have no inclination to watch this yarn but I did attend a play-reading related to O'Donnell at An Grianán Theatre in Letterkenny in Co. Donegal. I had the privilege of actually sitting on the stage along with a small number of other spectators to listen to *Making History*, written by the aforementioned, great Irish playwright Brian Friel. I had never been to a play-reading before but it left a deep impression on me. The lack of a visual context leaves the listener hanging on to every word uttered by the actors as they vividly enacted a meeting in Ireland between the two earls. It transpired that O'Donnell and O'Neill sailed to Spain. The former then made his way to Valladolid to plead for help with an invasion of Ireland from the new Spanish king, Felipe III. The city was the capital of Spain at the time. O'Donnell died in Simancas Castle on 10 September 1602, supposedly poisoned but more likely to have suffered from tapeworm. A plaque in Spanish and Irish beyond the moat and just inside the castle walls commemorating his passing was unveiled by one of his descendants in 1991.

The immense satisfaction I have gained with regard to my research into de Leyva would not have been possible without the link to Dad. I have much to thank him for and this is yet another example of how his influence has led me into areas of experience which I would never have imagined. He was an avid reader of *Time Magazine* as well as *National Geographic*, two excellent periodicals which undoubtedly broadened his depth of knowledge of world events. In researching this book, I discovered an extensive article in the latter written by Sténuit about the dives that uncovered the *Girona*'s treasures[13]. The issue coincided with the years in which he had a regular subscription to the magazine.

NOTES

1. See www.nationalarchives.gov.uk/palaeography/doc3_popup/transcript.htm – lines 42-45.

2. **Treasures of the Armada** by Robert Sténuit, Cardinal edition published in 1974 by Sphere Books Ltd., p.45.

3. As above, p.253.

4. **The Armada in Ireland** by Niall Fallon, Stanford Maritime Ltd. London, p.87.

5. See website www.ecured.cu

6. **In Conall's Footsteps** by Lochlann McGill, p.78. which borrows this quote from Dept. of Irish Folklore, ms. 1735, P.52.

7. See note 1, lines 22-29.

8. As above, lines 30-33.

9. See article written by Pat Conaghan in the Donegal Democrat newspaper, 31 August 2015, pp.18-19.

10. **The Armada in Ireland** by Niall Fallon, p.90.

11. See above, pp. 81-82.

12. Archivo General de Simancas, document reference K-1570 B63, Estado Francia, doc 7, Appendix doc 39.

13. See National Geographic, Vol. 135 No. 6, June 1969.

CHAPTER 20
"2017 PILGRIMAGE PART 1 – SINGAPORE"

"First view of St Andrew's Cathedral's partly exposed white spire emerging from behind buildings as we climbed up the steps from City Hall MRT Station. Thrill of re-connecting with Dad…Padang. Also re-connecting with Villana. Long chats in evenings. Snippets during day of recalled childhood, adolescence, teenage memories."

Diary entry day 1, Tuesday 3 October 2017

Villana is the eldest of my three sisters. She readily agreed to join me in Singapore for a week in 2017 to literally walk in our dad's footsteps. As I once again take up the direct link to his time in the Far East, his example of carefully penning his daily thoughts and observations for Mum encouraged me to do the same as I had already done during my Caminos. The highlights of our visit are instantly recalled as are those moments of extreme emotion but it is the smaller minutiae contained in my 55-page diary covering Singapore and Japan that would be wiped from my memory if I had not sat down each day with my intimate friend. The Irish poet, Patrick Kavanagh, whom I have mentioned in chapter 12 beautifully described these little details thus: "Ordinary things wear lovely wings."

I had three principal aims in visiting Singapore. Firstly to contact the families of Krish Nair and George Reuneker, secondly to meet David Marshall's widow, Jean, and their son Jonathan, and, finally and most importantly of all, to commemorate Dad's walk and those of the thousands of other POWs into captivity by following their footsteps from the centre of Singapore to Changi. In order to achieve the first of these, the British Embassy in Singapore helpfully suggested I email the *Singapore Straits Times* newspaper. They immediately offered to publish an article about our visit[1]. There then followed a couple of phone calls and an exchange of emails with their Heritage and Community Correspondent, Melody Zaccheus. These continued when we arrived in Singapore and the three of us also met for coffee to touch base. Later that morning, we were joined by Alphonsus Chern, the paper's award-winning photographer, who took some pictures and made arrangements to cover our departure from St Andrew's Anglican Cathedral the following Saturday on our trek to Changi. We chose St Andrew's as it was in the grounds of the cathedral where our dad was billeted in February '42 and was also adjacent to the Padang from where many other prisoners would have set out. In another amazing coincidence, Alf told us that his other passion was music and that he is the organist at the Catholic Cathedral of the Good Shepherd, the second stop on our pilgrimage walk.

To gain a better perspective on the days before the Japanese invasion of Singapore, Villana and I spent our first morning at the award-winning Battle Box Museum. This is built into the hillside of Fort Canning Park and is the site of the underground bunkers from where the defence of the island was conducted. It was only rediscovered in 1988, sadly 11 years after Mum and Dad's visit to Singapore. I'm sure they would both have been fascinated to relive a key period in the island's history. Here we were as their offspring and at roughly the same age as our parents on their one and only visit together to the country. The most striking exhibition is the room with life-size models which depicts Percival's meeting with his senior staff when the decision to surrender was taken. Newsreel footage shows what, for me, is the intensive, aggressive stare of the Japanese commander – General Tomoyuki Yamashita.

Later that morning we met Eric Chin, formerly the Director of the National Archives, and Patricia Lee, who is in charge of oral history. They gave us a conducted tour of the National Archives' building which was being temporarily mothballed and due for renovation on the same site. They insisted on taking us for lunch to a restaurant in 'Little India' off Serangoon Road through which we would pass on our walk. As our hosts drove us to the Anjappar Restaurant on Syed Alwi Road, the colourful displays announcing the forthcoming Deepavali Festival of Lights vividly drew our attention to the Indian community in Singapore. Combining with the Eurasian, Malay, and Chinese populations, one certainly gets the impression that this is a country where West meets East. I was brought down to earth with a bang by nearly choking on a green chilli hidden in a yoghurt dish, much to the amusement of Villana and our two dining companions!

A visit to the Changi Museum with the tour company Viator introduced us to Helena, our knowledgeable guide. She is from the Chinese community and spoke movingly about her father who was spared death in the infamous Sook Ching massacre. (*Sook Ching* comes from the Chinese for "purge through cleansing"). All Chinese males aged between

18 and 50 had to report to the Japanese military police, the Kempeitai, in screening centres round the island. According to Helena, the key to whether they lived or died lay in the appearance of their hands. Those who had labourers' hands or any tattoos on their bodies were separated from those with smooth hands. The Japanese feared that any insurrection from the Chinese, their traditional enemies, would come not from the workers but from the latter so-called 'intellectual' class. Estimates vary between 5,000 and 25,000 as to the number who were executed over a two-week period at the end of February and the beginning of March '42. At the Researching FEPOW History Group's two conferences in Liverpool in 2015 and 2017, I was privileged to meet the former director of the Changi Museum and coincidentally now the director of the Battle Box, Jeya Ayadurai. He provided each attendee with a most informative booklet issued by the Singapore National Heritage Board. The following description of the massacres on Changi Beach is quite horrific: "Bound by ropes in rows of eight to 12, victims at this site were instructed to walk towards the sea in batches. Japanese soldiers would then machine-gun them as they reached the shallow waters. While many died on-site, some managed to swim away or seek temporary refuge underwater as the ropes binding them loosened in the waters. The ensuing bayoneting of the victims after the initial firing by the Japanese soldiers meant that there were few survivors. The bodies of the Sook Ching massacre victims on Changi Beach were buried within the area in mass graves dug by a work party of 100 British and Australian POWs from Changi Prison. POW accounts reveal that some of the victims were still alive. However, the Japanese soldiers ordered them to be drowned. As the soldiers threatened injury to those who disobeyed, the POWs had little choice but to comply".[2]

As Helena addressed us by the small plaque which commemorates the massacres on Changi Beach, the upsetting images she painted contrasted with the noisy intrusion of 21st century transport, the giant passenger planes directly above our heads queueing in orderly fashion to swoop like ungainly albatrosses in their final run-in to Changi International Airport. It was 4 October, the feast of St Francis of Assisi and five years to the day since I walked north on day one out of Seville.

The booklet goes on to mention the selfless part played by a Japanese civilian administrator, Mamoru Shinozaki, who used his position to save the lives of over 2,000 Chinese civilians during the time of the occupation[3]. Before I left Singapore I made sure I bought a copy of his book,

Syonan My Story. In another ambit of World War II he joins a select pantheon inhabited by the likes of Raoul Wallenberg[4] and Oskar Schindler
(the subject of Steven Spielberg's 1993 film *Schindler's List*) in Nazi-occu-
pied Europe.

Earlier in our tour back at the Changi Museum, Helena had recounted
the story of the Changi Murals, the replicas of which hang in one of its
rooms. The originals were painted by the British POW Stanley Warren
in St Luke's Chapel in Roberts Barracks and depict five life-size murals of
biblical scenes. Warren changed the faces he painted from events in the
New Testament to those of some of his fellow comrades. The originals
have been conserved at the Changi Air Base by the Ministry of Defence[5].
When Villana and I met up with Jeya later in our stay, he said that Helena
was one of the best guides at the museum. As we listened to her description, her voice momentarily faltered revealing her emotion during one of
what must have been hundreds if not thousands of the guided tours she
has given. This was a memory that will stay with me always. At the end
of the tour we thanked her and shared with her one of our reasons for
coming to Singapore. She responded by saying she would have loved to
accompany us on our pilgrimage but unfortunately would be working.

That evening Villana and I were invited to dinner at Jean Marshall's
home where we also met her son, Jonathan. He had asked if he could
walk with us to Changi and we had readily agreed so the evening was
a good opportunity to firm up the route. At the time, Jean was 91. We
found her to be a remarkably alert and engaging lady. Two stories relating
to David stood out. She pointed to a beautiful Ainu carving of a brown
bear with a fish on its shoulder. The sweeping grooved style reminded
us immediately of a similar black bear that Dad had brought home from
Japan. Tradition has it that friendly bears carried fish to lost travellers in
the woods. David had been presented with the gift by the mayor of Nishi
Ashibetsu when he made a three-week private visit to Japan in June 1956
en route to China as part of a trade delegation from Singapore. He had
by then resigned from his role as first minister due to his disappointment
at Britain's unwillingness to move more swiftly to granting Singapore
self-government. He wryly commented to the mayor that he never came
across that bear. The note of provenance with the bear goes on to mention a disturbing encounter in Nishi Ashibetsu: "In the town David went
to a pharmacy to buy aspirin and found he was being served by a man
who suddenly blanched and stuttered. David recognized him as a rather

nasty guard of the POWs. David left the shop without comment." I cannot imagine how traumatic this unexpected meeting must have been for him. Unlike Dad who steadfastly refused to ever return to Japan, David did go but this was to be the only occasion. When he got back to Singapore, he told Jean that he had done his duty and that he was never going back.

By now, we had spent two full days in Singapore and the worst effects of jet lag had finally gone. However, my sleep patterns continued to be erratic and I found myself waking around 2.30 each morning, unable to sleep for a couple of hours as I mulled over the events of the previous day. The song I kept returning to on my iPod was Coldplay's '*Til Kingdom Come*'[6]. The symbolic unlocking of a door in the lyrics seemed so apt. I thought of Dad settling down each evening to write his letter to Mum as he pondered his future life, comforted by the unswerving belief that they would one day be reunited. The connotations of the original biblical reference in the title were not lost on me as I listened to the simple but catchy tune and the unadorned lyrics of the ballad. Chris Martin, the lead singer, effortlessly hits the high notes in the chorus as he pleads for understanding and patience.

Mum certainly did wait for Dad and I like to think that, were she alive, she too would have enjoyed the song. Like me, she loved singing and was a soprano in the local church choir of Our Lady of the Assumption in Newcastle. Villana too has emulated her as a soprano in her church choir in Ottawa.

The next morning we had a date with Patricia Lee on an upper storey of the huge National Library building. In her role as oral historian, she was keen to interview both of us as the offspring of a POW as opposed to prisoners themselves. She announced that this was a first and we felt suitably honoured. Her warm and engaging personality put us totally at ease as we sat down in front of a microphone for what turned out to be two hours without a pause. The time flew. She was keen to know how Dad's imprisonment had affected him and what life was like for him and Mum in rearing us and our three siblings particularly when the Troubles began in our teenage years. The questioning was incisive but always delivered and listened to in Patricia's unique, empathetic style. There were some highly emotional moments and Villana and I were grateful for each other's support. (I have since listened on-line to some of the fascinating interviews given by both David and Jean to the Oral History Department of the National Archives. There is no doubt that Singapore is a country that greatly values its heritage and which we would do well to emulate in these islands.)

That afternoon, we were pleased at how well we negotiated the MRT subway and buses, not to mention sheltering from a sudden downpour, in order to reach Bukit Timah. This suburb lay directly in the path of the advance of Japanese troops towards the centre of Singapore. Our destination was the Former Ford Factory where the surrender document was signed by Percival in the presence of Yamashita on 15 February '42. The clock on the wall in the same room where the surrender took place shows the time as 6.20 on that fateful Sunday evening. The art deco building houses a World War II exhibition gallery. The factory itself opened in '41 and was the first motorcar assembly plant in south-east Asia. The Japanese used it to manufacture motor vehicles for their army and it returned to producing motor vehicles after the war until it closed in 1980[7].

Saturday finally dawned, the day of our memorial walk to Changi. After an early and substantial breakfast in our hotel, we joined Jonathan outside St Andrew's Anglican Cathedral and an ever-smiling Alf who got us to pose for pictures in front of its pristine white spire. We looked resplendent in our COFEPOW (Children of the Far East Prisoners of War) polo-shirts. A short video posted by the reporter Melody on YouTube[8] shows us walking through the gates of the Catholic Good Shepherd Cathedral at a sprightly pace with our small backpacks. (The video also shows me reading some extracts in our hotel room from Carl's word-processed version of our dad's letters.) I can faintly hear the soothing sound of my scallop shell as it sways from my backpack and brushes against the miraculous medal given to me by a nun during my first Camino as Keith and I crossed the Meseta. The shell was a gift from Kiko which I will always treasure. It has a section missing from it, the result of me stupidly placing it beside my metal water bottle in my rucksack at luggage check-in at Heathrow back in '98. For me it is also a symbol that none of us is perfect and we all have our faults. Some people view the scallop shell as the obligatory paraphernalia of pilgrimage but for me it is a sacred amulet which helps to protect me. From my rucksack I also hang a short blue ribbon known to the inhabitants of Zaragoza in Spain as the *medida del Pilar*. It comes in various colours but always measures 36.5 centimetres, the height of the tiny statue of the Virgin Mary who appeared to St James on a 'pillar' and is revered by the people of the city in their cathedral. The ribbons are frequently seen tied to car steering wheels, prams, and helmets.

We had earlier posed for photographs taken by Alf in front of the high altar at the Good Shepherd as the cleaning ladies went quietly about their chores behind us. The folly of carrying Dad's officer hat crushed in my rucksack and adding to the weight was remedied by Alf offering to place it in his locker overnight for safe-keeping. Then Villana and I said a short prayer remembering our dad. His diary entry for 15 February '42, following the heavy fighting in the days before the fall of Singapore, includes the following lines: "I was not afraid once; I always did my duty and many times it was done under shellfire and aerial bombardment. Somehow I always felt that He was watching over me because you had asked Him to do so. I was at Mass this morning at our Cathedral and also at Communion. The church still stands though many buildings around are in ruins. God bless you, Eileen." The day also marked what would have been my mother-in-law's 100th birthday, another lady for whom I had great affection and who was prominently in my thoughts as we set off. My father-in-law had also seen action during the war in Greece.

It was 9 o'clock by the time we reached the 'Little India' district of Serangoon Road. We made two stops for refreshing drinks of coconut milk swigged from the giant fluorescent green fruits themselves. A machete lay beside a food stall in one of the bars reminding Villana and me that we were most definitely in an alien environment. Jonathan enjoyed a more substantial snack at the second bar and, on the terrace as the road slowly came to life, I regaled them both with a rendition of Irish folk singer Cara Dillon's version of the song 'Bright Morning Star'. It contains some poignant references to deceased mothers and fathers. The original was sung by the American country singer Emmy-Lou Harris. I have always enjoyed singing on my Caminos, usually on my own towards the end of a long day's walking and to take my mind off aching feet and shoulders. Dad often mentions performing his repertoire in front of small groups of fellow POWs. His 'party piece' was the amusing Irish folk song, 'Phil the Fluter's Ball', which he always sang at family gatherings and of which we all have fond memories.

Once past the end of Serangoon Road and the former red light district of Lavender Street, our route opened out into wide thoroughfares where we had to negotiate several pedestrian bridges high above streams of noisy traffic. We stayed close to MacPherson Road and were guided by the GPS on Jonathan's mobile phone. It was reassuring to be walking with a local otherwise we would have become totally lost. When the traffic finally began to thin out and we could hear each other better, we told him stories about our dad's experiences in the war and he in turn answered our questions about the many queries we had during our five days in Singapore. As the youngest of three older siblings, we had the impression that he knew little of what his father went through in Changi, the *Wales Maru,* and the Hokkaido Camps and he was so grateful for the information we imparted.

Further along the route, Paya Lebar is now an air base so we were forced to loop to the south, the rubber, rice and banana plantations long since gone. We then followed a path close to a canal. I spotted a group of swarthy-skinned Indians working on the bank and thought of Dad's great empathy towards his field ambulance unit as they prepared for war in the jungles of Malaya.

Not long afterwards, we ground to a halt as some recently trimmed overgrown bushes blocked the canal path. We reluctantly retraced our steps back to the dreaded concrete pavements, so often the undoing of long-distance walking pilgrims as their unforgiving surface frequently induces blisters and tendinitis. There was no bar to be seen for a drink and a toilet-stop as we reached the large suburb of Tampines. However, totally unexpectedly, we came across a table and some chairs by the pavement where we eagerly slumped to rest in the shade of some bushes from the searing heat of the midday sun. The high humidity had also taken its toll on me though less so on Villana who is used to similar conditions in the summer in Ottawa. Perhaps I need not have chided her in our hotel lobby that morning for not carrying enough water. Before we moved on, I went to investigate what appeared to be some artificial fruit at the base of a tree clump. Jonathan then told me that it was not artificial but an offering left by Buddhist families to the gods to pray for a family member who had changed religion, possibly to Christianity. Furthermore, touching it was associated with bad luck! In spite of my ignorance of local customs, I found the incident quite unnerving.

Eventually we reached a bus stop about 11 miles into the 14 of our walk. My one-year-old prosthetic knee had thankfully given me no trouble but I knew the pain in my lower back caused by my ankylosing spondylitis was slowing me down and, what was worse, it was forcing Villana and Jonathan to frequently stop to wait for me. It was unfair delaying their steady pace and I knew that the time had come to take a taxi and meet them at Changi Museum. I was disappointed at not finishing the pilgrimage but resigned to the fact that it was the right decision. It was a salutary experience and my mind went back to '98 and the young pilgrim at Puente la Reina having to give up. I then thought of those serene moments of acceptance at Frómista on my first Camino when I too had made plans to exit my pilgrimage.

The heavens opened soon after the taxi dropped me off at Changi and I quickly sheltered from the deluge under the eaves of the chapel. Despite the warm welcome from the staff who had been expecting us, it was still a lonely couple of hours as I waited for my two walking companions. I busied myself reading the tributes left by grateful visitors on the notice board by the altar. A colourful display of feathers adorned one wall. Poignantly they came from the Japanese School of Singapore. It was so good to see visual confirmation of reconciliation. I searched the plaque listing all the clerics in Changi Camp. This is located at the chapel entrance. Sure enough I found Fr Richard Kennedy's name among them. I wondered how far away from where I now stood had the assault on him taken place. How disturbing it must have been for Andy Coogan and Dad who were powerless to intervene and how many thousands of other unprovoked beatings were witnessed by the POWs in south-east Asia.

It was a powerful moment of reunion when Villana and Jonathan arrived. I was so proud of my big sister who was nearly 30 years older than Jonathan and had done so well to complete the 14-mile walk in the intense heat and high humidity of an equatorial climate. As we had arranged to meet Jonathan the following evening at his mum's, we forgoed a celebratory drink and went our separate ways. We all felt we had done our dads proud.

In the true spirit of ecumenism, Villana and I attended two places of Sunday worship the next morning. The service at St Andrew's began at 8. The celebrant's words and the large congregation's responses were shown on a big screen which was a first for me. The sermon contained no anecdotes relating to everyday life, something that I admit always makes me lose interest, but the welcome drink and chat with parishioners in the covered area afterwards more than made up for it. Not only did I meet an ex-pat who was keen to walk the Camino Francés in Spain but we were introduced to the brother of my contact at the British Embassy. In addition to being one of the deacons in the cathedral, it turned out that he was an orthopaedic surgeon at the School of Medicine at the National University of Singapore. He had noticed my ankylosing spondylitis wrist band

and gave me his card saying he had treated patients with the condition.

Needless to say, Villana and I knew exactly how long it would take to walk to the Good Shepherd for church service number two. There was an even bigger congregation there for the 10.30 Mass and we had to separate to find seats after I was chided for sitting on one of the air-conditioning units at the side. The singing (the words again appeared on giant screens) and Alf's organ-accompaniment were magnificent and the whole atmosphere with Dad's attendance in the same building uppermost in my mind combined to make me very emotional. The 'Lamb of God' made me particularly tearful as I received Communion. As often happens in Catholic churches, some of the parishioners vacated their seats afterwards to forego the final blessing and make a speedy exit. I hadn't noticed Villana slip in beside me to offer a hug of comfort. Reunited with Dad's hat and with a promise to Alf that I would see him again back at the Good Shepherd in two weeks after the second leg of my pilgrimage, we headed to a nearby shopping mall.

That evening, Jean was keen to hear our news and our impressions of the walk. Villana had decided not to accompany me to Japan as my busy itinerary involved five different hotel stops in the space of 10 days. I promised Jean I would call with her when I returned to tell her how I had got on. Jonathan arrived feeling much refreshed after a massage the evening before. We have remained in touch and he intends tackling one of the Spanish pilgrim routes in the future.

On the morning Villana and I split with her returning home to Canada after an extra day in Singapore and me flying to Tokyo, Melody texted to say that her feature in the paper was published that very day. Perplexed at not finding it, I texted her and she pointed us in the direction of the Home supplement. Sure enough, there was an entire page giving an outline with photos of Dad's experiences in Singapore and Hokkaido, the scroll of tribute, the 'love diaries', our parents' wedding, their meeting with David and Jean in 1977, and finishing with our walk to Changi and our appeal for the Nairs and Reunekers to get in touch (8). She had been meticulous in telling the story and it was the perfect send-off for what I knew was going to be an emotional roller coaster in the Land of the Rising Sun.

NOTES

1. *This duly appeared in their Home section on 10 October 2017. An on-line search entering '***Singapore Straits Times finding Dad's legacy***' gives a similar report with a short accompanying video.*

2. *See ***Singapore in World War II: A Heritage Trail*** published by the National Heritage Board. (www.nhb.gov.sg), p.39.*

3. *See ***Syonan My Story: The Japanese Occupation of Singapore*** by Mamoru Shinozaki, published by Marshall Cavendish Editions, 2011.*

4. *See ***To Save a People*** by Alex Kershaw, Arrow Books, 2011.*

5. *As note 2 above, p.38.*

6. *From the Coldplay album ***X & Y***, 2005.*

7. *As note 2 above, p.14.*

8. *See note 1 above.*

CHAPTER 21

"PART 2A, JAPAN – YOKOHAMA"

"On the train back into Tokyo, I found myself flicking through a book and being starkly confronted by a photo of a Japanese officer wearing what looked for all the world like a Gestapo SS uniform. I was finally looking at Lt Kaichi Hirate, commander of Muroran and Nishi Ashibetsu POW Camps…a quite seminal moment in my journey."

Diary entry Wednesday 11 October 2017

Thanks to Carl, I first contacted Taeko Sasamoto, secretary general of the POW Research Network Japan[1], a full two years before I went to the Far East. It had been my intention to combine my pilgrimage to Singapore with the re-enactment walk to Changi on the 75th anniversary of the Japanese invasion on 15 February. This would also have meant visiting Hokkaido during the middle of the winter when she warned me that we would be encountering deep snow, especially in the interior, making travel more problematical. Two of the older men whom she had contacted declined her invitation for me to meet them due to the prospect of being out of doors in freezing temperatures. However, my recuperation from my knee replacement operation enforced a delay until later in the year. Both Mum and Dad would have called this providential. I was definitely not to regret the enforced postponement.

Taeko offered to be my guide and then secured the services of Chris Holmes as my interpreter. I had met his mother, Keiko, at the annual reception for reconciliation at the Japanese Embassy earlier that summer. She is the founder of Agape World, an organisation which aims to promote greater understanding between Britain and Japan in relation to the POW families. She impressed me with her strong Christian beliefs and the serenity of her personality.

A chance conversation with a fellow guest at breakfast on the last morning of a holiday abroad had flagged up the *East Anglian Daily Times* newspaper as an appropriate conduit to contact the relatives of some of the Suffolks and Cambridgeshires who figured prominently in the list of the 'Thirteen'. A phone call with one of their journalists led to an article by Adam Howlett in the paper[2]. Thanks to this, I was thrilled to be contacted by two of the nieces of Pte Raymond Suttle. Carl and I met one of them, Diane Burgess, and her husband in London prior to my journey to the Far East at which she gave me a small cross carved from the pews of Hadleigh Church which her uncle regularly visited as a young man. I added this very special little cross to the 13 poppy crosses I had purchased from the gift shop at the National Memorial Arboretum in Staffordshire where Jan and I had gone to attend the 75th anniversary remembrance service back in February. All the crosses were destined for the men's graves in the Commonwealth War Cemetery at Yokohama.

One key figure I have only mentioned briefly until now is Lt Colonel Shigeo Emoto who was appointed as the second high camp commandant in March '44 with responsibility for all the POW camps on Hokkaido. This is because I want to devote a whole chapter to the individual who, I am convinced, saved the lives of hundreds of British, Dutch and American POWs on the island. His tenure was brief – a mere 14 months – but the impact of the reforms that he introduced was immediate as well as far-reaching. Two years before my visit, Taeko gave me the address of his son, Susumu. He was emeritus professor at Aoyama Gakuin University in Tokyo. This is a private Christian-based institution in the capital. Like his father, Susumu was a fluent English speaker and had welcomed to the country some other ex-POWs and their families. I sent him a four-page hand-written letter expressing my strong desire for us to meet while I was in Japan. I did not receive a reply but this was explained the year after when Taeko heard from Susumu's wife that he had been hospitalised with a heart problem. She asked me to resend the letter in typed form. This included a sentence which emphasised my belief that "our fathers were two men who shared a common goal in caring for their fellow-man." Susumu sadly passed away in April 2016 but Taeko heard from his widow that he had read my letter. I was so very glad.

I then asked Taeko to write and tell his widow that I was hoping to visit the graves of her husband and father-in-law. She replied to her saying that this would be impossible as they were situated too far away in Yamanashi Prefecture and she was, in any case, too old to guide us to the cemetery. The correspondence ended in what for me, as a westerner, was a most bizarre wish: "She appreciate your warmth very much and said that she would like to give your best regards to her husband and father-in-law in the other world." Another indication of the idea that the deceased in

Japan are still viewed in a real sense as being alive came when Taeko apologised for a delay in writing. This was most unusual as she was always most assiduous in replying to any of my queries. (I stress again that all the staff who work for the POWRNJ are volunteers.) She explained that Tokyo was in the middle of its annual 'Bon' holiday, the Japanese Buddhist festival celebrated at different times of the year in every part of the country. It is believed that this is when the souls of their ancestors return to visit their descendants. The nearest equivalent in the Christian calendar is All Souls' Day, 2 November, though it is not quite the same when it is we who remember the dead.

A year into preparations for my visit to Japan, I received a surprising email from Taeko which left me speechless. The five sentences about the camp commander were as follows: "The people in Muroran feel very sorry that Hirate was executed as a war criminal. Hirate was respected by many people. He was university graduate and spoke French and English. He was also honest and good at baseball. He was proud of hometown." It was obviously an impression she had gained in her research and did not necessarily reflect her own views. The locals' high regard for him in no way excused the way he ran the two camps for which he paid the ultimate price. One hundred of them had signed a petition appealing for clemency at his trial.

Besides the many general reasons for wanting to visit the country, I was keen to identify the Japanese medical officer who appeared in a photo in Mitchell's book sitting beside Dad with a samurai sword resting against his inner leg. It was taken inside Raijo Camp at liberation and includes Umeki and all the British, Dutch, and American medical personnel. I think it unlikely that the sword was the one that Umeki had purchased for Dad as he, Dad, would have deemed it insensitive to allow himself to be pictured with it. The impression it has always given me is that the officer has adopted a highly provocative pose.

Without Villana, I felt lonely as I arrived at Changi Airport for the flight north to Tokyo/Narita. On the plus side, it was satisfying that Dad's story was finally receiving attention in Singapore. However, I never imagined that there would be such media interest in the Japanese leg of my pilgrimage. In seven hours on my Japan Airlines flight, I covered what it took Dad over three weeks to travel on the hellship, ferry and train. What most struck me in the immigration queues at arrivals was the helpful marshalling by elderly non-uniformed staff, all proudly displaying their name tags. Remunerated or not, it impressed me that they were most definitely playing a part in Japanese society. The closest equivalent in the UK is the army of volunteers in National Health Service hospitals who direct patients to appointments if they are lost. I dutifully filled in my landing card and put the reason for my visit as being neither leisure nor business but rather following my father's footsteps to his POW camps. The young immigration official did not bat an eyelid as she waved me through.

As both the Commonwealth War Cemetery and Taeko's home were in Yokohama, it made sense to book a hotel in this huge metropolis. It was also the venue for the war trials in 1946 though I had forgotten this fact. Narita Airport is 66 km from the centre of Tokyo and Yokohama lies even further beyond it. My delay in purchasing a *suica* travel card from a machine in the adjacent station concourse meant that I missed the train Taeko had calculated that I could catch. I had no idea whether the next Tokyo-bound train would stop at Tsurumi, my ultimate destination in Yokohama's suburbs. Most of the passengers alighted in central Tokyo and I took advantage of the now spacious carriage to study the list of stations above the doors. I was delighted when I was able to pick out my stop and even more to glean the number of minutes it took to travel between stations. Looking at my current station and the time on my wrist watch I could then work out in my head at what time I would reach my destination. How efficient was this!

Ninety minutes after leaving the airport station, I arrived at nightfall in Tsurumi. Unfortunately, I exited the station into a part of the suburb which led into a dimly lit street. It seemed like a scene from an oriental film and I hastily retraced my steps to thankfully emerge into more modern surroundings. As a linguist more accustomed to addressing people in Spain and France in their mother tongue, it was an understatement to say that this totally alien language to me was going to limit my ability to communicate. The first person I stopped to ask for directions to the Best Western Hotel spoke a little English and used his mobile phone to accompany me all the way on the five minute walk. Not for the first time that day *"Arigato go zai mas"* (thank you very much) issued forth from my lips.

The porters and receptionist bowed and, following check-in, the latter handed me a lovely letter of welcome from Taeko which outlined the times and stations of the two local trains I should take the following morning to reach the cemetery. I was so impressed by the trouble she had gone to in order to organise our first meeting. Although I had no photograph of her, I recognised her as she had appeared in an Irish documentary film, *A Doctor's Sword*[3]. The story of the Irish RAF doctor, Aidan MacCarthy, greatly resonates with me and I recently had the immense privilege of meeting his two daughters – Nicola and Adrienne – in the bar they run on the main street of Castletownbere in Co. Cork. The film also features Nicola going on a pilgrimage to Japan and is given assistance by Taeko, coincidentally at the same cemetery. We were joined by Yoshiko Tamura, an English teacher and volunteer from the network. We paused at the cemetery entrance at the top of a hill in the most idyllically peaceful surroundings. A plaque reads "The land in which this cemetery stands is the gift of the people of Japan for the perpetual resting place of the sailors, soldiers and airmen who are honoured here."

Two local gardeners busily attended the graves. There are over 1,500 and are arranged in blocks of 10 rows of 16. They are immaculately maintained and I couldn't help wondering if the complete lack of any vandalism or graffiti would be afforded any foreign cemetery back in the UK, particularly if it contained the graves of enemy soldiers. I had actually brought 14 poppy crosses to Japan as one was destined for placement in front of a giant urn inside a small shrine. The granddaughter of Edgar Harold had contacted me after the newspaper article in the *EADT* to tell me that his ashes, along with those of 334 other British, American and Dutch service personnel, were in the urn. I found his name on a large roll of honour on the wall of the shrine. He had disembarked on 25 November '42 at Moji, the port where Dad had landed seven months later. Well over half the POWs in Edgar's hellship, the *Singapore Maru*, died during the voyage and Edgar himself passed away in the local quarantine station on 12 February '43.

Thanks to the excellent Yokohama Commonwealth War Cemetery website, we were able to easily locate all 13 graves. As I placed the individual poppy crosses with the names, ranks and ages in the rich brown soil in front of each, I noticed that most of them had epitaphs inscribed. They had obviously been chosen by relatives but three were sadly blank and I wondered if they could not have been contacted or had simply decided not to respond. (In preparing to write this book, I revisited my photographs of each of the graves. The words on Sapper Richards' immediately struck a bell: "Blessed are the dead which die in the Lord, for they rest from their labour." They come from the *Book of Revelation* and also appear in the chorus 'Lux Aeterna' of the English composer John Rutter's beautiful *Requiem* which my choir have recently sung.)

I had half expected the two railway crossing victims, Angell and Durrant, to be buried next to each other but realised that they were also immediately to the right of Raymond Suttle. There they stood in a line... ND8, ND9 and ND10, three men whose totally needless deaths had so angered Dad. Suttle's epitaph read "Into life's mosaic this precious piece was laid". Laying the special cross from Hadleigh Church at his graveside was the first of three very emotional moments for me on my pilgrimage to Japan. I wished his nieces could have been there to share the moment but, when I texted Diane, she replied by saying they had been following my itinerary and were so grateful. (The same journalist from the *EADT* subsequently wrote a second article[4] about my visit to the cemetery after I returned from the Far East.) The warm, moist soil reminded me of Dad's flower beds back at the bungalow which he always kept carefully weeded. In later years, when he was no longer able to tend to them, my siblings and I would set to work. The sandy soil always meant the weeds came away without a struggle.

A Japanese daughter pushing her father in his wheelchair took a picture of Taeko, Yoshiko and me. Did he know any of the POWs or was this special place somewhere they would regularly come on a routine walk? The three of us were volunteers, the ladies with the network and me with the CSJ, but I also discovered that they had been awarded the MBE for their work in helping the families of POWs. (As I have mentioned already, Dad had been the recipient of the military MBE by King George VI in June '46.) Both had attended a wreath-laying ceremony by Prince William in the cemetery in February 2015, 20 years after his mother – Princess Diana – had visited the same sacred place. Yoshiko related how, as a young woman, she had wandered quite by chance into the cemetery and had been fascinated to discover the history of a place that was on her doorstep. Like Taeko, she has dedicated her life to the process of reconciliation.

As we walked back down the hill to find a restaurant for lunch, I reflected on a very special morning. I felt privileged to have had the opportunity to lay a tribute at each of the graves of the 'Thirteen', the men whom Dad and the other British and American medical staff had fought in vain to save. Even though he never wanted to return to Japan, I felt sure that the visit this particular morning was one in which he would gladly have participated.

Taeko had asked me to prepare a talk to the network early that evening in a building in central Tokyo. While she and Yoshiko chatted together across from me in the train carriage, I spent the time perusing a Japanese book[5] which they had lent me. At one point, I suddenly realised that I was probably staring for the first time at a picture of Kaichi Hirate and this the ladies confirmed. The caption underneath stated that it was taken inside Muroran POW Camp. He seemed quite baby-faced, an impression that belied the decisions – or perhaps the lack of them – that he took in the camps. I scrambled for my mobile phone to take a picture of an image which will remain with me forever.

My talk was sparsely attended but there was much questioning and interest from the members who did come. These included Yukako Ibuki, an excellent English speaker, who works for a sister organisation called US-Japan Dialogue on POWs. They were so appreciative of my coming to speak to them and thanked me for sharing with them some of Dad's experiences in the Hokkaido camps. They looked forward to reading more in my book and to Carl's publication of the POW diaries.

The event lasted far longer than I had imagined and it was well after dark by the time we retired across the road for a meal. It was ironic that they should have chosen a Chinese restaurant. I tried jellyfish as part of a starter. It tasted far better than it looked! The thought of it took me back to Narin Beach in the '60s when they were regularly washed up on its golden sands and in the rocky coves beyond the distinctive promontory of Dunmore Head. Now I was actually eating one! My three female dining companions were particularly interested in Dad's 'dog-tag' which hung permanently around my neck throughout my pilgrimage to the Far East. It is circular, very thin, has a leathery feel to it, and identifies the wearer with a unique reference number. Yoshiko had earlier asked me if I knew where the second one was. I replied that I understood that the men only had one but she said that they all carried another which was carefully placed between the teeth to help identify the man in the event of death. The discovery of anecdotes such as this convinced me more than ever that I had made the right decision to come to Japan. We all took the same train back towards Yokohama afterwards but the ladies would not alight until they were absolutely sure I knew which was my stop for Tsurumi. It had been an exhausting day and I was greatly looking forward to the morrow which was to be my only complete day-off during my Far Eastern journey.

For the second morning in succession, I had breakfast with Andy, a young Taiwanese managing director of a ladies' shoe company. He was in Tokyo to attend a trade fair and I again enjoyed his company and his quietly attentive and interesting manner of chatting. He was probably of a similar age to our own son, Andrew (known to all his friends as Andy). Savoury food was very much in evidence at meal times in Japan though I did notice the surprising lack of bread and cheese. Convenience stores did not seem to stock fresh fruit and there was less of a choice of cakes and chocolate. This tied in with less cases of obesity judging by what I had seen of people on the streets.

I spent the entire morning in my hotel room sending emails to family and friends. Occasionally, I would rise from my chair to do my stretching whilst gazing down at the hive of activity in the streets below as trains constantly crisscrossed the thoroughfares. One sight above all others remains etched in my mind. Three young men, all dressed smartly in suits and ties, were busy sweeping the footpaths. I presumed this was voluntary communal work undertaken before they went to their places of work. This pride in keeping their area clean was mightily impressive and added to my perception that Japan truly is unique.

Following Yoshiko's suggestion that I check out the *Hikawa Maru* ship at its permanent mooring in a quieter part of Yokohama port, I took the train to Kannai. Evidence of the Bay Stars' baseball team begins right at the train station with two giant blue helmets adorning the main entrance. The area was a pedestrian's dream in that the signage to Yamashita Park and the ship beyond it was copious. Reminders of the US abounded in addition to the imposing structure of the baseball stadium and the stunning floral arrangement of a game in the adjacent garden. The red brick architecture of many of the buildings made me think of a busy downtown American metropolis. The fact that so much was new is explained by the 1923 earthquake which killed more than 40,000 of Yokohama's population, a fact I only discovered later in my visit. The main park entrance is via a mini dome, a gift to the city by the local Indian community to commemorate the deaths of their loved ones during the war.

The 300 yen (just over £2) entrance fee for the magnificent ship with its art-deco interior was incredibly good value. As I explored the sumptuously decorated dining room and a first class cabin with silver dining service neatly laid out beside an ornate bed, I thought nearer to home of what the *Titanic* would have looked like. Most impressive of all were the stained glass windows which caught the evening sun and one particular design of some colourful parrots. The bowels of the ship contained the engine room and some displays about the ship's history. Launched in 1930 as a passenger vessel between Yokohama and Vancouver and Seattle, she once again returned, many years after the end of the war, to ply her trade between the three countries. The voyage took 13 days. Her owners were very keen to maintain the patronage of one Charlie Chaplin and would employ a famous local chef whose speciality was tempura prawns, Chaplin's favourite, whenever he travelled. I had been curious to read about the history of the *Hikawa Maru* as a hospital ship but there were scant details about this in the exhibition which simply stated that it fulfilled the role between '41 and '53 and that a total of 30,000 Japanese soldiers were treated on board.

It was back in the park that I discovered Yokohama is twinned with San Diego in California. A sister city society was established in '57 to promote student exchanges and reconciliation between the two and, 60 years later, it is still active today. In view of the American atomic bombings of Hiroshima and Nagasaki, the creation of such a society must have indeed been a brave undertaking. A giant stone statue of a woman carrying a pitcher of water was a present from the city of San Diego in 1960 and further into the gardens I couldn't fail to miss a large replica bell, also donated by San Diego, which commemorates those erected in the 21 mission settlements of California. The latter were established by Franciscan monks along the 600 mile Camino Real (Royal Road). Caminos, Franciscans…would the coincidences never cease! I then remembered Mum and Dad had visited some of the settlements during one of their two visits to Max Andler and his family.

I braved McDonald's on my walk back to Kannai Station. Fortunately, there were pictures of all the food and drinks available on the menu (this was something I found everywhere I ate in Japan) which certainly made ordering easier. However, a fluorescent green drink which I had mistakenly taken to be a lemon Fanta had a quite disgusting taste. I had to draw a line at finishing that green concoction even though I had a raging thirst. Jean Marshall had shared a story of David entering a McDonald's for the one and only time in his life. Of all places, it was in Dublin where they had gone to attend the graduation at Trinity College of one of their daughters, Sara. I vividly recall our dad taking Carl and me to the city by train on a spring Saturday in 1965 to watch our first rugby international,

Ireland versus the South African 'Springboks'. Even more of a treat than Ireland winning 9-6 in what I remember as a dour game was sitting down at a table in an upstairs' restaurant in O'Connell Street and devouring a peach melba. We had him all to ourselves amid the carefree surroundings of the nation's capital.

NOTES

1. See website *www.powresearch.jp*

2. Article appeared in **East Anglian Daily Times** on *16 February 2017.*

3. *The documentary film,* **A Doctor's Sword** *(2015), is directed by Gary Lennon and produced by him and Bob Jackson.*

4. *This second EADT article appeared on 10 November 2017 to coincide with the annual Remembrance Day commemorations.*

5. *The book is entitled* **Shokei; Aru BC kyu senpan no sei to shi** *(Execution; the Life and Death of a class BC war criminal).*

CHAPTER 22

"PART 2B, JAPAN – HAKODATE, YAKUMO, MURORAN"

"Woke at 5. iPod time is usually 2 but had an anti-inflammatory last night. Need more exercise. Will try and get a walk again this p.m. Discovered I have a version of 'Molly Malone' by Dublin City Ramblers, another one of Dad's party pieces! Pyjamas courtesy of the hotel with Noguchi written on them."

Diary entry Monday 16 October 2017

I was disappointed for Andy at breakfast when he told me that he had secured no orders at the trade fair. He was returning to Taiwan. Like him, I too was leaving. The newly mounted Halloween display in the hotel lobby made me realise that 31 October was fast approaching. My thoughts had been elsewhere and I confess I didn't expect them to celebrate it in Japan. It was a much more confident me that negotiated my way through the election campaign volunteers in the square in front of the local station.

I was now heading for Tokyo Central and my first experience of the country's high speed 'bullet' train, the *shinkansen*. Preparations for boarding went like clockwork as travellers for the 9.20 train on my platform queued in the first orange lane while my train to Hakodate-Hokuto on the 9.36 queued in the second green lane. The lanes were angled to allow descending passengers plenty of space to alight. Even more impressive was that carriage number seven with my reserved seat pulled up at the exact spot at the head of my lane. Incredible!

I had always planned to mirror Dad's journey to Hokkaido by taking the train and to then return to Tokyo by plane from Sapporo. Our journey north passed Fukushima, far off to the east and close to the epicentre of the horrific 2011 tsunami which caused the explosion at the town's nuclear power plant. Later I recognised the name Sendai as one of the stations we passed on the speedy journey north. It housed one of the many POW camps on Japan's main island, Honshu. Eventually we reached Aomori and prepared to enter the 54-kilometre Seikan Railway Tunnel which goes under the sea to eventually emerge on Hokkaido. It had taken Dad four hours to make the crossing by ferry between the two islands. I was relieved to transfer to a more modest local train for the short journey to Hakodate. He had arrived in the middle of the night. It was early afternoon for me and I instantly felt connected to a much less built up environment than what I had experienced back at Yokohama and Tokyo.

At the station I was met by Chris Holmes who was to be my translator for the week. Our shared passion for football was something I came to value in the moments when we were able to relax. We both support London clubs, me as a lifelong fan of West Ham and Chris of Arsenal. Taeko had elected to fly and later that evening the two of us ate out at a local restaurant while Chris made arrangements to put winter tyres on his four-wheel-drive as he was expecting colder conditions when we moved to the interior of the island.

Thanks to Taeko's organisational skills, two men were waiting to meet me in the hotel lobby the following morning. The first was Daisuke Nakagawa, the junior editor from the Hokkaido *Shimbun* newspaper. The other was 86-yearold Masatoshi Asari, a botanical scientist who was to act as our guide to what remains of the Hakodate POW Camp. He is famous in the area as a propagator of cherry trees and has planted many of them at the Matsumae Castle Garden, an area at the southern tip of the island from which he comes. Taeko told me that, thanks to his efforts, 58 varieties of cherry trees are growing back in England at Royal Windsor Great Park and Kew Gardens. This he arranged in 1993 as a gesture of reconciliation between the two countries after his attempt to have a memorial at the site of the main Hakodate Camp was refused.

On a gloriously sunny autumn morning our small convoy of cars set out round the bay. We were heading for a small building lower down on the slopes of Mount Hakodate looking across at the port. The idyllic setting contrasted greatly with the horrific impression of "human skeletons" that greeted Dad on his first morning treating the sick. The area around the building was quite overgrown and it was an effort to keep up with the amazingly sprightly Mr Asari as he took us on a brief tour. A sketch map produced by an ex POW in 1989 called Chapman shows just how extensive the camp was. (There are further details in a book written by Alan Carter[1], another British POW, who was only 19 when he was first taken prisoner). We had been joined by a young reporter from NHK TV, Nobuyuki Hanaoka, and his female assistant who did the filming. (Nobuyuki had stepped into the breech vacated by another reporter who had asked me earlier in the year if I was interested in meeting Hirate's sister. I had thought long and hard about this – how it might be portrayed in the media, and her possible antipathy towards me as the son of an Allied officer whose testimony contributed towards her brother's execution. In the end I decided that I would like to meet her but, as it happened, nothing came of it.)

A plaque in the grounds explained that the building was constructed as a quarantine station during a cholera outbreak in 1885. It also saw use as a place for recovering tuberculosis patients to be housed. Significantly, there is no reference to its more sinister usage during the war. Perhaps this was not surprising as it is currently a café. Apparently, it is the only building of the 10 camps on the island which still stands on its original spot.

It was a strange feeling as I crossed the threshold of the quaint wooden structure. An even stranger occurrence was to follow. Along with most of the elderly gentlemen I was to meet who as young people had lived through the war, Mr Asari spoke not a word of English. Neither did he leave time for Chris to translate for me what he was saying nor for me to either give a reaction, ask a question or offer any of the details in Dad's letters. (I would carefully annotate relevant parts of Carls' word-processed version of them in each hotel room the night before. I had saved all of them to my tablet.) I hasten to add that this tendency is not confined to the Japanese but to many elderly people. Communication with foreigners can, however, often be a one way process. Nonetheless, our tour to that point had been quite frustrating. Poor Chris had the unenviable task of quietly attempting to summarise for me the gist of what he was saying while simultaneously lending an ear to what Mr Asari was next communicating. Naturally he was keen to tell his story to a wider audience and this I could understand.

I sat down opposite him in the café and, in an effort to create some point of contact between us, produced Dad's officer's hat from my backpack. Everyone I had met in both Singapore and Japan had respectfully asked if they could examine it and the reverence with which they handled it was both humbling and moving. I expected him to do the same via a gesture of permission but, instead of this, he lifted it gleefully and placed it on his head! He was so animated and both Taeko and I wanted to capture the moment with a photograph. Later that morning I was to discover even more of what this elderly gentleman was doing to foster a better relationship between the two countries but my immediate reaction was to share his delight at trying on the hat. Suddenly the reality of a photo circulating in the media back home of a Japanese citizen posing in a POW's hat hit home. My diary entry read "Sometimes one is swept along in an adrenalin-filled frenzy and you lose contact with reality and how easy it is to offend." Fortunately, the film crew and newspaper editor were temporarily nowhere to be seen and I was satisfied the event had not been captured on film by them. I quickly hit the delete button on my camera and, fortified by my coffee and sugar-filled mini donut, went back outside with Taeko, explained my misgivings, and asked her to delete the image she also had taken. She understood but I still stood over her to watch her do it, relieved in the knowledge that the image could not now be manipulated. The whole incident taught me to be circumspect of the media and also to keep myself grounded, much in the manner of our dad.

As well as the Chapman sketch map, Mr Asari provided Taeko and me with a number of other photocopied articles. The letter dated 7.8.86 from the diplomat C.E.A. Ripley already referred to in chapter 7 contains a short description of a daily ritual and is illuminating on many fronts: "My most vivid memory of Hakodate Docks was after a day's work we would march back to the camp SINGING to let the people know that we were happy! If we did not sing loud enough we were turned round and made to run back to the docks to start again." Ripley goes on to describe the hazards involved in the town's cement works: "At the factory there were huge silos. When the cement was getting low they opened a door in the base and we were made to get in and shovel the cement down on the worms. If we did not shovel fast enough the workmen below would hammer to make us go faster. The only lighting was a single light bulb in the roof of the silo. It was a very eerie feeling working among hundreds of tons of cement not knowing if you would be buried in cement at any moment." Insights such as this as to the POWs' working conditions add immeasurably to the information that is beginning to emerge about the camps. I was so glad I had come to Japan.

Following our visit to the site of the camp and another to the docks, our third destination was a modest wooden building back in the town which looked inside for all the world like an undertaker's with its neat lines of black marble headstones. As I passed through the middle, I did wonder why they all looked the same until the penny finally dropped. We were in a temple and these were the gravestones containing the ashes of families. Not only that but we were in the original hospital of Hakodate's main camp which had been dismantled and reconstructed. Mr Asari led us to the far end of the Eizenji Temple and stopped in front of a bronze memorial at waist-height and framed in grey marble. Inscribed on it was a selection of 128 of the hundreds of British and Dutch POWs who had lost their lives in the camps on the island. It was easier for me to squat on the floor in order to read the names. Six of the 'Thirteen' I spotted straight away – Suttle, Jardine, Glover, Durrant, Bond, and Angell – each with the date of their death accurately recorded. It transpired that Mr Asari had been to the British Embassy in Tokyo 30 years before to explain his plans for a memorial. He may not have succeeded in siting it at the camp but, tucked away in the original hospital in this non-descript suburb of Hakodate, this brave elderly gentleman had kept alive the memory of those foreign prisoners of war who never came home. Next to the plaque was a stone carving and a further engraving with the simple words "Peace and Reconciliation." I paid a quick visit to the temple's shrine on the first floor before our convoy, now minus the TV crew, headed for the *Shimbun* newspaper building.

In Daisuke's office, Mr Asari removed his hat and coat to reveal an immaculately tailored suit which complemented his white shirt and pink tie. This dapper man also used to be a school teacher and to this day visits local schools in an attempt to inform young people about what went on in their country during the war. He unfurled a long white banner with lots of Japanese writing in black and the names in English along the top of the three high camp commandants who had responsibility for all the Hokkaido camps. Beside each and also in English was a noun he had chosen to best summarise their chief characteristics: Toshio Hatakeyama "danger", Shigeo Emoto "affection", Tokuro Hosoi "uneasiness". Despite the impediment of our language barrier, I strongly identified with an individual who carries such a strong message. Since my retirement in 2011, I have gone back into St Peter's every year to deliver a talk in Spanish to their A level students on the Camino de Santiago. Before he left, he presented Taeko, Chris and me with a beautiful hamper of apples and grapes. On the subject of gifts, Taeko made sure that everyone who assisted us on our tour of the camps received a box of chocolates as a thank you. This was typical of her thoughtfulness.

The visit ended with a short interview. I felt very relaxed in Daisuke's company and was grateful once again for Chris' hard work as my inter-

194

preter. The short newspaper report the next day carried a photo of me sitting on the floor beside the plaque at the temple and a quote from Mr Asari: "I really felt the meaning of the history being recorded. I hope the British people understand our thought for the dead prisoners of war and it will help the relationship between the two countries."[2] (The week after I returned to England I received an email from Daisuke which said "I was strongly impressed by your behaviour at the Eizenji Temple Hakodate. You was deeply touched by seeing the monument which was engraved with names of dead POWs. I never forget that scene.") The perfect antidote to yet another amazing day came that evening when Chris located a bar which was showing Manchester United v. Liverpool. It was actually a karaoke bar with the threat of the live coverage of the match being pulled if the clientele so wished. This they could have done at any time and, to tell the truth, neither of us would have objected as it was a dreary 0-0 affair. How good it felt to talk over matters not related to my pilgrimage.

Four days into their incarceration at Hakodate the men must have been terrified at a series of sudden earth shudders: "Horrible earth tremors by day and by night. A large volcano a few miles across the bay." This was Dad's description and he saw it at closer quarters on Wednesday 16 June '43 when he and many of the new arrivals were moved round the bay to the second camp at Yakumo. He thought the name was "Komatchka" but it was actually Komagatake and we ourselves passed it the following morning off to our right as we drove out of Hakodate. My research has since told me that it is one of the most active volcanoes in Japan, had erupted in '42 and most recently in late 2000!

We arrived at some deserted farm buildings on flat land near the coast. There we were met by Nobuyuki, this time with two cameramen in tow. Our guide was a 79-year-old local historian, Shoujiro Takai. The young curator of the local history museum, Shigeyuki Ouya, was also in attendance though he spoke very little. Mitchell gives the camp's dimensions in his meticulously drawn sketches as 87 yards by 54[3]. More interesting was our decamping further inland where we stood on some higher ground to survey the runway the prisoners built. This is now used by the Japanese Airforce and is a restricted area. Mr Takai was only five years old back in the summer of '43 but still recalls the POWs wearing khaki caps, stripped down to their shorts, and "walking with ropes tied at their waists"[4] as they set about clearing and levelling the large area of farmland. When he spotted our party close to his farm we were joined by another elderly local,

Hiroshi Takeuchi, curious to see what was happening. Inviting us back to his adjacent outlying farm building, he recalled as a 10 year old having to make a long detour to get to school once the runway was completed. I have since discovered that the Battle of Attu, the furthest west of the US's Aleutian Islands in Alaska, hastened the construction of such airfields throughout Japan. This occurred in May '43 and was the only battle to be fought on North American soil with heavy casualties on both sides. Japan had occupied the island for almost a year.

We retraced our route back past the camp and on to a graveyard closer to the coast. The same black marble headstones that I had seen at the temple in Hakodate were much in evidence though now exposed to the elements. A chilly sea wind was blowing off the Pacific though the sun was still shining. Mr Takai took us to a rougher patch of land in the plot. There, in an unmarked grave, he said that three prisoners had been buried (though records show that only one died at Yakumo.) I knew that this included Stan Faunch, whose ashes now lie at Yokohama along with the other 12, but why was he not initially cremated like all the others and his ashes returned to a Buddhist temple as I have quoted in chapter 7 by Ripley? Did Yakumo, because of its smaller size, not have its own crematorium? This seemed unlikely given that the cremated remains of locals were in graves all around but perhaps these were more recent. One can only arrive at the conclusion that the Japanese considered that, as an early casualty of the camps, Faunch did not merit a cremation (in a similar fashion to the Chinese who were unceremoniously buried under the sand at Itanki Beach in Muroran). The only saving grace was that he had originally been buried in hallowed ground.

Although Mitchell had not been allowed to attend his friend's burial, he was one of a party of 20 who were permitted to visit the graveyard on Sunday 24 October '43, their weekly *yasume* day and the eve of their departure to Muroran[5]. His description of the area exactly matches my memory of the surroundings: "The party left camp with two guards who knew the way, and followed dirt tracks and narrow paths between empty paddi fields to a tiny unfenced graveyard, lost amid low tumbling dunes of sand and marram grass. Windswept and lonely, it was an unhappy place at the back of beyond: far from human habitation and useless for any other purpose…One unmarked square remained. Stan's last resting place – a very 'far corner of a foreign field', which hopefully would be 'forever England.'"

Dad's diary entry states that no Mass was said at the camp that Sunday. This was probably because the padre, his friend Fr O'Mahoney, was otherwise occupied and is indeed reported by Mitchell as saying a few words in prayer over the grave. Here I was standing on the same spot virtually 74 years to the day since the men's tender farewell to their young comrade. I was immensely grateful for Mr Takai giving me a bunch of flowers to lay on the grave. In an amusing touch, he also handed me a tin of milky tea. This proved a good photo opportunity for the assembled media. Unlike the day before with Mr Asari, I knew that at this point I would be the main focus of the filming. The camera crew's presence was becoming quite intrusive, especially in this sacred setting. Both the NHK national and international television reports filmed over the two days show me blessing myself over the grave[6]. I was determined not to cry and had earlier anticipated this moment as we approached it. I quietly asked Chris for his help. My words were "Chris, don't let me cry." I have no idea in what context he translated the figure 1969 but, to make light of the situation, I whispered to him "FA Cup Final 1969, Manchester City beat Leicester City 1-0. Neil Young scored the goal." He chuckled at the association. He didn't reciprocate immediately but took a few seconds to utter his non-sequitur: "Have you seen my new trainers? There's a hole already in the sole of one of them." I have never been so grateful for the timing of a comment. His alleviation of an emotional situation got me through and it was with immense relief that I grabbed a few minutes on my own as the party returned to their vehicles. I looked up at some rays of brightness poking through a dark sky and prayed quietly for Stan's soul. The words on his epitaph at Yokohama, his final and deserved resting place, read "God is love."

After a meal in a local Italian restaurant, Nobuyuki asked if he could do an interview with me before he filed his report. Both subsequent broadcasts in November and the following January presented a reassuringly balanced viewpoint. The Japanese one, for example, referred to Dad "writing down the terrible, cruel and barbarous treatment of the prisoners of war by the Japanese military." The later English one, essentially similar in content, included the sentence "The Japanese Army appear to have ignored the Geneva Convention standard on the treatment [of foreign prisoners]." Both drew attention to the circumstances of Raymond Suttle's death but the English one used a narrator's voice to read Dad's unequivocal stance in his 1988 summarised version of the diary: "Pte Suttle died today. I was forced at bayonet point to omit the cause of death! But in our own hospital I recorded the real cause – 'Exposure to intense cold and neglect while incarcerated by the Japanese.'" However, there was one notable exclusion from both reports. Dad had added "The camp commandant was responsible for the death of Pte Suttle". My aim had always been to present a balanced point of view and the broadcasts naturally focused on my praise for Lt Col. Shigeo Emoto and the reforms he introduced (the subject of chapter 24). Nevertheless, although I cannot recall if I specifically mentioned the name of Lt Kaichi Hirate, I find it at best unfortunate and at worst blatantly censorial that this sentence was excluded during the television station's editing process. This was in contrast to Daisuke Nakagawa's article in the Hokkaido *Shimbun* on 5 October, prior to my arrival in Japan. He reported on Dad's affidavit from January '46 which directly blamed Hirate as bearing responsibility for crimes against prisoners.

In fairness to Taeko and in the context of her surprising email to me about Hirate the year before, she gave me a hand-written note after the film crew left requesting further help from me for the broadcast. It read thus: "The local people in Hokkaido sympathised with Lt Hirate that he was executed although he made efforts to treat POWs humanly [humanely]. They believe that Hirate was tried [put on trial] to take a responsibility for poor supervision of his men. Your father's diary will disprove this common view." This last sentence gave me immense comfort.

The interview itself lasted a full 15 minutes, Nobuyuki thanked me and he and his camera crew responded to my request for a photo before they took their leave. Genuine smiles beamed from their faces. On reflection, they had been doing their job and if my visit was highlighting the past and the plight of foreign POWs for another generation in Japan, then the filming was a price worth paying.

Chris, Taeko and I continued our clockwise journey further round the bay to its southern-most point. We were heading for the port city of Muroran, scene of the third camp and the 20-month incarceration where all the men were to experience their worst treatment. It was the place I least looked forward to visiting but where, paradoxically, encounters with two men lifted my spirits. On the way, Chris pointed out the exclusive Toyako Windsor Hotel perched high on a hill-top and the setting for the July 2008 G8 Summit attended by Gordon Brown as the British prime minister and other world leaders. The impressive Hakucho Bridge, opened in

1998 – a further link to my first pilgrimage – , spans Muroran's sheltered bay. We were heading for a quieter part of the city and our accommodation at the Prince Hotel. I stretched my neck as we passed the huge girders at different heights to catch my first glimpse of the Wanishi Steelworks which dominate the skyline.

By now it was 3.30 in the afternoon and I had another media appointment but this time with BBC Radio Gloucestershire's Richard Atkins, their 'Faith and Ethics' producer and presenter of their Sunday morning breakfast programme. Richard had interviewed me several times in connection with two of my Caminos but never in quite such a faraway place. It was 7.30 in the morning back in the UK. The mobile signal at the back of the hotel was poor and it was no problem moving to the lobby as there were no guests to be seen. Muroran is definitely not a tourist destination unlike Hokkaido's ski resorts, unspoilt interior, and undisturbed wildlife habitats further north. I chatted about my pilgrimage to the Far East but did indicate my apprehension at what was coming next. Knowing that Jan also would be listening from bed, I sent my special love to her, Andrew and the girl who is now his fiancée, Becky. There was just time left to squeeze in a mention for Philomusica's forthcoming concert of Rossini's *Petite Messe Solennelle* at Tewkesbury Abbey with a promise that I would be back to sing. After checking in, I wandered down to the dockside through the deserted, late Sunday afternoon streets. It was a relief to snatch a few moments of quiet time and to stretch my legs.

At the table for dinner at the hotel, Taeko and I were joined by 87-year-old Satoshi Motono, president of the Muroran Local History Study Group. He had been receiving treatment for cancer and had, understandably, been reluctant to meet me in the middle of winter. Aware of the effort this retired secondary school teacher had made to come, I was greatly looking forward to a meal in his company. With Chris unavailable, it was left to Taeko to interpret. Unlike any of the men I had met to date, he patiently waited for her to assimilate what he had said as she translated for me in her broken English. This gave me plenty of time to react with a follow-up question or to impart information from Dad's diary. Like Mr Asari, Mr Motono was a retired teacher. His subject was history and he is one of a number of contributors to an illustrated book about the city's past entitled *Muroran no utsuri kawari* (Changes in Muroran). He told us that his wife had sadly died 36 years before, leaving him with two sons.

Dad's diary entry from Thursday 11 January '45, the men's second winter in Muroran, includes the following afterthought to Mum: "Did I tell you that some Japanese medical orderlies visited us the other day and a funny little lad began singing a song about Ireland in Japanese (march time). He came again today. He always gives me a very special salute." (This had echoes of Dad's frequent friendly gesture to me as a teenager). As I already knew from Taeko that Mr Motono had met some of the prisoners as a young boy, I was keen to know if the boy in question was him. He replied that he only met the POWs when he was working at the steel furnace and not inside the camp. Under no circumstances were the boys allowed to talk to the prisoners. He started there in '43 when he was only 13 and worked until April '45. Initially, he had worked part-time and this consisted of separating the coke from the coal. Then it became full-time. I must confess I had not expected to hear stories about child labour before I went to Japan. He then talked about the poor diet and the food that he ate with his parents after work each evening when he would recount what he had seen during the day. He strongly maintained that their diet at home was no better than what he observed the POWs were eating. The next day he presented me with a copy of his book.

He then went on to describe the shelling of Muroran by three American warships – the USS *Wisconsin*, *Missouri*, and *Iowa* – on 15 July '45. There was no reply from the Japanese as the ships were beyond the range of their defence artillery which only extended to 7,000 metres. (Nobuyuki subsequently emailed to say that a weapons' factory as well as the steelworks were the targets and that battleships were employed by the American navy as the island was outside the range of the B29 bombers). The casualty figure among the local population was 400. This was a story of which I knew nothing. However, one period of history he spoke about and of which I had some knowledge was the war between China and Japan following Japan's invasion of Manchuria in 1931. This was based on part one of the PBS America documentary series, *WWII: China's Forgotten War*. Casualty figures were enormous and this was the guards' background at Muroran, the majority of whom were war-wounded. Mitchell describes two of them as being "mono-wings"[7] after each lost a left arm at the shoulder. It transpired that the then 25-year-old Lt Kaichi Hirate had very little experience of military combat when appointed camp commandant in November '42. (Before he enlisted in the army and served in the transportation of troops, he had worked as a librarian in the Korean government library.) One can imagine, therefore, the low opinion the guards had of him and the impunity with which they acted on the many occasions when he left the camp to go to Hakodate[8].

Two days later I was to meet the only person who has written a book about the POWs on Hokkaido. In it, there is a reference to a civilian called Masayuki Yamato who describes the cruel training he underwent before starting work in the factory as "a living hell"[9]. This was meted out by discharged soldiers from the war in China. He comments: "It is no wonder that these disgraced soldiers gave no mercy to POWs when they did not even give it their own people." Furthermore, the guards would have despised the POWs whom they viewed as inferior because they had surrendered. A reference to Hirate in the same book comes from Toyozoo Murakami, a guard sent to Muroran seven or eight times up to July '44, and reads: "The gentle camp commander gathered the guards each day and explained international law to them, that they were to treat the POWs kindly, but this attitude was totally incomprehensible to the guards." (*Onko* is the Japanese word for 'gentle' and also translates as 'even-tempered' and 'mild-mannered'. I wonder how many of the POWs would have concurred with this description of Hirate.)

In the relaxed atmosphere of the hotel's first floor dining room, I felt it important to share, albeit a very small fraction, Dad's diary with Taeko and Mr Motono. I produced my tablet and showed them the nominal roll, the transcribed version of the diary, and a sample of the original hand-written one which Carl had scanned. (Nobuyuki had also used an extract from the latter in his report). With the help of a magnifying glass, they both carefully examined Dad's dog-tag. They seemed so pleased as was I at an evening when I had engaged with a local man on such a meaningful level. Even though I appreciate it was not him, Satoshi Motono will always embody for me the little boy who sang the Irish song and gave our dad that friendly salute.

As for the meal itself, our chef was a former student of Mr Motono and we were treated to an extra serving of sushi. Although tasty, I was surprised at how much rice lies under the fish. Sake wine is a favourite tipple of Taeko's but was definitely not a hit with me. As we stood up to go, a diner at a nearby table came over to greet Mr Motono. He was an ex-colleague and taught English. He wished me a happy stay in Muroran. When I explained the reason for my visit, his eyes began to well up. I quickly proffered him my hand and inwardly admonished myself for upsetting a stranger.

Knowing that the following day would be very difficult, I took an anti-inflammatory capsule before I went to bed in order to get an uninterrupted night's sleep. As I headed for the lobby after breakfast, I noticed a beautifully intricate brown wooden carving of a myriad of tiny horses. They were all sculpted out of a single block of wood. It was in the same Ainu style of Dad's and David Marshall's bears. In addition to Mr Motono, we were joined by Seiji Taninaka, the curator of the local Tontenkan Museum, and Mikio Suda, a Muroran reporter from the *Shimbun*. Our first destination on another sunny but chilly day was a viewpoint high on the slopes of Mount Sokuryo behind the hotel. The high chimneys of the Wanishi Steelworks down in the main city to the north-east continued to spew out fumes in much the same way they would have continued night and day with POW slave labour from '43 to '45 and presumably ever since.

Mikio's article in the paper the following day referred to the condolences I expressed to Mr Motono over the high civilian casualty toll arising from the shelling of the city. As director of an upmarket skiing company at Niseko, Chris was meantime having to juggle phone enquiries and text messages from prospective clients with what was an extremely busy day interpreting for all of us. He coped admirably. Mr Motono thanked me and was then "at a loss for words" as reported by Mikio. I was only aware of Taeko's reaction to my expression of sadness in the same article when I read her quote: "I heard the words of sympathy from a person on the side of the Allied Forces for the first time."

There was, however, one question I was asked and on which Mikio did not report. It left me frustrated to the point of anger. It related to the shelling and to Dad's letters. "Is there anything in the diaries to indicate the POWs knew Muroran was going to be shelled?" It was as if the prisoners themselves and not the Japanese took the decision five weeks before the bombardment to move inland for self-protection! The implication was derisory and my reply was brief and to the point. On a happier note, the idyllic vantage point and presence of a very special gentleman seemed the perfect opportunity to present Mr Motono with an enamel tea mug I had purchased as a gift for someone in Japan from the Imperial War Museum in London. The slogan on the side read "While there is tea there is hope".

We then followed the scenic road down the hillside towards some spectacular cliff scenery along the south-east coast of the city. The views reminded me of the contours of Howth to the north of Dublin which Jan and I regularly visit while killing a few hours before boarding the ship back to the UK after our visits to Newcastle and Donegal. Mum and Dad also loved their day out to the suburb's pretty harbour during their honeymoon. Many times have we stood on beaches staring across either side of the Irish Sea. Pausing to gaze at Ireland's magnificent Atlantic west coast always makes me think of the 3,000 miles that separate us from America. (On a personal note, Carl's interest in family history has shown we have many relations on our dad's side in the eastern United States). At one point, our little convoy parked by a viewpoint to take in the scenery of the city's cliffs and beaches. This was my first view of the stunning cobalt-blue waters of the Pacific stretching out eastwards towards the west coast of America. Ireland seemed so very far away. I identified very strongly with Dad's presence in the same area when he too caught his first glimpse of Muroran's majestic east coast. It was Wednesday 30 August '44. He would not have been there at all were it not for the fire the day before at the local crematorium where the bodies of the previous nine British POWs had been cremated and where Sapper Richards was due for cremation. For the second time in three days he accompanied the body but on this occasion to the main crematorium. Paradoxically his spirits were lifted: "We went all along the coast road and oh it was lovely." From his vantage point at the crematorium perched on top of the hill he wrote: "It was a lovely sight to see the blue Pacific down below us and accompanied by the dull tolling of the temple bell, it was perfect."

Another reporter joined us by the, for me at any rate, infamous Itanki Beach at the foot of the hill. The crematorium had stood there until 1955. This would have meant that David Marshall would not have had the opportunity to visit it the following year. The man did not introduce himself but was very keen to get up to speed with events as he furiously scribbled down notes. Then the other reporter, Mikio Suda, had a phone call saying that, following publication of the *Shimbun* article in the newspaper the day before and the photo of me at the shrine in the temple, they had received a call from a reader claiming to have met Dad. This was intriguing and I hoped for a follow-up. I was not to be disappointed.

Our extended party now headed back towards the uglier parts of central Muroran and the site of the former camp. Unlike Dad after Richards' cremation, we did not travel as the crow flies. He wrote "We came back a short cut through the factory – it is a terrific size and does turn out a lot of finished iron goods." The steelworks' brooding presence made me think of the POW slave labour as well as the civilian, not to mention the child, labour all toiling within its confines in the most abject conditions. Now I was even more aware of the brutality suffered by many at the hands of the guards. The city's population has dropped from 120,000 at the end of the war to the current 87,000. Much of the centre seemed run-down with few people and cars about. Shortly after we passed the factory complex, we parked up near a small bridge that separated us from a waterway and the adjacent railway line. A barrier at the level crossing is now in place at the scene of the tragic deaths of Angell and Durrant. Fate had dealt them such a heavy blow when liberation – though the prisoners did not know it at the time – was within touching distance. (I have since discovered a little of the background of Cpl Alec Angell[10] who worked as a secretary at the Papworth Village TB Settlement in Cambridgeshire. If he was also on the *Wales Maru* and at Hakodate, I wonder if he ever became aware of the main camp's former use as a recovery site for TB patients.) The sound of a passing train alerted us to the need for evasive action, a poignant reminder of the story of the accident.

I knew that the site of the camp was close at hand. The hill which now boasts the Hatcoh Daira Observatory forms the backdrop. Mitchell's sketch shows a parade ground at the top end of the camp. Dad wrote in an entry in August '44 that there was "quite a gallery of Japanese kids up on the hill watching me" during some shot and discus practice. Earlier that same month he heads for the rising ground to spend "an hour in the misty evening dreaming on my little hillock of grass." A short climb to a favourite spot must have helped him cope with the daily medical traumas at the camp not to mention the pressures of leadership. Mitchell's description of the camp is "An oddly shaped enclosure about 150 by 40 yards at its widest point, built on the extreme edge of the town and surrounded by an eight-foot close-boarded fence with smooth side inward. No barbed wire. Two, possibly three guard towers had been built but were not used."[11] (The boarded fence with no gaps is illustrated in a Christmas card sketched by a Dutch POW on which Dad wrote to Mum on 23 December '44.) Sure enough, we pulled up within a matter of a few minutes. It was not a residential area. We got out of the vehicles in a wide, quiet thoroughfare between two large warehouses. I was told that the one on the right is a nail factory built in 1947 on the site of Muroran Camp. By 1959 virtually nothing remained of the camp, scene of the deaths of 53 British and Dutch prisoners of war. Although it was a sombre moment for me, Chris' delayed translation – whether under instructions from Mr Motono or his own decision – as to the use of the unit on the left showed a sensitivity that I admired but which did not particularly upset me. He told me it is now a casino though nothing from the outside indicates the activities within. I checked a photo I took later of a car park sign beside the name Maruhan. It turns out that they are the country's biggest entertainment conglomerate and provide gaming machines, arcades and bowling alleys.

Soon afterwards, a small white pick-up truck arrived. Out stepped a short elderly man in a baseball cap with Venezia (Venice) across the front. He introduced himself as Yoshikazu Yamamoto, the earlier phone-caller to the newspaper. He carried a walking-stick and promptly sat down on a small bank of dried grass by the road. He had recognised Dad in me from the photo at the Eizenji Temple in Hakodate. Chris' face beamed from ear to ear as he translated the man's observation that I was as handsome as my father! I too was highly amused. I asked him when he had met Dad. He replied that it was in August '44. Never expecting to come across anyone in the Far East who had actually met our dad as a prisoner, I followed up with the question "How do you know it was August '44?" It turns out he was a farmer and knows exactly the height of the potato crop at that month of the year. He and another teenage boy had been walking past Dad and another officer sitting on a bank and the former had briefly engaged them in conversation under the watchful eye of a guard. It was a good photo opportunity for the two reporters though, surprisingly, his appearance did not merit a mention in Mikio's article the next day. Mr Yamamoto seemed particularly pleased when I showed him Dad's officer's hat. Taeko was keen to share aerial maps and articles about the camp at Muroran with him, Mr Motono and me. The camp had been highlighted in an elongated 'L' shape, the narrowness of it thus confirming Mitchell's account. This was 'living history' in its truest sense in our little huddle linking the past with the present and in the exact location where so many distressing events had occurred.

To get a better idea of the camp's extension, we drove up a narrow twisting road in the direction of the observatory. When we halted, Mr Yamamoto kept a discreet distance which convinced me that he had not simply turned up for a few minutes to share in the media limelight. I was asked for the umpteenth time during my visit to Hokkaido how I felt. *Shimbun* reported that I had said "War is sometimes needed as a necessary evil but there are stories in both countries". I went on to say that I come from another generation and wanted "to understand and have a peaceful relationship between the two countries." Although I was thinking of the terrible atrocities committed in the camp, into my mind had also come images of the indescribable suffering of the residents of Hiroshima and Nagasaki. It was with some relief that I then spotted some 20 nursery school age children running towards their teacher in the playground of their school on the other side of the nail factory from the casino. Jumping for joy in the warm autumn sunshine and sporting their smart light blue baseball caps, they reminded me that life goes on. I'm sure Dad would have been delighted to know what now lies next door to the site of the former camp as would Mum with her dedication to her pupils back in the Omagh of the early '40s.

I thanked Mr Yamamoto for taking the time to come and tell us his story. I was delighted to be allowed to pay for lunch at an award-winning noodles' restaurant but was glad that I was not wearing the museum curator's white shirt which emerged speckled with pork noodles' sauce at the end of the meal! That evening Mr Motono, Mr Taninaka, Taeko and myself gathered at another typical restaurant near our hotel. For the second time in the space of a few hours, I marvelled at their double-jointed dexterity in squatting around a table which measured a mere 28 cms (about 11 inches) above the floor (I know because I took a picture of my West Ham cap standing on its end!) As for me, I sat at an angle with my legs fully outstretched. Mr Motono insisted I try some *gobo* (burdock), a root vegetable associated as a basic foodstuff in the war years. By the end of the evening I had shared three meals with this placid and likeable gentleman. We had exchanged fascinating stories. Taeko emailed me the following year with the news that his cancer had finally caught up with him. He died on 25 August 2018.

The plan for the following day was for us to arrive at Bibai early in the afternoon. This large town lies in the interior and many prisoners from Hakodate were transferred to the main camp there to work in the coal mines. Although most of the Muroran POWs were sent elsewhere in the same vicinity, i.e. to Nishi Ashibetsu/Raijo, Taeko had arranged for me to meet the author of the book about the Hokkaido camps and resident of Bibai – Hitoyasu Shirato. Chris had calculated that we would need to leave our hotel in Muroran by 10 o' clock. This gave me a window of two hours to meet him and Taeko near the site of the camp from the day before. It was too good an opportunity to miss. Taeko was sceptical but I was desperate to stretch my legs and felt confident enough in my sense of direction to set off on foot from our hotel. Chris lent me a mobile phone with a tracking device so he could locate me at the allotted time.

There was a real spring in my step at 8 as I set off which reminded me, albeit with only a small bag on my back, of my Camino walks. Early on I took a wrong turn and ended up on the wrong side of the railway line which would have entailed going through the steelworks' complex. Avoiding the city's bypass through a tunnel proved the next obstacle but at least I was hugging the contours of the bay on the busy commuter road I was following. Not including the many faces that stared at me from the general election posters, there was only one other pedestrian over the 90 minutes it took me to reach what I now calculate must have been the deserted Wanishi Railway Station. One solitary car was parked up at the station forecourt. It was a taxi and I knew this was the only way I was going to arrive anywhere near the camp let alone be on time for my lift. I eagerly clambered in to sit on its brightly coloured patterned rear seat. It was impossible to make the driver understand where I wanted to go so I showed him an advertising leaflet from 'Second Street'. On Chris' advice, we had gone to this shop the day before for me to purchase a woolly hat and thermal gloves for the colder days ahead. Everything in the store is second-hand, in excellent condition, and at affordable prices. The nearest equivalent in the UK and Ireland would be a charity shop though in Japan the merchandise is not donated. Not even a flicker of recognition from the driver. Then I recalled we had all driven past the Super Arcs Shopping Centre. That did the trick. I reached another deserted car park 20 minutes before opening where he dropped me off. I spied a small convenience store beyond it where I promptly headed for the toilet, cereal bars, and a rendezvous with Chris and Taeko.

At Bibai I was curious to find out why we were meeting Mr Shirato at the town's sprawling municipal offices. He too was short and elderly and spoke no English. We followed an employee into a lift and eventually emerged on the roof-top where we enjoyed an extensive view of the town and its wooded surroundings which once held the coal mines. He pointed out the site of the former camp which is fenced off and is now a Japanese army base. In a conversation with him later on at the office of a small museum, we were joined by Jun Fujinami from the Ashibetsu branch of the Hokkaido *Shimbun*. The former began by thanking my brother Carl for taking an interest in the story of the British POWs on the island. Carl had sent him several photos to include in his book which he later presented to me. He mentioned the 14,500 Korean prisoners in camps throughout Japan and the 15,000 Chinese. Of the 440 Chinese imprisoned on Hokkaido, a staggering 160 died in the first three months of captivity. I was now beginning to get a perspective on the fate of other foreign nationals. What happened to the Chinese in the Nishi Ashibetsu Camp particularly upset Dad and I was keen to discover more the next day when we visited the area.

The name of Colonel Toshio Hatakeyama, the "danger" first commander from Mr Asari's banner back at Hakodate, came up. A written reply by Hatakeyama to an Australian prisoner in April '43 that is still in the possession of the man's family in which he, the prisoner, cites the terms of the Geneva Convention, is dismissive of such claims and states that the POWs should be grateful they have food. In an article in the *Stars and Stripes*, an unofficial American army newspaper, it is claimed that 1,400 British, Dutch, and American POWs died during his two years of tenure. "When petitioned by Allied prisoners to lighten their burden, Hatakeyama declared that in America Japanese were being treated inhumanly."[12] (One week before England's first lockdown began, I attended a production at the National Theatre in London of the powerful drama, *The Seven Streams of the River Ota*, which deals in part with the atomic bombs. One scene is set in a tenement block in post-war New York. A new Japanese tenant is called a "banana" by one of the other occupants. His quiet dignity in the face of much prejudice left a deep impression on me.)

Mr Shirato claimed that General Higuchi, the army commander of northern Japan at the end of the war, ordered his troops to defend the area from an American invasion. He cynically made no provision for food to be sent to them as there was no point because they would fight to the death anyway, this being the likely outcome. On a lighter note, he told us that the prisoners who worked on some of the local farms were given the nickname "pumpkin hands" due to them turning yellow as they handled the vegetable. Before we left, I asked him out of curiosity how many visits he had received from former POW families interested in the experiences of their loved ones. In view of the relative proximity of Korea, I was not surprised to hear that some 300 had come from that country. I was only the fourth to make the trek from Britain and Ireland to Hokkaido. Even given the high cost of travelling to such a far-flung corner of the world, the number seemed disappointingly low.

By the time we left Bibai it was dusk. As we later pulled up at the car park of the Onsen Starlight Hotel on the outskirts of Ashibetsu, the first snowflakes of the oncoming winter were gently falling on the windscreen of Chris' people-carrier. It had been another day of discovery and copious note-taking. There only remained one more day in the media spotlight. The envigorating air of our new surroundings next to a wood augured well for my visit to Dad's final three camps.

NOTES

1.   See **Survival of the Fittest, A Young Englishman's Struggle as a Prisoner of War in Java and Japan,** Alan Carter *published by his son, Paul Carter, and printed by Russell Press, Nottingham 2013, p.70.*

2.   *Published in Hokkaido Shimbun newspaper Sunday 15 October 2017.*

3.   *See Mitchell p.122.*

4.   *As in note 2, published Sunday 22 October 2017.*

5.   *See Mitchell pp. 140-141.*

6.   *The first report was broadcast on NHK National TV on 21 November 2017 and the second on NHK International TV on 24 January 2018.*

7.   *See Mitchell p.151.*

8.   *See* **Hokkaido no Horyo Shuyo Jo (POW Camps of Hokkaido)** *by Hitoyasu Shirato, published in 2008, p.110.*

9.   *As above, p.103.*

10. *See article by Wendy Roberts on www.trumpingtonlocalhistorygroup.org/sub-jects_ww2notes.html*

11. *See Mitchell, p.149.*

12. **Stars and Stripes,** *3 November 1946.*

CHAPTER 23

"PART 2C, JAPAN – NISHI ASHIBETSU/RAIJO, UTASHINAI, AKABIRA, SAPPORO"

"It was a steep, slippery slope at Akabira down to a flat football pitch and 'giant' golf area. I set off on my own, determined to get to the river before the newspaper reporters, in order to have a few moments of reflection. Chris followed shortly and recorded a tearful tribute to Dad from me on his mobile phone. The bend where I stood probably marked the spot where he nearly drowned on 29 August 1945."

Diary entry Wednesday 18 October 2017

Like Muroran, the population of Ashibetsu has dwindled from 75,000 in 1960 to 14,000 at the present day. This probably reflects the closure of the coal mines in the surrounding area in 1992. Fortunately, the history of its past is faithfully recorded in the remarkable Hoshi no Furu Sato Hyakunen Centennial Museum. The name translates as "a beautiful starlight sky at night over the village". Even bearing in mind my limited knowledge of Japanese, the propensity of its people for indulging in poetic spirituality puts me in mind of my native Ireland and its Gaelic language. A pre-learnt phrase for my O level oral exam somehow remains with me to this day: *"Bhí na deora liom agus é ag imeacht thar sáile"*. This translates as "The tears were with me and him going off over the sea". The engaging curator, Takahiro Haseyama, had a basic command of English and acted as our guide in the museum. His knowledge of the POW camps in the area was a huge bonus which I had not been expecting.

This was a day when I took many photographs and made lots of connections. The variety of exhibits was a particular source of fascination. A weaving loom that could have been straight out of the Dunlewey Visitors' Centre in another Gaeltacht area of north Donegal was the first thing to catch my eye. Ainu jewellery, tapestry, and robes adorned one area and a selection of wooden clogs was reminiscent of the more remote rural settlements in Galicia through which the pilgrim passes on the road to Santiago. I must admit to an element of foreboding when I saw the pelt of a black bear hanging full length off a wall. An Ainu carving of a brown bear with a squirming fish between its teeth took me right back to David

Marshall's and Dad's collections. A model of an ancient circular burial ground could have easily been the Newgrange Stone Age Passage Tomb from the Boyne Valley in Ireland such were the similarities. Next to it was another model with a tiny figure interred in a foetal position. Immediately young Stan Faunch sprang to mind. Intriguingly, the figure was clutching a flower pot.

Inevitably, there were items from the war. These mainly consisted of Japanese army caps, woolly hats, long coats, and cap badges from many different units. Poignantly, in the middle of these, was a basic metal dish inscribed with the name of a Dutch POW called Schreuder together with his identity number – 92701.

At the end of the tour Takahiro took us up to his office to show us a series of photographs and maps with crosses pinpointing the exact whereabouts of the local Allied POW camps. On a desk in the middle of the room was a model of Raijo Camp which was based on a site map in the country's national library. In response to my query about the presence of an American B29 in the middle of the camp, he explained that it was there to represent the dropping of relief supplies to the prisoners. As an aside, he also pointed out that some 300 of them were used in the bombing of Tokyo on 10 March '45 which resulted in the deaths of 140,000 of its citizens and a million who were made homeless. (Wikipedia puts the casualty list at between 90,000 and 100,000 but it was still an appalling loss of life and, again, an event about which I knew nothing.) As for the model, it was significant that it closely resembled Mitchell's sketch[1]. Takahiro was able to identify the guard in the provocative pose that Mitchell had incorrectly labelled a "Japanese medic officer" in the photo of the POW medical staff at liberation. In fact he was the officer in charge of finances – Sgt Major Sakurada Tsunezou. I find his presence totally unjustifiable. My diary that morning read "His [Takahiro's] illustrations and evident knowledge transformed the visit in a way the guides to the other camps had not managed. They gave me a real appetite for the afternoon tour, this was truly living history and in the hands of an expert." Taeko too took copious notes as she did every day.

Thank goodness there were no low tables for lunch at the nearby local restaurant overlooking the Ashibetsu River! The town is dominated by a huge white statue of the Buddha which is in view literally everywhere you go. Another feature of the skyline which Chris pointed out as our little troupe headed for the camps was the vapour trails left by aircraft now tracking north-west rather than west on a flight path towards Europe.

The new direction is due to the threat from North Korea's dictator, Kim Jong Un. My immersion in the past received a temporary but chilling jolt back to the present.

We were now joined by a local retired teacher, Akihiko Sato. There were, in fact, nine camps in the immediate area – five for allied POWs namely Bibai, Nishi Ashibetsu, Raijo, Akabira, and Utashinai, and four Chinese[2]. I was particularly interested in finding out more about one of the latter as Dad had taken such an interest in it in the days following liberation. Another family who had previously come to Hokkaido to visit Muroran and attempt to locate the whereabouts of Nishi Ashibetsu/Raijo Camp were three generations of the descendants of A.J. [Jack] Ford, yet another of the many Suffolks who were imprisoned with Dad. The youngest of these was his great-grandson, Joe Cross, who has written a blog about their visit. Chris had also acted as their guide and had asked Joe for some photos to be emailed before we set off. Unlike Joe, his father and his grandfather, we were fortunate to be in the hands of Takahiro who brought his tablet so we could compare old photos of Nishi Ashibetsu with the quiet but sadly run-down community it is today. I remembered a photo of the old railway station we had seen that morning at the museum and recalled Dad's description of the train's short journey from Ashibetsu on the Japanese version of what he had romantically referred to as the Lough Swilly Narrow Gauge Line in Donegal. It is still there though it now serves as some sort of goods' storage building. Nearby, Takahiro pointed out a dilapidated private house which he thought was once the chemist's, the probable scene of David Marshall's distressing encounter with the former camp guard. His sketch maps showed the position of Nishi Ashibetsu Branch Camp 4B not far along the road. This was a new camp set up later in the month of June '45 which housed 52 American, 45 Australian, and three British POWs. The name is confusing for people like me who are tracking the movement of the prisoners from Muroran Branch Camp 1B. Like Dad, they all left on Tuesday 5 June, travelled on one train to Ashibetsu to be greeted by "terrific crowds", then on the minor train to Nishi Ashibetsu where "more crowds greeted us". They were then marched the three miles up the Ashibetsu River to Raijo which is also confusingly labelled on the POW Research Network Japan website as 1B[3]. None of the POW diaries emanating from Raijo ever mention this name. It is always referred to as Nishi Ashibetsu.

Most of the men in both camps worked in the coal mines in the valley though there is little evidence of them now. We drove along the main road high above the path by the meandering Ashibetsu River that Dad and the 348 British, 155 Dutch and five American prisoners would have followed on their first day. Stopping on a viaduct, we spotted beyond the foliage of the trees the wooden bridge they would have crossed. I imagined that the steady afternoon drizzle overhead matched the sombre mood of the men after Durrant and Angell's deaths two days before. Shortly afterwards, we pulled up at an area of spindly trees and light undergrowth which marked the position of Raijo Camp. Mitchell described it thus: "Built especially to Emoto's design this camp was on an area of disused paddi-fields and covered about 43 by 20 yards. Such a compact area gave each man far less space than in previous camps, but this had in mind winter conditions when such closeness would help conserve heat. In summer heat it was far too warm. The fence was again close boarded and about eight feet in height, but was less well made than at Muroran."[4] Emoto had been relieved of his post as overall commander of the Hokkaido camps the previous month but Dad confirmed Mitchell's conviction of his contin-ued involvement[5] when, back at Muroran, Hirate read out Emoto's fare-well speech to the prisoners on Monday 28 May. "He [Emoto] expressed his sorrow at leaving us so very suddenly. He would like to see us all when the war is over – as friends. There was great gloom in camp. He mentioned about the new camp – the good arrangements he had made for our comfort there."

Takahiro again produced his tablet, this time to compare the wooded horizon in the background in front of us to the group photo of British POWs at liberation. The similarity was striking. I imagined the parade ground in front of the long line of British huts that housed the 349 POWs where Elizabeth Hallett's father, Sgt Eric Davies, noted, in turn, the pre-sentation of the three scrolls of tribute – on 26 August to Max Andler, 28 August to Jan Jongsma, and 6 September to our dad – each so beautifully composed by David Marshall. As we stood by the quiet traffic-free road-side, an elderly man walked past taking his daily exercise. I wondered if he had any idea of the secret past of this isolated woodland. There is nothing to mark the spot where the POWs first heard the rumours of their release after 42 months. However, Dad was not one of them. We were next on our way to the two remaining camps where he had been unceremoniously moved on his own after a mere three weeks at Raijo.

At a nearby community we made a detour past a smarter-looking house which marked the site of a brothel used by former Korean civilian guards and prisoners in the days immediately after the war. Takahiro insisted we not stop due to sensitivity in the area even all these years later. That evening he emailed Taeko and me three photographs belonging to a local woman who was 20 when the war ended. They were probably taken by someone from the International Red Cross. Her mother owned a field next to Raijo Camp and was asked by two of the Japanese guards after surrender if she would be willing to lodge them in return for protection "from sexual violation by POWs." I hasten to add that at no stage while I was on Hokkaido was this form of abuse an issue with regard to Allied prisoners. Two of the photos showed a Sgt Abe and Sgt Umeki (the medical officer who spoke good English and had purchased the samurai sword for Dad) standing on top of a hut at Raijo with the letters PW hammered into the slanting roof on planks so as to guide American aircraft dropping relief supplies. I had earlier learnt that a mass brawl had taken place on the bridge downstream involving released Korean and Chinese POWs with each group vying for patronage over the brothel. One man had tragically drowned.

As Akabira, Dad's sixth camp, is located before Utashinai, his fifth, we aimed for it first. In contrast to Nishi Ashibetsu and Raijo, we were in a more populated area. Back in England I had enlisted the help of Tim, a friend from Philomusica, in analysing the aerial photos from the planes on the USS *Nehenta Bay* aircraft-carrier. He had downloaded current images of the bend in the Sorachi River which indicated the location of the camp. This helped in orientating myself in advance of the *Shimbun* reporter towards the point where I reckoned Dad had entered the water to rescue the men on the opposite bank. Chris knew of my intentions, followed me swiftly down the bank, and filmed my emotional tribute to our dad. On another note, the land was so low-lying I could see why he had described it as a quagmire with mud everywhere.

On my tablet the night before in my room at the Onsen Starlight, I had re-read Dad's diary entries to Mum over the two months he had spent at Akabira. Its idyllic setting had helped to soften the blow of his separation from the men back at Raijo. Here are four of them:

Tuesday 24 July 1945

"There is a lovely view from the camp – wooded hills, and a broad river which is one of the camp boundaries. Darling, yet another dream about you. I am optimistic these days and I love you. God bless you, Eileen."

Wednesday 25 July

"I sat today for ages looking down at the river and dreaming of you. God bless you, Eileen."

Saturday 28 July

"The river brings me great consolation because then I can be alone with you and nature. God bless you, Eileen."

Friday 10 August

"My darling. I have been sitting by the river and dreaming of you and home and the wonderful times that lie ahead of us. It makes me so deliciously happy, Eileen, that I could almost cry. We shall be so happy. God bless you, Eileen."

As I gazed at the tumbling waters of the fast-flowing river, their mutual love of nature and Mum's key role in his survival were never more evident.

Utashinai was off the main road. Dad had spent barely 12 days there. His kit only arrived four days after he left Raijo. Significantly, it contained his secret diary which was not found despite a check at the main gate. Evidence of open-cast mining lay beyond a fence with some now over-grown slag heaps. Then it was time to head back to Ashibetsu and a meal that evening when Chris, Taeko, the reporter Jun Fujinami, and I were Takahiro's guests. I wore Dad's RAMC tie in honour of the occasion. I had learnt so very much from a man who is now retired as the museum curator. I felt so very relaxed in the company of friends, two of whom had been my constant companions for nearly a week. The friendly staff at the town's Polo Restaurant took some lovely photos of our celebration together, visual depictions of the reconciliation which had always been my cherished goal.

Unlike the overcast weather of the previous day, my final full day on Hokkaido dawned with beautiful sunny weather and a cloudless sky. The three of us had no media commitments. I felt my own private sense of freedom as we retraced our steps back to Nishi Ashibetsu. We passed the sites of the Mitsui Corporation's Officers' Club and the Mitsui Ashibetsu Chinese POW Camp. According to Takahiro's maps, they were both situated closer to the Ashibetsu River than the Allied POW camp in the town. I reflected sadly that I had found no information about any Chinese POW camp in Japan either on the POW Research Network Japan website or in any media searches I had done prior to coming. This was in marked contrast to their meticulously logged information about Allied POWs and lists of fatalities. It was as if they never existed. However, after I returned to England and emailed him the letter of thanks that Dad received in '46 from the man in charge of the Hakodate Branch of the Chinese Association, Takahiro emailed me a statistic about the Chinese who worked in the Mitsui Ashibetsu Coal Mine. They had been sent there the previous August, a full year before the end of the war. 171 of the 610 had died. (Based on the 1946 records of the Japanese Foreign Ministry, the figures in Mr Shirato's book[6] put the losses even higher at 273 out of 600 or 45.5 per cent. This appalling figure is easily the highest of the four Chinese camps in the area). Ki San Lee whom I have already mentioned in chapter 9 in relation to his letter of thanks to our dad, remained in Ashibetsu after the war, married a Japanese woman, had a child, and passed away in 1952. I'm sure Dad would have been interested in finding out what had happened to a man who had gone to a lot of trouble to contact him. Two extracts from his letter I reproduce below:

> *"I want to thank you from the bottom of my heart for all that you have done for me and my friends while we were imprisoned in Ashibetsu. Thanks to you, they have all regained their health and most of them returned to their homes in China…I also want to thank you for the clothing that we have received from you and they certainly came in handy."*

As we were all keen to inspect the symbolic bridge upstream at close quarters, Chris parked up his people-carrier on a minor road and we strolled down to the river passing an American-style fire hydrant and a can recycling centre. We had the peaceful surroundings of the wood and the river all to ourselves. Ten-foot-high barriers blocked our access but there was a way round to one side. Piles of fallen autumn leaves obscured the lethal gaps in the slats. We had learnt from Takahiro that the bridge was constructed in 1920 following the drowning of some children when the river was in spate. This recalled for me 12-year-old Norah Ryan, the heroine of the novel *The Rat-Pit*[7], as she crosses what I always think of as the Gweebarra River in south-west Donegal. The book is set in the early 1900s. She, along with many other women, waits for low tide before crossing the treacherous river to pick up yarn for knitting socks at the nearby town. This was their sole form of income. One of our family's visits to Portnoo in the '60s coincided with the unveiling of a new bridge across the river. (On a personal note I remember an unusually quiet traffic-free evening in the same decade when my second cousin Geraldine Murphy and I cycled from Portnoo to the bridge. Known to everyone as 'Gerry', she was the chief stewardess on Pan Am 103 which exploded in mid-air over Lockerbie in December '88. She was our parents' goddaughter and one of our favourite relatives. Gerry had a unique gift for relating to young people.)

We drove further upstream to cross by another bridge in an attempt to view the old one from the far bank. This proved impossible as the barriers were much further away but what we did come across before this next impediment was a simple shrine. Two small Buddha-type figures draped in red cloth, an incense container, and artificial flowers adorned it. I asked Chris and Taeko if they could pick me up on the road back to Nishi Ashibetsu while I stayed by the shrine for a while to fully take in what for me symbolised the children's drowning. There were many other things to fill my thoughts as, complete with rucksack and swinging scallop shell, I then retraced part of our drive back up towards a clearing in the forest. I suddenly found myself staring at a large statue of what I have now learnt is a 'Kannon'. In the Buddhist religion she is the goddess of compassion and mercy. I was particularly struck by the precision with which her left hand was raised with her thumb and forefinger touching – a gesture related to the teachings of Buddha. The statue or *jizo* in Japanese is in the grounds of the Buddhist temple of Shinshoji.

By now it was lunch-time and a welcome bench offered me the perfect setting for a picnic. I waved a greeting at a woman busy washing her dog outside a nearby house. She reciprocated. At this isolated spot there was no other sign of life. Soon I heard the sound of Chris' vehicle and, intrigued by the black and white figure in pilgrim garb on a poster outside the temple, I asked Taeko if we could visit. There was also a tree adorned with ribbons such as I had seen as a *hospitalero* at Rabanal in the garden after the departure of some Korean pilgrims. Removing our shoes, we were duly invited in by the monk, Denkyo Fujikawa, who made us feel really welcome. The temple lies on a pilgrim route which traverses the whole of Hokkaido and takes in 88 shrines in all. Shinshoji is number five. I purchased my pilgrim passport and received my first stamp from a constantly smiling Denkyo as I posed for a photo with him on the matted floor in front of a low, ornate altar. As for the poster of the pilgrim, the staff he carries is called a *shakujo* which is nowadays ceremonial but was once used in self-defence[8]. On his left wrist was draped a set of Rosary beads with what may be Buddhist scriptures wrapped in the palm of his hand. The coincidences in our short visit I found quite remarkable on this very special day. Nor did they end there. After his death, half of Ki San Lee's ashes were buried at the temple while the other half were handed over to China when the mayor of Ashibetsu visited the country in 1956. This was indeed a fitting recognition of the small part played by one Chinese citizen in helping his fellow countrymen who stayed behind on Hokkaido after the war.

I'm not sure how I found out about the nearby Canadian World Theme Park but, with time on my hands in the afternoon and my curiosity piqued, I was determined to get there. The staff at the hotel reception advised taking a taxi but I couldn't resist the walk. The pure mountain air and riot of autumn colours created the perfect antidote to the built up areas I had been experiencing for nearly two weeks. I thought of Dad and his diary entry the day after the men arrived at Raijo: "There are beautiful wooded hills all around us here and the men should be healthier and safer here than in Muroran."

After a 45-minute stroll with a steeper climb towards the end, I reached the brow of a hill to be met by the impressive vista of the huge park. Built in the early '90s, it has as its theme the main character from the Lucy Maud Montgomery novel, *Anne of Green Gables*. Hokkaido is twinned with Prince Edward Island in Canada and the book is set on a farmstead there. It was virtually deserted save for a couple of gardeners and, even allowing for the fact it was no longer the tourist season, the entire complex seemed very run-down. This was epitomised by a totem pole half-buried in the grass. There was no-one on duty so I was able to wander round at will and take in the black and white timbered hotel, the train station, chapel, clock tower, woodman's house, and a knitted woolly creature mounted on a scooter in front of a log cabin. The buildings were all locked-up but were certainly not empty shells as I peered through the windows at the authentic furnishings within. Villana would have loved it. The park was so vast I had no time to reach the recreated town nestling by a lake at the bottom of the valley. I knew I would have to make it back to the hotel before dusk as the last vestiges of sunlight were bringing a decidedly autumnal chill to the air. Reluctantly, I took my leave of the colourfully-drawn matchstick figures of Diana, Gilbert, Anne, Marilla, Matthew, and Mrs Lynde on the hoarding above the entrance. It had been a quite magical experience and reminiscent in its unexpectedness of a special evening listening to the 'Boss' and his band in Santiago at the end of my second pilgrimage. No setting could have been further removed from the dark history of the POW camps just down the road.

It was to be Taeko's departure next morning for her flight back to Tokyo from Sapporo. I hadn't expected to be anywhere near the camps on our journey south towards the airport but suddenly we were crossing the Sorachi River and, then on the main highway, I could make out the flat terrain of what was once Akabira Camp as well as the turning to Utashinai. We were now imitating Dad's route to what he believed was 'Kamikoge' Aerodrome at Chitose. There was a squadron of *kamikaze* pilots based there and he probably confused the name. This is now New Chitose Airport at Sapporo. (The city was the venue for England's opening match against Tonga in the 2019 Rugby World Cup.) The approaches to Hokkaido's international airport go past what is now Okadama Army Airbase and I recognised the naval aerodrome hangars that form the backdrop to Lt Edmunds' photos of the men's departure on 13 September '45. Dad must have looked forward to his maiden flight with a mixture of relief that he was finally going home and apprehension about boarding an aircraft.

We dropped Taeko off outside the main terminal building. My *Lonely Planet* Japanese phrasebook and dictionary describes the custom of bowing as relating to "timing, posture and movement" as they are "a reflection of sincerity, respect and maturity."[9] She deserved all of this and more besides. I ensured my bow was deep, heart-felt, and reached my waist in front of this diminutive lady who, from the moment she knew my list of priorities, had co-ordinated my entire visit to her country. She, Yoshiko who met me for a coffee at Haneda Airport in Tokyo the next day, and Yukako, along with countless other volunteers continue to strive ceaselessly to bring to the attention of their own country and the rest of the world the story of the POWs.

All too soon I had to say goodbye to my favourite Gooner (Arsenal supporter). We embraced in the lobby of my hotel near the airport. For a whole week and, in the midst of making arrangements for forthcoming ski bookings over his mobile phone for his company's clients, he had given his time generously. Not only did he interpret for me but he kept me grounded with his stories of football trivia at the moments when emotion would certainly have got the better of me in an alien world of photographers, camera crews, and reporters.

I make two more observations before catching the airport bus to follow Dad's journey back to Honshu, albeit to Tokyo rather than Yokohama. Already in the lift as I went down to breakfast was a young woman. On reaching the ground floor, she was most insistent that I exit the lift before she did. She was closer to the opening doors than me and it was polite to let her go first. She was uncomfortable with this and was obviously unused to the gesture but, at my insistence, she reluctantly agreed. I had found Japan to be a very sexist country. (Dad makes a similar observation in his reflection which I have transcribed in my epilogue.) I was told that many younger women either marry older men or emigrate abroad. *Okusan* is one of the many words for 'wife' and is used in the context of other people's wives. *Oku* means 'far back inside', possibly suggesting a kitchen where a dutiful wife is expected to spend a lot of her time. (In terms of language, Japanese is not unique in this respect. When I first went to Spain in the final years of the Franco dictatorship, a woman's married name carried the preposition *de* as in 'of' in front of that of her husband.)

My second observation relates to giving my room number before entering the breakfast room. Without the services of Taeko and Chris, I practised 1027 (*ichi, ray, ni, shichi*) several times in advance. I was pleased when the person in charge ticked the number off the list without me having to repeat it. It then struck me how the prisoners too would have had to shout their number twice daily at *tenko*. Dad's was *ichi, ichi, ray, ni* (1102) and Gerald Sketchley's *ichi, san, ku, ray* (1390) as he reminds the reader in the title of his article *The Captive Guest*. In a very reflective mood, I tucked into my copious breakfast buffet with guilty thoughts uppermost of half-starving POWs.

POSTSCRIPT 1

Lt Kaichi Hirate was tried as a Class B war criminal. The trial lasted 11 days and was conducted by the military commission appointed by the headquarters of the United States Eighth Army. At its conclusion, the solicitor general read out a telegram from Pte Raymond Suttle's parents calling for the death penalty[10]. He was hanged at Sugamo Prison on 23 August 1946. Hirate was held responsible for the deaths of 53 POWs at Muroran, the highest number at any camp on the island apart from the main one at Hakodate. He was the only Japanese officer on Hokkaido to be executed. Among the charges he faced was that he "did unlawfully disregard and fail to discharge his duty as camp commander and restrain the members of his command, permitting them to commit cruel and brutal atrocities and other offenses against allied Prisoners of war held in said Camp."[11] In chapter 7 I have already referenced Dad's affidavit which was used in the trial, particularly in relation to his belief that Hirate bore full responsibility for the death of Pte Suttle.

After I returned to England I enlisted the help of Miriam Davis, a new member of our choir who is a fluent Japanese speaker. Among her translations of some of the chapters from Mr Shirato's book on the camps, I learnt that the camp interpreter, Lt Oswald Wynd, wrote a letter pleading for clemency following the sentence. (There were, in fact, 100 such pleas.) Part of this letter was quoted in a book about Hirate by one of his (Hirate's) friends, Shigemi Tamura[12] Bearing in mind Wynd's resolve never to return to the country where he had spent his formative years[13], I found this intercession surprising. It could be explained in that Tamura wanted to paint his friend in a more positive light or Wynd may genuinely have felt pity for the young camp commandant who was held in such low esteem by the guards due to his lack of military experience. In this context, I turn to Dad's diary entry of Friday 6 October '44. When hearing of Wynd's sudden transfer out of Muroran Camp, he wrote of his mixed feelings: "There was a bombshell today when Wynd was detailed to proceed to Hakodate tomorrow morning. As an interpreter he will be badly missed, but otherwise I think not! We didn't see much of him as he never ate with us but spent his day in his room." How sad that this was ultimately to be Dad's low opinion of someone with such a key role in the camp.

Wynd's fictitious description in his novel of the fate of the Japanese officer in charge of the POWs on board the *Oshima Maru* hellship reads as follows: "Tokyo, Aug.27,'46. The first Japanese to be sentenced to death by the War Crimes Tribunal, Major Eichi Hirado, was today hanged at Sugamo Prison. Hirado was convicted of having personally executed, by the sword, an American sailor Albert Janus on board a ship carrying prisoners of war from Singapore to Japan."[14]

The factual description of the trial runs to nine pages and I have only recently become aware of it. It is both fascinating and disturbing in the detail it provides. In addition to his responsibility for the death of Suttle, a charge is also brought against Hirate for denying Sapper Ernest Glover treatment at a nearby local hospital in Muroran. Dad's affidavit is cited in the case for the prosecution. When Hirate is recalled to the witness stand by the defence, he outlines his reasons for punishing Suttle. His version of conditions in the guardhouse are diametrically opposed to Dad's and must be upsetting, if not insulting, for Suttle's relatives to read. The commission's summing-up includes the following statement: "Several prisoners, now dead, would probably be alive today if the accused had properly concerned himself with their welfare and had availed himself of those facilities which were available."

POSTSCRIPT 2

Seeing Yoshiko's smiling face at Haneda Airport arrivals was a welcome boost before my bus transfer across Tokyo for my second flight of the day, this time from Narita Airport. I thanked her for the expertise with which she had interpreted my talk to the Research Network the week before. As she knew I was heading back to Singapore for a short overnight stop, she drew my attention to the story of the first Japanese officer to be hanged following the war crimes' trials at Singapore. The man's son had contacted her group to show them letters he had received from his father while stationed in Singapore during the war. In them, he made no reference to the executions he had ordered of prisoners. She empathised with me at the prospect of my imminent flight heading in the direction of typhoon Lan. The Singapore Airlines plane did experience some severe buffeting. I tried to block out the hysterical sobbing from a passenger on the row in front of me as we made our approach.

It felt strange the next day to be back in Singapore without Villana. I walked past Raffles Hotel which was partially closed due to renovation and St Joseph's Catholic Church where our dad had knelt in front of its tabernacle on Tuesday 20 January '42 to pray for our mum on her birthday. The church was undergoing a complete refurbishment so, alas, I was not able to enter. After Mass at The Good Shepherd Cathedral, I met up again with Patricia Lee from the National Archives. She and her husband passed on their thanks from their football-mad son who had swopped his allegiance from Manchester United to Manchester City! I had got Andrew to email him a photo of him interviewing City's famous Argentinian forward, Sergio Agüero. They kindly drove me to Kranji Cemetery which Villana and I had sadly not had time to visit. There were hardly any visitors that Sunday afternoon but I was particularly struck by the presence of two young Chinese women laying flowers and playing music from a mobile phone in front of a grave near the entrance. At the top of the hill, I sought shelter from the sweltering sun high overhead in the scant shade offered by the huge concrete monoliths that depict the names of thousands of Commonwealth soldiers. I rang Jeya, the director of the Battle Box, to recount the story of the Japanese officer and his son. He said he would be keen to contact the women from the Research Network. Providing him with this was an unexpected by-product of my pilgrimage to the Far East and one which I was delighted to facilitate. The young women were still at their vigil as I left.

There was just enough time to catch up with Jean Marshall[15] and update her on my experiences in Japan before I returned to Changi Airport to board my midnight flight back to Heathrow. My ultimate terrestrial pilgrimage was at an end. It was 'ultimate' in the sense that it was so very special and never to be repeated. To walk in the footsteps of where our dad walked during the most traumatic period in his life was such a privilege. However, on another level, it is my belief that life is an ongoing pilgrimage which prepares us for another existence in an everlasting world to come.

NOTES

1. *See Mitchell Fig.8 sketch, p.240.*

2. *Hitoyasu Shirato in his book **Hokkaido no Horyo Shuyo Jo (POW Camps of Hokkaido)** lists the Chinese in a grid on p.177 as Mitsui Bibai, Mitsui Ashibetsu, Sumitomo Ashibetsu, and Hokutan Sorachi.*

3. *www.powresearch.jp/en/archive/camplist*

4. *Description as in note 1.*

5. *Mitchell reproduces the whole speech on pp.231-232.*

6. *As in note 2, p.177.*

7. ***The Rat-Pit** by Patrick MacGill, Birlinn Ltd, Edinburgh, 2001.*

8. *See www.eastlondonkempo.co.uk/blog/the-staff-of-the-mountain-monk-history-and-meaning-of-the-shakujo*

9. *See **Lonely Planet Japanese Phrasebook & Dictionary**, 7th edition, March 2015, p.113.*

10. *Source of this information on the trial comes from an information sheet by the POW Research Network Japan who honoured Suttle and two other deceased Allied POWs at their annual commemoration in the Commonwealth War Cemetery in Yokohama on 3 August 2019.*

11. *See www.legal-tools.org/doc/15acea/pdf*

12. *The book is **Tomo-sono sei to shi no Akashi-B kyuhan senpan Hirate Kaichi taisa no shogai** (The Proof of Life and Death of my Friend, B Class War Criminal, Kaichi Hirate's Life) by Shigemi Tamura.*

13. *See Oswald Wynd obituary at www.independent.co.uk/arts-entertainment/ obituary-oswald-wynd-1169874.html*

14. *See **The Forty Days** by Oswald Wynd, Collins, St James's Place London, 1972, p.248.*

15. *Jean sadly passed away on 29 March this year.*

CHAPTER 24

"LIEUTENANT COLONEL SHIGEO EMOTO"

"My feelings during my interview with the High Commandant were those of awe and admiration for his dynamic personality. His superb command of the English language was a pleasant surprise to me. His views on international politics and Japan's part in them were interesting. The modesty of the Japanese people was very well described and it was novel to me. The High Commandant's ambition to make this the best prisoner-of-war camp in Japan will receive all my possible support and co-operation. He has shown a close personal interest in every man in camp, listening attentively to their difficulties and complaints and carried out improvements without delay. He gave a patient hearing to the medical questions which I raised and attended to them on the spot. He has granted privileges to the Red Cross personnel which is a big step towards fulfilment of the spirit of international Red Cross. I wish the new High Commandant every success in attaining the lofty ideals with which he is imbued."

To date, neither Carl nor I have been able to ascertain the context in which our dad wrote this description of the Japanese officer who did most to improve the conditions of the prisoners in Muroran POW Camp. It is headed "No.1102 [Dad's POW number] Major F.J. Murray" but was not among his possessions when he returned after the war. Shigeo's third son, Susumu, passed on a typed copy of it to Taeko who in turn emailed it to Carl back in 2007. I have no doubt, however, as to the veracity of this glowing testimony.

The contrasting mortality rates among Allied POWs under Toshio Hatakeyama, the first commandant of the Hokkaido camps, and Shigeo Emoto, his successor, speak for themselves. With regard to the Yakumo and Muroran camps, the Research Network puts the figures at 39 Dutch and eight British prior to the beginning of Emoto's tenure on 3 March '44, and only one Dutch and three British (Lumbers, Quarterman, and Jardine) from then until late May '45 when he was relieved of his post. The reason given by his superiors for this was that they felt he was being too lenient. The confirmation of Emoto's enlightened attitude towards the POWs is shared by at least seven other men whose accounts I have read namely Max Andler, R. Keith Mitchell and Eric Davies who were all with Dad at Muroran, and Dan Brown, Alan Carter, C.E.A. Ripley and Eric Cooper[1] who were imprisoned at either Hakodate or at another nearby camp at Kamiiso. An indication that Emoto took his responsibilities seriously is evident in Dad's letters where he logs nine occasions in the commandant's 14-month period in charge when he visited Muroran. These were not cursory day visits. Four lasted between three and four days and on one occasion he spends an entire week at the camp.

The men first met Emoto on Tuesday 14 March '44. It was evidently a short fact-finding mission to establish contact. Dad, along with four other officers, attends a two hour-meeting with him. They must all have been impressed with his "perfect English". The tone is relaxed: "He declared that Japanese women were the best in the world – I was bold enough to differ and declare Irish girls to be the world's best!"

His second visit is during the first week of May. On Wednesday 3rd, Dad significantly uses that same adjective, "dynamic", which I have quoted to describe the impact he makes: "My darling, the camp is being gradually transformed into a place of luxury. The High Commandant is a dynamic force in this place and makes things happen at high speed. I shall always remember these days. I feel so much more freedom now." On the Sunday, American Red Cross medicines and toiletries are released to the men. Were these the same ones the British and Dutch officers were forced to pose beside in the propaganda picture taken in February and to which they were cruelly not given access? The cynic in Dad comments that day that "The medicines were wonderful if we can keep them." Mitchell confirms that Dad was frequently threatened by having access to them withdrawn if he refused to toe the line. Emoto returns to Hakodate on the Tuesday, a full week since his arrival. Dad writes: "All the men have spectacles now; dental repairs and fillings daily." His 1988 abridged version records an American dentist called Brown melting down silver coins and filling teeth with the resultant liquid.

It cannot be under-estimated the effect Emoto's arrival had on the POWs after over two years of captivity when they had been subjected to the norms of inhuman treatment by nearly every Japanese *shoko* (commissioned officer), guard, and Korean civilian *hancho* (work party leader). Mitchell mentions the issuing of library books and blunt razor blades. Sgt Eric Davies makes reference to more rice and clothing. Dan Brown at Hakodate[2] talks of tea and a cigarette for the men he interviewed and new socks, towels and overalls. *Yasume* now takes place every Sunday instead of one in three. More significantly, in view of the insanitary conditions, the installation of a sewerage system reduces the cases of dysentery. No wonder the high death figures showed such a remarkable decrease.

Emoto is passionate about imparting his love of Japanese customs to the assembled ranks of prisoners who have a morning or an afternoon off work to listen to lecture topics as varied, according to Davies, as India, the Philippines, and the American Civil War. This tiring imposition must have been a small price to pay for what Mitchell terms "totally unexpected friendliness."[3] He also recounts a response to his invitation to the men to express their demands. One brave man gets to his feet and asks for an end to the beatings. Emoto promises that this would take place though the reality was that the guards gradually return to their old ways after his departure and Hirate continues to turn a blind eye to their misdemeanours.

On his fourth visit, Dad and the senior Dutch MO, Lieutenant Lutter, are interviewed by two Japanese journalists. It is Thursday 3 August. Emoto is also present. "I gave them an earful of woe about the frightful state of the men's health (British), about the poor food and the hard work. They were all furious but I *had* to do my duty. I spoke about the improvements and about the awful beatings before the Colonel arrived. It may cost me a lot but I *had* to do it." Two days later comes a second interview with Emoto. There is no hint of retribution from him for Dad's outspokenness. "I appealed again for the sick and he insists that no sick or weak men be sent out to work. It was a wonderful victory for me, no matter what the cost". This order is reinforced on Sunday 17 September when Emoto phones from Hakodate issuing the command that a further 30 men work for only half a day and do less strenuous work. On Friday 3 November during his sixth visit, he arranges for baths to be more frequently available and for fires to be lit as winter approaches. Dad ensures Emoto is aware of the men's gratitude: "I made my usual speech of thanks when he had finished and said how much we appreciated everything he had done."

On Sunday 12 November Dad is told by the brutal Japanese military doctor – Dr Shiba – that, in a letter written by Emoto, he (Emoto) is furious at the death of a man at Hakodate. Dan Brown's diary entry from 3 November confirms that the POW concerned was Driver Albert

Wilkinson.[4] Dad notes Emoto's anger that his Rule 5 that POWs should not die has been broken. I suspect that 'Rule 5' was one of a number that he drew up and are referenced in Max Andler's diary during the visit of a general from Tokyo (probably Hiroshi Tamura[5]) to Muroran. (Dad confirms the date as Tuesday 20 February 1945.) "He [the general] was… very upset when he saw the Colonel's policy up on the wall in English in all the groups and buildings."[6] Max's diary entry and Dad's differ in that Max specifies that Emoto accompanies the general. I think it likely that this was the case given the rank and importance of the officer. Dad does imply that Emoto is present in what can only be described as the pity he feels towards the commandant when the general condemns the camp for not sending enough men out to work: "Poor poppy has an awful time and lost much face during the inspection." Given the fact that Emoto was 57 in 1945 (many of the prisoners used to refer to him as "the old man"), I suspect that the nickname "poppy", presumably based on pop, was Dad's reference to him rather than to the young Hirate.

Back at Hakodate Camp, Eric Cooper states that there was a delay in implementing Emoto's reforms. Nonetheless, he describes him as "a very fair man" and backed this up by being "very strict and a great disciplinarian."[7] Doubtless these characteristics would have also been more appreciated by some of the guards at Muroran coming, as they did, from a mature officer with pre-war military service in the army. The mutual respect between Emoto and the British POWs is never more evident than in the following description in Cooper's book: "Each time we arrived back from work he [Emoto] would stand, together with the men on his staff, on the verandah of the administration block, then salute, and remain in this position until all men had departed to their respective huts, a very fine soldier. There was still much cruelty and degradation suffered by us all, but no prisoner spoke ill of the commandant. He had gained our respect." Sadly, Cooper too adds that guards and civilian *hanchos* took advantage of his periods of absence "to make things difficult and hard for some men."

During the commandant's second visit to Muroran in May '44, Mitchell rises from a squatting position at the end of a camp lecture on the history of the Samurai warrior caste to make a direct request to be given lighter work after bouts of amoebic dysentery and pleurisy. He is flabbergasted not only by Emoto's immediate assimilation of his past medical history but his promise to look into the request. The following morning he begins work in a warm casting shop supervised by "a good *hancho*". [8]

Mr Asari at Hakodate had given me a copy of a story about Emoto written by a British prisoner there called Danny Meaghan. (This also appears in summarised form in Nigel Brown's account of his father's experiences.) During work in a warehouse in the docks at Hakodate on 3 August '44, Danny saves the life of a young Japanese woman who is about to fall face down though a trap door. His number is taken by a guard and, eight days later, Danny is dismayed to hear it called out by Emoto who is standing on a specially erected platform. To his complete surprise, the commandant lauds him thus in front of all his fellow prisoners: "It is hard for a man to show bravery when he is a prisoner of war but there is one man whose bravery shines out like a light." He recounts the story and Danny is presented with a certificate, 100 cigarettes, and a dozen razor blades. This moving anecdote had added a new dimension to my own visit to the dock area.

It is easy to imagine the sense of loss and unease at an uncertain future the prisoners in all four camps under his command – Hakodate, Kami-iso, Kameda, and Muroran – would have felt at Emoto's transfer. He is not at Muroran in person to take his leave but Hirate reads out a letter from him on Monday 28 May '45 which is reproduced by Mitchell.[9] The move has taken Emoto by surprise but his tone of obedience is beautifully expressed in a quote he uses from the British author, Sir Arthur Conan Doyle: "It is not for the pawn to argue when the fingers of the player move him from the square." He concludes by saying "When I have the pleasure of seeing you again after the war is over I am in hopes that I shall be able to meet you as gentlemen each, in entirely different circumstances and I am always looking forward to this opportunity wherever I go. Before closing this address I wish to express my sincerest hopes for your permanent health and constant prosperity during and after this war. Goodbye and good luck to you all." Some ex POWs did, in fact, take up his offer to visit him. He died in 1966 and his son Susumu continued this invitation from his father right up until his own death in 2016.

It was entirely appropriate that Emoto should return to the camps and play some part in the men's evacuation. On Friday 24 August, he visits Bibai, Raijo and Akabira. The men are formally given the news that the war is over and a toast of beer is drunk. Dad had not been reunited with his men and was still at Akabira. His diary entry at one point indicates the pride he takes in the commandant's speech when "he paid great tribute to a certain Major Murray and I knew you would be proud, Eileen, to hear that I had done my job well." Taken out of context, this quote could be misconstrued as that of a 'Jap happy' British officer. However, the entire evidence from all the penned thoughts of the British POWs I have read point not just to the words but, more importantly, to the actions of an influential Japanese officer who transformed the conditions under which they were held (to say nothing about how he improved their mind-set). Putting this in context, however, I must agree with Nigel Brown in his tribute to Emoto that his was, sadly, "a lone voice". Nevertheless, it must still have taken empathy and understanding of the conditions under which the POWs toiled, in addition to the linguistic skills to convey his ideas, for him to be able to enact the massive improvements he brought to all the Hokkaido camps. As I recall my remarks on camera to Nobuyuki and the NHK film crew at the restaurant in Yakumo, I do not regret a word of my own personal tribute to Shigeo Emoto when I stated my belief that he saved the lives of hundreds of British, Dutch and American prisoners of war on the island.

NOTES

1. See **Tomorrow You Die by Eric Cooper**, *published by E.S.Cooper and Sons, Huddersfield, 1995.*

2. *www.nigelbrown.me.uk/pow-emoto.htm*

3. *See Mitchell, p.177.*

4. *Visit website in note 2 above.*

5. *General Hiroshi Tamura was the head of the Japanese Prisoner of War Information Bureau.*

6. **Letters Home, a Reflection of a Man's Survival, Maxwell M Andler,** *The Center Press 2005, p.153.*

7. *See note 1, p.40.*

8. *See Mitchell, p.181.*

9. *See Mitchell, p.231-232.*

CHAPTER 25

"AXIAL SPONDYLOARTHRITIS – DAD'S STORY... AND MINE"

"Getting AS was the best thing that ever happened to me."

A comment made to attendees at an annual NASS AGM and symposium by a physiotherapist prior to her conducting a stretching break, Frenchay Campus, Bristol University.

"Axial SpA (AS) affects around two to five adults per 1,000 in the UK. This means an estimated 200,000 in the UK have axial SpA (AS)."[1] My purpose in writing this chapter is to raise awareness of what some call a condition and others a disease. I would also like to highlight the great work done by the charity, the National Axial Spondyloarthritis Society (NASS), in the UK to support sufferers and their families.

What exactly is axial SpA? It is an umbrella term which covers both non-radiographic axial SpA (inflammation is visible on MRI but not on X-ray) as well as ankylosing spondylitis (AS). By contrast, the latter can be seen on X-ray. To explain its linguistic origin, I am borrowing the definition from a NASS booklet: "Ankylosing means fusing together. Spondylitis means inflammation of the vertebrae. Both words come from the Greek language. Ankylosing spondylitis describes the condition where some or all of the joints and bones of the spine fuse together."[2] It is a form of inflammatory arthritis which mainly affects the spine but can affect other joints in the body.

One of the biggest obstacles to confirming that someone has axial SpA is a delayed diagnosis. As the sufferer's doctor is usually the first port of call, NASS has been particularly active in recent years in raising awareness among GPs of the tell-tale signs of the condition. Increased lobbying at Westminster has resulted in the first ever parliamentary committee being launched at the House of Commons in December 2018.[3] In my own case, my GP on Merseyside in 1982 referred me to the local hospital where I was diagnosed as suffering from gout. As the medication I was prescribed brought no improvement to my condition, I sought a second opinion. I vividly recall a large group of medical students accompanying their professor at the Royal Liverpool University Hospital when I attended an outpatient clinic appointment. After giving him my symptoms and receiving a short examination, he told them that it was a classic case of misdiagnosis and that I had AS. (This was the name given to it in those days but it is now referred to as axial SpA.) I was 28. In our dad's case, the delay was decidedly longer. It came in 1980 when he was 68 and is confirmed in a footnote he wrote in the 1988 version of his POW diary. This was all the more surprising bearing in mind that he himself was a GP until he took early retirement in 1975.

Although I have a relatively mild form of axial SpA, my rheumatologist has always stressed the need for regular exercise, particularly involving stretching. This should be the watchword for all sufferers regardless of how much or how little they can manage and was why the physio's words at the Bristol Symposium especially struck a chord with me. A feature of axial SpA is that the sufferer feels better after exercise and, paradoxically, worse after rest.

The average age for diagnosis is 24. NASS's ambitious aim is to reduce the average diagnosis time from eight and a half years to a 'gold standard' of just one. Dad's early letters to Mum include a reference to "ten rheumatic weeks in bed in Beechwood" (the name of our home in Belfast). In Rawalpindi in February 1940, he spends six weeks in a hospital bed with rheumatic fever after twisting his knee playing cricket. Only three days after the march into Changi, he is hospitalised for five days with sub-acute rheumatism. This follows his first night of captivity spent sleeping on a bed of leaves under the trees. The next night he experiences awful pain in his hip and fever. These prolonged periods in bed will have undoubtedly helped to reduce his fever but will have certainly made his back stiffer and more painful. On 6 June '42 he is given an injection into his spine. On 25 June he is admitted once again to hospital in Changi with an arthritic spine. There he spends almost four weeks. It is the only period in the entire 42 months of his imprisonment when there is no diary entry to Mum. A month later on Friday 21 August, he plays in a cricket match in the camp and scores eight runs. "I could scarcely run at all, nor could I throw a ball! I discovered how really weak I am nowadays." There are no further references in the diary to his arthritis though I suspect the reason again was that he didn't want our mum to worry.

What were the chances of Dad passing on axial SpA to me or any of my siblings? "The risk of AS is considerably increased if an individual carries a particular gene called HLA B27". [4] The offspring of someone with axial

SpA has, on average, a 7 per cent chance of developing the condition but this rises to 13 per cent if the child inherits the gene. I expect I have the gene but do not know for sure. Our son Andrew is 36 and fortunately shows no symptoms. He still regularly plays competitive football and was a county-rated tennis player as a junior.

It was not in Dad's nature to complain about physical ailments but we all noticed how stooped he became as he got older. His 1980 diagnosis should have been accompanied by appointments with a physiotherapist but this was not the case. My diagnosis two years later did not involve any either. I guess it was at a time when less store was placed on the immense benefits of physiotherapy in the recovery process from injuries, quite apart from the permanent need for it in a condition like axial SpA. Before I left my third teaching post in the north of England in 1985, I was given a cortisone injection at the Royal Hospital in Liverpool into the base of my spine following a painful 'flare'. (It is interesting to note that the terminology has changed from a 'flare-up' to a 'flare' which I still associate with trousers!)

Since moving to Gloucester in 1986, I have been under the same rheumatologist at Gloucester Royal Hospital. She refers me for periodic physio which has really helped me to incorporate new stretching exercises into my twice-daily 15-minute routine. This has been particularly beneficial as the condition has spread from my lower back to my neck and shoulders. I no longer use armrests when I sit due to the pressure on my shoulders. High-backed seats spread the support for my back more evenly and I always aim to keep both my feet on the ground if I am sitting on a sofa or armchair. I never read in bed as it places too much pressure on my lower spine. I always avoid sitting in a deep sofa in other people's homes and opt for a chair instead. I have found using a lumbar cushion at home and when driving brings great relief. On long car journeys to Ireland and Scotland, I do stretching exercises whenever we stop. The long-haul flights to the Far East were particularly trying. Extended stands on concert platforms with my choir leave me scurrying off to a quiet part of churches and abbeys at the interval to perform stretching exercises from side to side – much to the amusement of several choir members. I now find golf and browsing round department stores take a painful toll on my lumbar spine due to the constant stopping and moving off again. I have given up the former but can manage shopping if I find a seat for five minutes. People who don't know I have the condition presume I am tired but, unlike many axial SpA sufferers, I always have plenty of energy and a short rest is normally all that is required. In complete contrast, others will question why I never keep still but movement, even if it just involves standing up for a matter of seconds, usually helps to reduce stiffness. I must stress that these are the coping strategies that work best for me but will not necessarily suit all sufferers.

As for medication, I realise I am extremely fortunate in only having to take two paracetamol tablets during the night to help me sleep. I walk for over an hour every day but, in the middle of a flare, this becomes more difficult. However, it usually improves if I persevere. If the pain is too great, I take NSAIDs (non-steroidal anti-inflammatory drugs) but even then I limit the dosage and frequency. The benefit from them, apart from reducing the discomfort, is that they enable me to free up my joints so I can do proper stretches. The alternative is a gradual spread of the pain and stiffness to my back, shoulders and neck.

I have not yet mentioned the part played by stress in the condition. The end of a long week in the classroom was not commensurate with playing five-a-side football on a Friday afternoon in the sports' hall at St Peter's. I used to find my ability to run was severely restricted with stiffness in one or other of the sacroiliac joints of my lower spine. This was so frustrating as I really looked forward to sport-related interaction with my colleagues not to mention the banter in the changing rooms and the pub afterwards. My rheumatologist always recommended hydrotherapy and I agreed to give it a go one summer term when the departure of exam classes always brings a reduced timetable. The warm waters of the pool at the local cottage hospital initially brought relief but having to return within the hour to teach made the whole experience too stressful and I gave up after a month.

I taught full-time for 31 years and continued part-time three days a week for a further two before opting for early retirement at the age of 57. During my final two years, the routine of updating Amaia, my job-share colleague, via email each evening certainly facilitated what for me was a new way of preparing lessons. Relinquishing my responsibilites as head of modern languages in a large comprehensive of 1,500 students has certainly reduced my stress levels and the frequency of my flares.

I am indebted to one of the physios at Gloucester Royal Hospital for two recommendations that greatly improved my ability to cope with the condition. To take some of the pressure off my back, I had gone through a spell of getting up every night at around 3 a.m. to go downstairs and sit for a while in the lounge. When Lisa asked me if I had tried lying on my tummy in bed for a few minutes, I replied that it made it worse as I inevitably tilted my head to one side so I could breathe more easily. This always made my neck really sore. She then showed me how placing a second pillow at a tiered level supporting the front of my shoulders meant that I could keep my head straight and breathe properly. Alleviating the pressure on my back, even if only for a few minutes, has transformed my sleep pattern.

Then she broached the subject of hydrotherapy. I told her of my scepticism as to its benefits but she encouraged me to give it another go. This time I went to a hydrotherapy pool in a nearby school for pupils with special needs. The weekly sessions were run by three trained physios and were designed for people with axial SpA. There were six of us and the classes were purposeful and great fun but they also had the added benefit of sharing coping strategies in the changing-rooms with fellow sufferers. Now retired, I no longer have to clock watch or worry about having to return to teach. The classes have been temporarily discontinued as a new pool is being built on the site but I have continued with 'self-help' hydro at Gloucester Royal. The half-hour sessions leave me tired but I will never again underestimate the physical and mental benefits of exercising my joints in warm water, a routine which would be otherwise impossible in any other environment on my doorstep.

I have already mentioned the curvature in Dad's back which became more pronounced as he aged. At the symposium in Bristol, I was shocked at the beginning of the day by the appearance of a man who arrived at the car park on the campus. He was so bent forward that he could barely look up to see where he was going. His was the classic profile of a sufferer whose body is literally in the shape of a question mark. On a metaphorical level, this punctuation mark is very apt as there is no known cure for axial SpA. The image has always remained with me. Just recently, I struck up a conversation with a man on the hills near our home whom I suspected of having axial SpA. He explained that he had been shielding during the Covid-19 pandemic. I felt quite humble when he explained that he had only 30 per cent lung capacity due to the compression on these organs caused by the curvature of his spine. By contrast, I am not as stooped as Dad was but this is an ongoing battle. Sadly for someone who rode his bike come hail or shine to school for 25 years, I am now finding it increasingly difficult to keep my head raised to watch the road ahead for oncoming vehicles and obstacles.

I have two further reflections on a condition with which I have lived for well over half my life. An anaesthetist had warned me that with axial SpA sufferers it was often difficult to insert an epidural into the lumbar spine due to the fusion of the joints in that area. Before I received my prosthetic knee, the last thing I remember before the operation was her remark that there was no sign of fusion when she inserted the needle. I felt elated that my constant exercising had contributed to this. On a more general note, in spite of the fact that I was carrying a rucksack that varied in weight between 10 and 14 kilos and walking over 2,000 kilometres on three Caminos in Spain, I never had any problems with back pain. Admittedly, I was walking in the summer during two of them but it was chillier in the spring and the autumn at the time of the third. Higher temperatures normally reduce the outbreak of flares unlike the winter period when the body becomes tense. The key difference in Spain, however, was the constant daily movement...not to mention the complete lack of mental stress as a pilgrim on the open road.

NOTES

1. *See NASS booklet from September 2019 Living well with axial SpA (AS), available from www.nass.co.uk*
2. *See NASS booklet from March 2015 Ankylosing Spondylitis Guidebook answers and practical questions.*
3. *On 17 September 2020, the newly elected Conservative MP, Tom Randall, spoke movingly during a 25-minute debate in the House of Commons about his first-hand experience with axial SpA.*
4. *As note 2.*

EPILOGUE

"I THOUGHT TODAY that all men should spend part of their lives as prisoners of war. I have learned so very much and please God profited by my experience. I have learned to appreciate all the little things of life, the things that I have always taken for granted – a good home, good parents, brothers, sisters, friends, and you darling; all these little luxuries that I have never regarded as luxuries before. I have learned self-restraint especially by word – it is easy to hurt people; I have learned not to sulk, to refrain from sarcasm. I have learned to mind my own business. I have been taught the spirit of true resignation to God's will; I have learned to suffer mentally and physically without showing it or inflicting it on others – it is grossly unfair to inflict these sufferings on others. I have learned humility – and yet I have been ruthless in my war against bullies. The weaklings always have my sympathy; they have no champion. I have learned to live in very close contact with men whom I disliked intensely; all the rotten things about them have jarred badly but I have conquered it all. I could never have believed this change possible – my method in the past consisted of avoiding people whom I disliked because I considered it hypocrisy to even try to be nice to them. I am more than ever determined to get out of here alive but it will not be at anyone else's failure."

Francis J. Murray
Muroran POW Camp, Japan
Friday 11 August 1944

"I THOUGHT TODAY that freedom is a very wonderful goal. Freedom of thought, of word, of action. Freedom brings a happiness that one cannot appreciate until one has seen what lack of freedom can do to people. I have known this country not a little – the people are slaves, they have no freedom of any kind, they have no soul, they belong to the government, they are an unhappy race. A few men rule the masses with a hand of iron. The ordinary people are good; the peasants are simple, kindly folk, yet when they are taken in tow by the military clique they become vicious and cruel. They have no enjoyment out of life. Woman is much inferior to man in all ways in Japan. Tyranny and oppression are hateful yet these people accept it with

their queer philosophy. They accept it because it is disguised as patriotism; because their religion teaches them to accept things that come from above. The freedom I experienced in England was amazing. Free speech, religious freedom; everything free and easy. 'An Englishman's home is his castle'. No-one ever interferes; no-one is interested in what his neighbour is doing. Freedom is surely worth fighting for – the Poles thought so, the Irish did too; English freedom was threatened in 1939 and now they are still fighting to maintain it. Pray God they will grant more freedom to others – that freedom which they so jealously guard with their lives. Oh! To stretch out my arms to the heavens and look into unbounded space from an Irish hillside and breathe that word 'Freedom'!"

Francis J. Murray
Muroran POW Camp, Japan
Saturday 12 August, 1944

My siblings and I read these two reflections with a mixture of pride and humility. Dad writes them at a time when he has had a dream about his deceased mother, and goes on to empathise with Mum as he fears for the safety of his future sister-in-law. 'Mattie', or Sister Bernadette as we knew her, had entered the novitiate in a Little Sisters of the Poor convent in German-occupied northern France. The first is a beautifully crafted summary of what he has learnt as a POW. In many ways it is a template for what he was to bring to his future life. The second is a passionate reflection on the Japanese people and serves as a warning to how nations in general can be swept along in a tide of destructive nationalism. Whilst admiring the tolerance he experiences in England, he is nonetheless forthright in what he views as Britain's hypocritical stance on colonialism. I should add that in later life he was never particularly vociferous one way or the other in the debate over Irish unity.

On a personal note, thanks to the restrictions of movement imposed by the Covid-19 pandemic, instead of it taking me three years to write this book it has only taken me two. No thanks to Covid-19, many sedentary mornings leaning towards a computer screen have not helped my posture but I will be forever grateful to Dad for giving me a daily focus during these many months of lockdown.

Continuing my reflective mood as I near the conclusion to my book, I set out to walk my first Camino in Dad's memory 23 years ago. When I began, I would never have expected to be penning a diary entry on day 34 (or any other day for that matter) coinciding with my arrival in Santiago that read "Prayers to be offered for Jesús from Estella, Inés from Castrogeriz, priests at Roncesvalles, and nuns at León." They were all people who had specifically asked me personally or the congregations at Mass to pray for them. Like Dad in the camps, I too had learnt many things about myself from my experiences on the pilgrim road in a foreign country – tolerance towards others, self-reliance, the importance of sharing, and a renewal of my faith, to name but a few. The trick, of course, lies in putting it all into practice. The 'ring of promises' etched on the monoliths before Zamora in 2014 would hold me to that!

Due to his reluctance to relive any of the memories of his captivity, Dad initially restricted meeting up with his fellow POWs to Finucane, Evans and Fr Kennedy, though 20 years later it would have been fascinating to hear what he spoke about with Fr O'Mahoney at our home in Belfast. Reunions with Max in Los Angeles would have been happier occasions, though less so with Mitchell in '83. Reliving this last shared experience upset him greatly. By contrast, my reunions over the years with Anne in Liverpool, Pierre at his home in the Béarn in France, and Javi and Bea in Burgos have been joyous occasions when our more challenging Camino days hardly ever came up for discussion.

I have heard anecdotally that there are nowadays more pilgrim-orientated services in churches along the Caminos in Spain. In 1998 I only received two pilgrim blessings – at Roncesvalles in the Pyrenees, and the same one at Santa María in Rabanal. At the end of 9.30 vespers in the village church and before everyone settles down for the night, the Benedictine monk, Padre Javier, approaches the many pilgrims who flock to this humble edifice across the square from our Gaucelmo hostel. He raises his right hand and utters these special words as he asks on their behalf for God's help in the days that lie ahead:

"Sé para ellos compañero en la marcha/
"Be for them a companion on their journey,
guía en las encrucijadas/ a guide at the crossroads,
aliento en el cansancio/ a breath in the midst of their fatigue,
defensa en los peligros/ a defence when they face dangers,
albergue en el camino/ a place of refuge on their path,
sombra en el calor/ and of shade from the heat,

luz en la oscuridad/ a light in the darkness,
consuelo en sus desalientos/
consolation in the midst of their breathlessness,
y firmeza en sus propósitos para que,/
and a place of strength in the quest for their goals so that
por tu guía, lleguen incólumes al término de su camino..."/
they may, through your guiding power, arrive safely at journey's end..."

In a metaphorical sense, so much of the blessing could have applied to the 36,000 Allied POWs who were transported to the Japanese mainland. They too faced difficult decisions – stand up to their captors or submit. They too faced the challenge of somehow finding the time each day to unwind from the daily grind of slave labour in the cement factory or the docks at Hakodate, the steelworks at Muroran, and the mines at Nishi Ashibetsu and Utashinai, not forgetting the thousands who built the 'death' railway in Burma or toiled in the Kinkaseki Copper Mine on Formosa, endured the tropical heat of Singapore, or the freezing winters on Hokkaido and, finally and most importantly, searched within themselves for the will to survive. Thousands never made it to Japan and died on the hellships from disease, malnutrition or as a result of 'friendly fire'. (Tragically the latter formed the biggest proportion of deaths on the ships.) The 'Thirteen' were among the 3,500 fatalities in the 130 camps in Japan but this figure would have been much higher were it not for the skill and dedication of men like our dad or Max Andler or, indeed, for the humanity of the few enlightened Japanese officers like Lt Col. Shigeo Emoto.

My admiration for the POW Research Network Japan and their volunteers is undiminished. A statement on their website[1] aptly summarises their empathy and their altruism: "We sincerely wish to express our profound sympathy for those victims who grievously lost their lives during the war, and at the same time, it is also our genuine wish that those lists [of deceased POWs] would be of help to their bereaved families, friends, especially to those who have little or no knowledge about what had become of their loved ones." The annual 'Listening to Voiceless Stories of POWs' Commemoration at the Commonwealth War Cemetery at Yokohama in 2019 organised by Taeko and Yoshiko featured Pte Raymond Suttle and two other prisoners. The preface in their information sheet affirms the organisation's commitment to the memory of all the deceased: "Whenever you come here to the Commonwealth

War Cemetery, Yokohama, you see the well-cared site of greenery and repose. Have you ever noticed that these 1,800-plus graves allocated in order have a different and very special story each? We have 'listened' to these stories of the men interred here, so far away from their homelands. Let us introduce three of these stories today." Taken out of context, these words could easily have been written by someone from the Royal British Legion or any other Allied war veterans' association.

Covid-19 together with the floods in England over the winter of 2019/'20 have put paid for the moment to my plans to walk the Camino Inglés (English Camino) from Winchester to Southampton, a distance of 25 km, and A Coruña to Santiago, a further 75 km. (I have, however, already received my first pilgrim blessing from Fr John O'Shea in front of the statue of St James in the church of the same name in Reading, the traditional starting point for the Inglés.) The combined 100 km walked in England and in Spain would qualify me for another *compostela* though, as with my other three, a piece of paper is not my primary motivation. The English leg incorporates the city from where Dad departed to the Far East and to which he returned on the Queen Mary five and a half years later. The Spanish leg begins in the town that I hold dearly in my heart and which taught me as a 20-year-old how to be independent. During research on the English leg of the Inglés, I discovered that Winchester Cathedral was the venue in 1554 for the marriage of Felipe II (four years later to become the 'Armada king') to Queen Mary of England. My pilgrimage will follow in reverse Felipe's route which began with Mass in Santiago Cathedral, the sea crossing from A Coruña to Southampton, and his wedding at the cathedral.

Mindful of the memorial at the port to the thousands of POWs who returned to Southampton across the Atlantic, it occurred to me that I should include in my pilgrimage a visit to St Michael the Archangel church where Jan and I had attended the repatriation service in 2013. What should I recently come across on their website but news of a weekly midday litany of the Community of the Cross of Nails. This association was originally set up following the destruction in November 1940 of much of the city of Coventry and its cathedral by German bombs. "Two of the charred beams [of the cathedral] which had fallen in the shape of a cross were set on the altar and three of the medieval nails were bound into the shape of a cross."[2] After the war, crosses of nails were presented to Kiel, Dresden, and Berlin in symbolic acts of reconciliation.

Of the 160 Cross of Nails centres throughout the world, there are four in Northern Ireland. One is a school and a very special one at that. Lagan College, as mentioned in chapter 1, was the first integrated school in the province. The school's foyer has its own cross of nails together with a prayer which reminds me of the peace monoliths at Castrotorafe Castle, two-days' walking from Zamora. I re-produce part of it here:

> For the hatred which divides nation from nation,
>
> race from race, class from class
>
> FATHER FORGIVE
>
> For the covetous desires of people and nations to possess
>
> what is not their own
>
> FATHER FORGIVE...
>
> For our indifference to the plight of the imprisoned,
>
> the homeless, the refugee
>
> FATHER FORGIVE...

The school's incredibly strong message of reconciliation between communities and nations is a powerful statement which epitomised part of the purpose of my own pilgrimage to the Far East. My memory of the Spanish castle will forever be associated with Larry Montagu, another champion of the self-worth of all young people and his belief in their ability to change the world.

Without dwelling on the politics or the religious zeal behind the conflict between Spain and England in the 16th century, I do think of the estimated 5,000 Spanish sailors and soldiers who either drowned in one of the greatest mass shipwrecks in history or were slaughtered on Irish soil. Like the 'forgotten army' in the Far East, it is gratifying to know that they too are finally beginning to receive the recognition they deserve. Perhaps the tiny, close-knit communities of south-west Donegal will one day also be able to boast, in an even more meaningful way, the stories of St Conall, Alonso Martínez de Leyva, and Beatrice McHugh.

I return, finally, to our dad. While Mum had a few days away in the month before he died in September '93, I flew home to give my sister Edmée a break for a week-end from her caring duties for our dad. Nothing was to prepare me for the physical and mentally upsetting demands of looking after a loved one who was confused and clearly unwell. He didn't speak much over those couple of days. I slept on a mattress on the floor beside his bed so I could more readily turn him on his side. At one point, he looked at me and said "You know what it's like." I knew immediately that he meant shifting my position in bed to relieve the pressure on my lumbar spine that all sufferers from axial SpA have to endure. I felt humbled and very emotional that he could be thinking of others at a time when his mental faculties were rapidly diminishing.

A few weeks later Mum was temporarily hospitalised and said her goodbyes to him at the bungalow. Dad slipped into a coma. It was a Monday and I continued to teach and set work for my classes at St Peter's in anticipation of my prolonged absence. Edmée was joined mid-week by Carl which then made hospital visits to Mum viable. I arrived on the Thursday to take my turn at the vigil by his bedside. Late on the Friday afternoon, Edmée popped up the main street in Newcastle to collect Carl's birthday cake. Dad had lain motionless on his bed for four days. Suddenly, and with a huge effort, he sat up and turned his head towards me before slumping back on the pillow. It was to be the final movement of a man who devoted his entire life to the service of others, an ordinary man who had lived, like so many, through extraordinary times.

I will finish by quoting the Prayer of St Francis of Assisi. The pilgrim saint links a philosophy cherished by our dad to oft-recurring themes and events in my life. The English composer, Jonathan Willcocks, set a beautiful tune to it in his choral work, *Lux Perpetua*, which my choir have sung on several occasions. Poignantly, it was chosen by John Hume's family as a prayer distributed to mourners at his Requiem Mass in St Eugene's Cathedral in Derry on 5 August 2020.[3]

Lord, make me an instrument of your peace:
Where there is hatred, let me sow love;
Where there is injury, pardon;
Where there is doubt, faith;
Where there is darkness, light;
Where there is despair, hope;
And where there is sadness, joy.
Divine Master, grant that I may
Not so much seek to be consoled
As to console,

To be understood as to understand,
To be loved as to love.
For it is in giving that we receive,
It is in pardoning that we are pardoned,
And in dying that we are born
To eternal life.

NOTES

1. *See www.powresearch.jp/en/archive/powlist/index.html They plan to publish a book about all 130 camps in December 2021.*

2. *See www.lagancollege.com/cross-of-nails*

3. *John Hume was one of the chief architects of the Good Friday Agreement in 1998 and, together with David Trimble, was the joint recipient of the Nobel Prize for Peace later that year.*

DAD: TIMELINE

- 4.12.1912, born in Belfast.
- 1929, meets Eileen O'Kane in Ranafast, Co. Donegal.
- 1937, graduates from Queen's University, Belfast, and begins work as GP in Birmingham.
- 9.1.40, leaves England for India to work in a military hospital in Rawalpindi, and Murree Hill Station.
- 20.4.41, arrives in Malaya.
- 5.7.41, receives cable from Mum agreeing to marry him.
- 16.1.42, appointed CO of a Motor Ambulance Convoy.
- 18.1.42, arrives in Singapore.
- 15.2.42, date of surrender of Singapore, becomes POW of Japanese.
- 21.2.42, imprisoned Changi POW Camp.
- 16.5.43, embarks on *Wales Maru* prison ship.
- 7.6.43, disembarks Moji, Japan.
- 10.6.43, arrives Hakodate POW Camp, Hokkaido.
- 16.6.43, transferred to Yakumo POW Camp, Hokkaido.
- 25.10.43, transferred to Muroran POW Camp, Hokkaido.
- 21.2.44, becomes CO of British POWs in Muroran Camp.
- 5.6.45, transferred to Raijo POW Camp, Hokkaido.
- 26.6.45, transferred to Utashinai POW Camp, Hokkaido.
- 7.7.45, transferred to Akabira POW Camp, Hokkaido.
- 2.9.45, returns to Raijo POW Camp.
- 13.9.45, flies from Chitose Aerodrome to Yokohama.
- 18.11.45, arrives in Southampton on *Queen Mary*.
- 4.2.46, marries Mum in Belfast.
- 1946 – 1975, works as a GP in north Belfast.
- 25.9.93, dies at home in Newcastle, Co. Down.
- 22.9.09, Mum dies at home in Reading, England.

ROLL OF HONOUR YAKUMO AND MURORAN POW CAMPS, HOKKAIDO

JUNE 1943 – JUNE 1945

RANK, NAME, AGE, DATE OF DEATH, AREA IN YOKOHAMA COMMONWEALTH WAR CEMETERY

1. Signalman Stan Faunch, 21	24.6.43	RA4
2. Private Robert Bivans, 25	13.11.43	CA1
3. Private Thomas Mayes, 39	1.12.43	LB2
4. Private Roland Braysher, 34	1.12.43	CA7
5. Private Raymond Suttle, 23	23.12.43	ND8
6. Private Francis Bond, 27	3.1.44	CA3
7. Sapper Ernest Glover, 39	3.1.44	AB7
8. Corporal John Lumbers, 27	9.3.44	JB9
9. Private Sidney Quarterman, 28	5.5.44	CC1
10. Driver William Jardine, 32	22.5.44	EB10
11. Sapper Richard Richards, 29	26.8.44	CC11
12. Warrant Officer Edward Durrant, 43	3.6.45	ND10
13. Corporal Alexander Angell, 29	3.6.45	ND9

All died at Muroran except Signalman Stan Faunch who died at Yakumo.

CONTACT: My email address is **mutil1@hotmail.co.uk**

I would be particularly interested in hearing from the families of George Reuneker, Krish Nair, and Stephen McElligott, as well as any further relatives of the 13 men who died on our dad's watch.

BV - #0009 - 120922 - C9 - 234/156/14 - PB - 9781913675165 - Matt Lamination